The Roman Games

Blackwell Sourcebooks in Ancient History

This series presents readers with new translations of the raw material of ancient history. It provides direct access to the ancient world, from wars and power politics to daily life and entertainment, allowing readers to discover the extraordinary diversity of ancient societies.

Published

The Ancient Near East
Edited by Mark W. Chavalas

The Roman Games
Alison Futrell

Alexander the Great
Waldemar Heckel and J. C. Yardley

The Hellenistic Period
Roger Bagnall and Peter Derow

The Roman Games

Historical Sources in Translation

Alison Futrell

Blackwell Publishing

BLACKWELL PUBLISHING
350 Main Street, Malden, MA 02148–5020, USA
9600 Garsington Road, Oxford OX4 2DQ, UK
550 Swanston Street, Carlton, Victoria 3053, Australia

First published 2006 by Blackwell Publishing Ltd

9   2014

Library of Congress Cataloging-in-Publication Data

Futrell, Alison, 1962–
    The Roman games : a sourcebook / Alison Futrell.
        p.   cm. — (Blackwell sourcebooks in ancient history)
    Includes bibliographical references and index.
    ISBN: 978-1-4051-1568-1 (hardcover : alk. paper)
    ISBN: 978-1-4051-1569-8 (pbk. : alk. paper)   1. Games—Rome—History.
    2. Games—Social aspects—Rome.   3. Amphitheaters—Rome.
    4. Rome—Social life and customs. I. Title. II. Series.

GV31.F88 2006
796′.0937′6—dc22
                                                                        2005013068

A catalogue record for this title is available from the British Library.

Set in 10/13pt Stone Serif
by Graphicraft Limited, Hong Kong

For further information on
Blackwell Publishing, visit our website: www.blackwellpublishing.com

Contents

Illustrations

Preface

The roar of the crowd, the screams of animals and victims, the smell of blood, sweat, and perfume, the flash of weapons within the last frantic, fatal movements, the colors of the charioteers glimpsed through the dust and jostling crowd as the horses round the last turn. Given the heady sensualism embedded in the original phenomenon, it is not surprising that Roman spectacle holds a prominent position in the modern imagination, becoming a site of contemporary social and political meaning. The bloody entertainments of imperial Rome are like the stereotypically luxurious bath-houses, the banquets, and the orgies, all central to the popular perception of Rome as a civilization devoted to sophisticated luxury, to personal pleasures, a civilization doomed by its decadence. It is true that the Roman world devoted an overwhelming amount of time, energy, money, and attention to spectacle, with politicians bankrupting themselves to provide games, towns giving over huge amounts of public space and public funds for the construction of venues. But this was hardly a matter of officially sanctioned hedonism, pure and simple. The games carried a complex nexus of interlocking meanings in imperial Rome; the organization, production, and presentation of these performances articulated social, political and cultural meaning and provided substance and setting for the playing out of Roman values. This book considers Roman spectacle from the perspectives of those who created, used, experienced, enjoyed, hated, respected, condemned, and found themselves in the games as an active, living institution. Rather than trying to extract The One True Meaning of the games, I have attempted to present Roman spectacle as multiple complicated experiences that touched different individuals and groups in different ways.

The ancient resources assembled here are of many different types. Typically, literary texts favor the viewpoint of the wealthy elite, those who produced and read this kind of material. Inscriptions in stone and high-quality artistic representations also tend to reflect upper-class expectations, as it required a certain financial status to pay for such items. The wealthy elite did not speak with one voice, however, as a range of agendas, regional backgrounds, and changes over time flavor the evidence. Graffiti and curse tablets are more ephemeral media and hint at motivations driving non-elites in the Mediterranean. The lived experience of performers leaks out in dribbles from fairly limited material, represented mostly in epitaphs and the Christian martyr acts. The interests of *editores*, imperial and otherwise, can be found in law codes and painted notices for games; these different texts spoke to different target audiences, however; the one offering practical precedents for administrators and the other celebrating a gathering of a specific social network, met for the purposes of exchanging honor and pleasure. The editorial introductions for each source attempt to locate the material in the ancient context, drawing out the distinctive points of emphasis and purpose.

The original inspiration for this collection came from Thomas N. Habinek, who organized a graduate seminar on the arena at UC Berkeley in the spring semester of 1991. The participants in the course provided much stimulating discussion and provocative perspectives. My gratitude to then fellow-students Martha Jenks, Haley Way, Judy Gaughan, Matt Roller, Eric Gunderson, John Harding, Trevor Murphy, and Mark Ryerson, and to Tom Habinek, whose discussions of the project in the years since have greatly influenced its ultimate framework and emphasis. The final manuscript owes much to the diligence and care of my two research assistants, Cynthia Ann Gonzales and Julia Hudson-Richards; Julia's help with the tedious minutiae is particularly appreciated, as is her wit. Thanks also to Jodie Kreider, who made me stop fiddling at a key moment. I'm also grateful for the support of Blackwell Publishing, particularly Al Bertrand and Angela Cohen, noteworthy in their patience and understanding. As always, the faculty, staff and graduate and undergraduate students of the Department of History at the University of Arizona have provided assistance, insight, and stimulation in bringing this effort to completion. A shout out to the U. of A. Classics Department as well. Finally, I extend enormous appreciation to friends and family for their continuing efforts to encourage me and maintain balance and sanity in my life.

Acknowledgments

The editor and publisher gratefully acknowledge the permission granted to reproduce the copyright material in this book:

1 Plutarch, *The Fall of the Roman Republic: Six Lives*, translated by Rex Warner with introduction and notes by Robin Seager. © 1958 by Rex Warner. Introduction and notes © 1972 by Robin Seager. Reproduced by permission of Penguin Books Ltd.

2 *Lives of the Later Caesars: The first part of the Augustan History, with Lives of Nerva and Trajan*, translated by Anthony Birley. © 1976 by Anthony Birley. Reproduced by permission of Penguin Books Ltd.

3 Pliny the Elder, *Natural History: A Selection*, translated with an introduction and notes by John F. Hely. © 1991 by John F. Hely. Reproduced by permission of Penguin Books Ltd.

4 Seneca, *Letters from a Stoic*, selected and translated with an introduction by Robin Campbell. © 1969 by Robin Alexander Campbell. Reproduced by permission of Penguin Books Ltd.

5 Betty Radice, *The Letters of the Younger Pliny*, translated with an introduction by Betty Radice. © 1963, 1969 by Betty Radice. Reproduced by permission of Penguin Books Ltd.

6 Petronius, *The Satyricon*, translated with an introduction and notes by J. P. Sullivan. © 1965, 1969, 1974, 1977, 1986 by J. P. Sullivan. Reproduced by permission of Penguin Books Ltd.

7 Seneca, *The Apocolocyntosis*, translated with an introduction and notes by J. P. Sullivan. © 1965, 1969, 1974, 1977, 1986 by J. P. Sullivan. Reproduced by permission of Penguin Books Ltd.

8 Juvenal, *The Sixteen Satires*, translated by Peter Green. © 1967, 1974 by Peter Green. Reproduced by permission of Penguin Books Ltd.

9 *Cassidorus: Variae*, translated with notes by S. J. B. Barnish. © 1992 by S. J. B. Barnish. Reproduced by permission of The University of Liverpool Press.

10   *Acts of Christian Martyrs*, translated by Herbert Musrillo. © 1972 by Herbert
     Musrillo. Reproduced by permission of Oxford University Press.

11   *The Digest of Justinian*, Latin text edited by Theodor Mommsen with
     the aid of Paul Krueger, English translation edited by Alan Watson.
     © 1985 Alan Watson. Reproduced by permission of The University of
     Pennsylvania Press.

12   Suetonius, *The Twelve Caesars*, translated by Robert Graves. © 1957 by
     Robert Graves. Reproduced by permission of Carnet Press Ltd.

13   Tacitus, *The Annals and The Histories*, edited by Moses Hadas, translated
     by Alfred Church and William Brodribb, 2003. Published by Random
     House.

14   Tertullian, *Apologetical Works and Minucius Felix*, translated by Rudolph
     Arbesmann, Sister Emily Joseph Daly and Edwin A. Quain, 1950. Repro-
     duced by permission of The Catholic University Press of America.

Every effort has been made to trace copyright holders and to obtain their
permission for the use of copyright material. The publisher apologizes for
any errors or omissions in the above list and would be grateful if notified
of any corrections that should be incorporated in future reprints or editions
of this book.

1

The Politics of the Arena

Origin and Growth of Games

The great games of the ancient Mediterranean grew out of religious holidays to become spectacular celebrations of the divine pantheon, events that not only called upon divine support to ensure continued prosperity for the state, but also offered an elaborate, formalized series of actions that encouraged, even required, the participation of an expanded human audience. These spectacles tended to follow a standard format of procession, sacrifice, and games. The procession, the first part of the festival, was, practically speaking, a means of conveying the worshipers, the officiants, and their implements of worship to the sacred space of the altar or temple. To enhance the ritual quality of the movement, the procession followed a specific, religiously significant pathway; the personnel were arranged in a specific order; the participants wore particular kinds of clothing, spoke or sang ritual words. These guidelines could involve sacrificial animals in the procession as well, who not only would be draped in wreaths or ribbons, to set them apart from "common" animals, to make them "sacred", but also were meant to conform to certain kinds of behavior: they had to seem willing to approach the altar, and cult officials who accompanied them made sure of this. The procession was followed by the sacrifice. Sacrifice was the basic act of Graeco-Roman religion, establishing a positive relationship between deity and worshiper through the offering of a gift; this could mean the immolation of an animal, the pouring of a wine or oil libation, or setting cakes or flowers on the god's altar for his enjoyment. In return, the deity would provide success and prosperity to the community of the worshipers. The sacrifice would be accompanied by prayer that often specified the nature of the relationship between divine and human, perhaps the declaration of a specific need or the acknowledgement of divine favor. Games were the third and, eventually, most elaborate, portion of the festival. Beginning perhaps with simple contests of athletic or musical skill, games can be understood as the offering of the best in human achievement in honor of the deity. As political systems became increasingly sophisticated, state sponsorship of an official religious calendar of festivals afforded an opportunity to celebrate not just the gods, but also to showcase the wealth and organizational talent of the state and its leaders. The games became more and more the dominant feature of the festival. More days could be added to accommodate more competitors and more events, presented in increasingly specialized venues to the delight of huge crowds of spectators, all recipients of a variety of powerful messages that went far beyond the pious acknowledgement of divine power.

Games and the Roman state

In Rome, the presentation of spectacles by state apparatus begins early in the Republic with the *Ludi Magni* or *Ludi Romani*, held in honor of Jupiter Optimus Maximus, chief god in the Roman pantheon. These were initially votive games, vowed on the field of battle as an extraordinary gift to Jupiter, if the god would grant victory to the Roman army. By adding *ludi* to the usual religious ritual, Rome's leaders ratcheted up the scale of the gift to the deity. The connection to victory is important as well. Roman military success was a major resource for the financial demands of Roman spectacle. Generals, by channeling booty seized from the enemy toward *ludi*, were able to present themselves as agents of pious duty toward the Roman state and as selflessly generous toward their fellow citizens who would take pleasure in these games. Chariot racing, *ludi circenses*, was the type of spectacle associated with the *Ludi Romani* from an early period. By the middle of the fourth century, *ludi scaenici* or theatrical presentations had been added to the spectacle repertoire of Rome. Until this time, the *Ludi Romani* were still "extraordinary", i.e. they were not held on a regular basis as part of the ordinary religious calendar. In 366 BCE, they became the first set of *Ludi* to receive annual sponsorship by the Roman state, to be organized by the curule aediles each year as part of their duties to protect the well-being of Rome, a link clearly stated by Cicero some three centuries after the regularization of the *Ludi Romani*.

Source: Cicero, *Against Verres* 2.5.36:[1] I am now an aedile elect; and I understand the position in which the nation's will has placed me. With the utmost diligence and solemnity I am to celebrate the holy festival of Ceres, Liber and Libera. By holding the solemn festival of our Lady Flora I am to secure her favor for the people and commons of Rome. In the most worthy and devout fashion, I am to perform the most ancient festival, the earliest to bear the name of "Roman" in honor of Jupiter, Juno and Minerva. I have been made responsible for the safeguarding of our sacred edifices and for the protection of the whole of our city.

Despite the serious tone of Cicero's declaration of duty, it is clear that the presentation of aedilician games became a real opportunity for an ambitious man relatively early in his career. A set of spectacular games would make a memorable impression on the people and establish the reputation of the aedile as a skilful administrator, a savvy and stylish auteur, and a generous benefactor, whose own resources would top off any gap in the funding supplied by the state. Scipio Africanus, the conqueror of Hannibal, for example, first comes into public view as the *editor* of impressive *Ludi Romani* in 213 BCE.

The late third and early second century saw a frenzy of multiple additions to the ritual calendar, including the *Ludi Plebeii* (for Jupiter), the *Ludi Apollinares* (for Apollo), the *Ludi Megalenses* (for the Great Mother) and the *Ludi Florales* (for Flora). A number of overlapping influences shaped spectacle and its importance in Rome at this time. This was a period of intensive overseas involvement for Rome. There was a huge influx of wealth into the hands of primarily Rome's elites, who, as military leaders, claimed control of war booty. Senatorial political power increased rapidly alongside this economic power, as the Senate was in control of administering and coordinating Rome's overseas interests. As the stakes were raised, the competition among leaders of the elite for access to the benefits of empire intensified. There was increasing contact with other peoples, particularly Greece, with its prestigious and highly appealing cultural achievement. New perspectives on life and new ways of expressing cultural values were infiltrating the Roman mindset, although not without generating some tension. Rome's ambitious leaders were interested in accessing innovative public displays, like the spectacles sponsored by contemporary Hellenistic kings and states in the eastern Mediterranean. There was concern, however, that Rome retain her distinctive identity, that leaders not be perceived as sacrificing their old-fashioned Roman morality for the sake of flashy and luxurious foreign ways. Spending newfound wealth on games was "safer" than personal expenditure and had the benefit of positive audience response. Ordinary games, however, were controlled by the aediles, a mid-range magistracy. Those at the top of Rome's political ladder therefore opted to present extraordinary games, often associated with the commemoration of their success in war, and private games, such as gladiatorial combats, which had the benefit of being less susceptible to carping criticism by one's rivals.

One such sponsor was Marcus Fulvius Nobilior, who celebrated his triumph over the Aetolians in 187 BCE with an extravagant triumphal procession, permanent monuments to his success, and ten days of impressive games that incorporated the first wild animal hunt as part of the extended spectacle. He had to struggle to do so, however. M. Aemilius Lepidus led a number of Nobilior's rivals in trying to suppress his triumph, challenging the military leadership that had won the victory in the first place. Other alleged irregularities were contested, as will be seen below.

Source: Livy 39.22:[2] Then for ten days, with great magnificence, Marcus Fulvius [Nobilior] gave the games which he had vowed during the Aetolian war. Many actors too came from Greece to do him honor. Also a contest of athletes was then for the first time made a spectacle for the Romans and a hunt of lions and panthers was given, and the games, in number and variety, were celebrated in a manner almost like that of the [late first century BCE].

Origins of gladiatorial combat

Sponsorship of gladiatorial combat began in the private sphere, as part of Roman funerals, a means of embellishing the public obsequies of Roman nobles. Although ostensibly these were unofficial spectacles, the *munera* were intended as a public demonstration of the prestige and importance of the noble Roman who had earned the acclaim of the public funeral. As was the case with many symbols of Roman authority, such as the toga, the *fasces*, and religious panoply and ritual, the origin of this custom was attributed to the Etruscans. Nicolaus of Damascus wrote a history of the games during the reign of Augustus, emphasizing the Etruscan connection.

Source: Nicolaus of Damascus, *Athletics* 4.153: Romans presented the games of gladiators . . . a practice they were given by the Etruscans.

Paintings from the tombs of Etruscan nobility point to their custom of commemorating the dead with extensive funeral games, which seem to incorporate a variety of contests, including combats. Others suspect the Roman *munera* developed under strong influence from the area of Campania to the south, where from 343 to 290 BCE Rome fought three wars against the Samnite people, expanding Roman influence and being influenced by local customs in return. There is some indication that gladiatorial-style combats were a feature of banquets in this area. Later Roman accounts of the practice, like those of Livy and Silius Italicus, tend to criticize it as an excess of luxury, rather than demonstrations of skill and control. This habit may, however, underlie the location of gladiatorial schools in the area of Capua, known from a later date.

Source: Livy 9.40:[3] The war in Samnium, immediately afterwards, was attended with equal danger and an equally glorious conclusion. The enemy, besides their other warlike preparation, had made their battle-line to glitter with new and splendid arms. There were two corps: the shields of the one were inlaid with gold, of the other with silver . . . The Romans had already learned of these splendid accoutrements, but their generals had taught them that a soldier should be rough to look on, not adorned with gold and silver but putting his trust in iron and in courage . . . The dictator, as decreed by the senate, celebrated a triumph, in which by far the finest show was afforded by the captured armor. So the Romans made use of the splendid armor of their enemies to do honor to the gods; while the Campanians, in consequence of their pride and in hatred of the Samnites, equipped after this fashion the gladiators who furnished them entertainment at their feasts, and bestowed on them the name of Samnites.

Source: Silius Italicus 11.51:[4] Then too it was their ancient custom to enliven their banquets with bloodshed and to combine with their feasting the horrid sight of armed men fighting; often the combatants fell dead above the very cups of the revelers, and the tables were stained with streams of blood. Thus demoralized was Capua.

The Roman sources that document this practice, however, do so from a fairly hostile perspective. Capua was an early ally of Rome during the era of its expansion in Italy in the fourth and third centuries. When the Carthaginian general Hannibal invaded Italy in the late third century, Capua shifted allegiance to him, opting, perhaps, to maximize an opportunity to become the leading Italian city under a new Punic hegemony. Rome took Capua's decision badly, to say the least, and forced Capua to return to the Roman hegemony, severely punishing the Capuans for abandoning their Roman allies. This relationship has shaped the accounts of Campanian gladiators in the literature, as they are connected with what the Romans saw as Capuan decadence and luxury, the lack of ethics and self-serving political maneuvering leading up to Capua's betrayal of Rome in the Hannibalic war.

Tertullian, one of the more prolific surviving early Christian writers, objected to the spectacles for a number of reasons (see chapter 5), which he explained in his hostile survey of the games. His description of the origins of gladiatorial combat points to Etruria as the source of the practice; he expands on this by giving a negative interpretation of the early funerary context of such events.

Source: Tertullian, *On the Spectacles* 12.1–4:[5] It still remains to examine the most prominent and most popular spectacle of all. It is called *"munus"* [obligation] from being an *"officium"* [duty]. For *"munus"* and *"officium"* are synonyms. The ancients thought they were performing a duty to the dead by this sort of spectacle after they had tempered its character by a more refined form of cruelty. For in time long past, in accordance with the belief that the souls of the dead are propitiated by human blood, they used to purchase captives or slaves of inferior ability and to sacrifice them at funerals. Afterwards, they preferred to disguise this impiety by making it a pleasure . . . Thus they found consolation for death in murder. Such is the origin of the gladiatorial contest.

The original purpose and meaning of such funeral games may be understood as a form of human sacrifice: men fought to the death at the funeral of a much-valued leader, whose spirit benefited from the spilling of blood. More importantly, the slaying of human victims acknowledged the importance of the loss to the community and enhanced the public reputation of the deceased in a way which transcended his mortality. The combats also demonstrated the capacity of the heir, who arranged the obsequies in pious duty and exercised the authority necessary to command death itself. The need to make such acknowledgements, to benefit the dead and the living, could be particularly strong in times of crisis for the community. The earliest Roman examples of *munera* took place during the conflicts with the Carthaginians, Rome's most serious opponents of the middle Republic.

Source: Livy *Summary* 16: [in 264 BCE] Decimus Junius Brutus first gave a gladiatorial *munus* in honor of his deceased father.

Source: Livy 23.30: (216 BCE) And in honor of Marcus Aemilius Lepidus, who had been twice consul and augur, his three sons, Lucius, Marcus and Quintus, gave funeral games over a period of three days and presented twenty-two pairs of gladiators in the Forum.

The gladiatorial combats thus began to grow at a time when Roman spectacle as a whole was expanding, and no doubt for similar reasons. The risks of warfare heightened tensions in Roman society; new festivals and *munera* both countered this anxiety by engaging supernatural support and demonstrating the continuing capability of Rome's leadership, even in a time of crisis. Gladiatorial combat was also perceived as "Roman"; it carried none of the questionable cultural baggage of some other forms of spectacle and, further, had moral value (see below).

Gladiatorial games grew in size and complexity from the third to mid-second century BCE. All were associated with public funeral celebrations of the noble dead, with gladiators a part of the *munus* or obligation owed to the deceased. At first these combats were staged as part of the funeral itself, within a few days of the death of the person commemorated; later, they were often held some time after the actual funeral, but with the stated purpose of celebration of the deceased still intact. As the panoply surrounding the games, the number of participants, the special accommodations required all grew more lavish, an extended period of time was required, in order to make all the arrangements, not just for the show but for accompanying feasts and huge quantities of funeral meats.

Source: Livy 39.46: (183 BCE) On account of the funeral of Publius Licinius[6] meat was distributed, and 120 gladiators fought. Funeral games were given lasting three days and, after the games, a public feast in which . . . dining couches were spread across the entire forum.

Source: Livy 41.28:[7] (174 BCE) Several gladiatorial games were given that year, and other small games; one was noteworthy beyond the others, that of Titus Flamininus, which he gave on account of his father's death[8], with a distribution of meat, a public feast, and theatrical shows lasting four days. The climax of the show, which was big for its day, was the fact that 74 men fought over a three-day period.

Origins of wild animal shows

From fairly early days, animals had been a part of the religious festivals of Rome, incorporated into ritual as part of the sacred performance meant to guarantee the good-will of Rome's gods. The grandiose display of exotic animals in Rome, however, is connected to the spread of Roman hegemony; Romans encountered unusual and intimidating beasts and gained access to supplies of such rare animals as part of the expansion of Roman authority. At first, animals were displayed as living war-booty, symbols of the acquisition of distant territories, living embodiments of the far-flung landscapes of the Roman empire. At first this symbolic value was enough; eventually Romans made use of exotic animals in a more dynamic way.

This happened very directly in the case of elephants; Romans met war-elephants, regularly featured in Hellenistic armies, on the field of battle. In spectacle these animals carried imperial meaning, partly because of their colossal size, partly because of the tradition of politically significant symbolic value of these animals: elephants were the special mounts of eastern powerbrokers, of Alexander and the Seleucid and Ptolemaic monarchs, as well as the affiliated deity Dionysus, carrying along with those kings messages of unstoppable conquest in the east. Elephants were also thought to have particular moral value because of their own characteristics. Pliny tells us about elephant piety, elephant patriotism and sense of duty, and the elephant's special capacity to recognize human sociopolitical categories. At the triumph celebrated by M. Curius Dentatus in 275 BCE, elephants captured from Pyrrhus were the highlight of the *pompa*. A few years later, L. Caecilius Metellus took this one step further; Pliny tells us that he captured and brought to Rome some 140 formerly Carthaginian elephants, who not only marched in the triumphal parade but were chased in the Circus as well. The description, however, acknowledges the relatively primitive state of Roman spectacle management at the time.

Pliny, *Natural History* 8.16–17:[9] A large number of elephants were captured from the Carthaginians in Sicily by the victory of the pontifex Lucilius Metellus in [252 BCE]: there were 142, or, as some authorities state, 140, and they were ferried across [the straits of Messana] on rafts which Metellus had made by putting a layer of planks on rows of wine-jars secured together. Verrius records that these elephants fought in the Circus and were killed by javelins, because the Romans were at a loss what to do with them, since they had decided not to look after them or give them to local kings. Lucius Piso says that the elephants were simply led into the Circus, and, in order to increase the contempt for them, were driven round it by men carrying spears tipped with a ball.

Elephants were the first exotic animals to serve in spectacles as the executors of the Roman will, the agents of public execution, a duty surely appropriate to animals with an innate sense of justice. Spectacle executions can be traced to 167 BCE, when Aemilius Paullus, newly victorious over Perseus, ordered that deserters from the Roman troops be crushed by elephants. Valerius Maximus says that this reinforced army discipline even more because of the spectacular nature of the punishment. In 146, a similar set of spectacle executions, the squashing of foreign deserters by elephants, was part of the triumphal games of Scipio Aemilianus, using North African elephants, symbols now of Carthaginian defeat, to carry out the imperial will of Rome.

Source: Valerius Maximus 2.7.13–14: For the Younger Africanus, after having destroyed the Carthaginian Empire, threw foreign deserters to the wild beasts as part of spectacle he offered to the people. And Lucius Paulus, after King Perseus was vanquished, for the same fault (desertion) threw men under elephants to be trampled . . . And indeed military discipline needs this kind of severe and abrupt punishment, because this is how strength of arms stands firm, which, when it falls away from the right course, will be subverted.

Roman spectacle overseas

Rome's intensified production of spectacle was associated with expansion of Roman influence outside Italy and increased involvement with the other powers in the Mediterranean. To some extent, Roman presentation of lavish events was meant to demonstrate Roman capacity beyond the military, to show that, culturally, Rome was fully able to engage in leadership. Romans adopted and adapted politically charged spectacle techniques developed by Hellenistic kings. When Scipio Africanus presented *munera* in Spain in 206 BCE, he commemorated his uncle and father, who had died five years earlier. More significantly for Scipio, 206 was the year in which he settled the Iberian front of the Second Punic War on Rome's behalf. The games made use of local performers; note, however, how political competition is imported into the arena itself, a literalization of the fight for public office that Livy finds reprehensible.

Source: Livy 28.21:[10] Scipio returned to [New] Carthage to pay his vows to the gods and to conduct the gladiatorial show which he had prepared in honor of his deceased father and uncle. The exhibition of gladiators was not made up from the class of men which *lanistae* are in the habit of pitting against each other, that is, slaves sold on the platform and free men who are ready to sell their lives. In every case the service of the men who fought was voluntary and without compensation. For some were sent by their chieftains to display an example of the courage inbred in their tribe; some declared on their own motion that they would fight to please the general; in other cases rivalry and the desire to compete led them to challenge or, if challenged, not to refuse . . . Men also of no obscure family but conspicuous and distinguished, Corbis and Orsua, being cousins and competing for the post of chief of a city called Ibes, declared that they would contend with the sword. . . . Since they could not be made to give up such madness, they furnished the army a remarkable spectacle, demonstrating how great an evil among mortals is the ambition to rule. The older man by his skill with arms and by his cunning easily mastered the brute strength of the younger. In addition to this gladiatorial show there were funeral games so far as the resources of the province and camp equipment permitted.

Aemilius Paullus was in charge of the Roman military when it defeated Perseus, King of Macedonia, at the battle of Pydna in 168 BCE. The Macedonian Kings had been, since the time of Philip II and Alexander the Great, preeminent creators of the kingly image in the Mediterranean. Macedonia itself was a major player in contemporary diplomacy until the Roman victory entailed the establishment of a Roman administrative presence and the end of the monarchy. In the months following Pydna, Aemilius Paullus engaged in a number of image-building activities as Rome's agent in the Greek east, including the presentation of elaborate games at Amphipolis, which would be the Roman capital in the new Macedonia. These demonstrations were meant to impress the Greeks with the high level of Roman cultural sophistication, Rome's facility with the Greek symbols of power, as well as assert that Rome's leaders were not simply brutal generals but astute producers of impressive political theater. Paullus' pithy remark was meant to drive this last point home.

Source: Livy 45.32–33:[11] The serious business was followed by an entertainment, a most elaborate affair staged at Amphipolis. This had been under preparation for a considerable time, and Paulus had sent messengers to the cities and kings of Asia to give notice of the event, while he had announced it in person to the leading citizens in the course of his tour of the Greek states. A large number of skilled performers of all kinds in the sphere of entertainment assembled from all over the world, besides athletes and famous horses, and official representatives with sacrificial victims; and all the other usual ingredients of the great games of Greece, provided for the sake of gods and men, were supplied on such a scale as to excite admiration not merely for the splendor of the display but also for the well-organized showmanship in a field where the Romans were at that time mere beginners. Banquets for the official delegations were put on, equally sumptuous and arranged with equal care. A remark of Paulus himself was commonly quoted, to the effect that a man who knew how to conquer in war was also a man who would know how to arrange a banquet and to organize a show.

Gladiatorial games were incorporated into spectacle by some non-Romans, most prominently by Antiochus IV Epiphanes, King of Syria, whose long stay in Rome as a hostage for his royal father's good behavior may have influenced his choices. Significantly, his time in Rome overlaps with the early second-century massive upswing in spectacle, when frenzied expenditure on ever more lavish shows became thoroughly embedded in elite political competition. When he returned home to take up his family's throne, Antiochus introduced significant Roman-style innovations into his panoply of royal symbols, including the construction of a Capitolium or Temple of Capitoline Jupiter, use of the toga, use of a Roman magisterial chair, Roman-style banqueting, and gladiatorial combat. Livy notes that Antiochus had to gradually acclimatize the locals in Antioch to this type of spectacle. The results are perceived as valuable, not only in enhancing Antiochus' connections with powerful Rome on a politico-cultural basis, but, as Livy points out, to promote militarism.

Source: Livy 41.20:[12] In regard to the splendor of his shows of every sort [Antiochus] surpassed earlier kings, his other spectacles being given in their own proper style and with an abundance of Greek theatrical artists; a gladiatorial exhibition, after the Roman fashion, he presented which was at first received with greater terror than pleasure on the part of men who were unused to such sights; then by frequent repetitions, by sometimes allowing the fighters to go only as far as wounding one another, sometimes permitting them to fight without giving quarter, he made the sight familiar and even pleasing, and he roused in many of the young men a joy in arms. And so, while at first he had been accustomed to summon gladiators from Rome, procuring them by large fees, finally he could find a sufficient supply at home...

The best description of how the *munera* were used by Antiochus is in Athenaeus' account of his celebration of victory over Ptolemy VI in 166 (a victory significantly shaped by Roman active interest). Antiochus saw these games as an opportunity to establish his own reputation as a leader of international prominence, specifically competing with Aemilius Paulius, recent presenter of remarkable games, in so doing. Having sent announcements of this extraordinary event to cities all over the Mediterranean, Antiochus was personally involved in arranging the enormous procession to open the games, showcasing thousands of soldiers, sacred paraphernalia and luxury items, and in their midst 240 pairs of gladiators. This was followed by feasts and shows, all meant to demonstrate the wealth, power and international influence of Antiochus.

Source: Athenaeus, *Philosophers' Banquet* 5.194–195:[13] This same king, hearing about the games instituted in Macedonia by Aemilius Paulus, the Roman general, and wishing to outdo Paulus in magnificence, dispatched envoys and delegates to the cities to proclaim the games which were to be given by him near Daphne . . . [the parade] was led by certain men in the prime of their youth, five thousand in number, who wore Roman armor of chain-mail; after them came five thousand Mysians; close to these were three thousand Cilicians equipped in the fashion of light-armed troops, and wearing gold crowns. After these came three thousand Thracians and five thousand Celts. These were followed by twenty thousand Macedonians, ten thousand of them with gold shields, five thousand with bronze shields, and the rest with silver shields; close upon these came two hundred and forty pairs of gladiators . . . The games, gladiatorial contests and hunts took thirty days to conclude; during the first five days in which spectacles were carried out, all persons in the gymnasium anointed themselves with saffron oil from golden basins . . . For a banquet on one occasion there were spread a thousand *triclinia*[14], on another fifteen hundred, with the most extravagant deckings . . .

Spectacle and Roman Politics

Politics and shows

By the late Republic, gladiatorial matches had become public entertainment like the ordinary holiday games, votive games, and the triumphs, a powerful political tool for attracting voters and enhancing one's reputation as a public benefactor. The funerary association had become merely a pretext by this time; *munera* would be offered years after the death of the alleged honoree. The primary motivation was political ambition. The *munera* thus were presented as "extraordinary" games, like those offered by triumphators as part of the celebration of victory. *Munera*, however, anticipated "victory", helping politicians to secure success in the battle for public office. L. Licinius Murena, as praetor of 66 BCE, prepared for success by sponsoring games; not having presented spectacle prior to this had been a real obstacle in his recent campaign, just as his deluxe praetorian games would be an asset far into the future.

> Source: Cicero, *For Murena* 37–39:[15] There were two things which Murena, in his campaign for the praetorship, suffered seriously from the lack of, but which were both of considerable benefit to him when he came to stand for the consulship. One was games, the expectation of which had been brought about by certain rumors and by the deliberate suggestion of his rivals for office . . . Both of these advantages fortune held back for him until he stood for the consulship . . . as for his not having put on games, a factor which had hampered Murena in his campaign for the praetorship, this deficiency had been made up for by the extremely lavish games he put on in the course of his year as praetor . . . It may be that you . . . attach more weight to the urban vote than to that of the soldiers. But, if so, you can hardly show the same contempt for the high quality of Murena's games and the magnificence of the spectacle, since this was unquestionably of enormous help to him. Do I need to point out that the people and the ignorant masses adore games? It is hardly surprising that they do.

Innovation in spectacle was a means of distinguishing oneself from the pack of candidates; devising novel means of enhancing the games was becoming increasingly difficult as Roman tastes became more sophisticated through familiarity. The aedile for 65 BCE, Julius Caesar, offered spectacles which became legendary for their rich and exciting production values. Caesar maximized the impact of the games by mounting in addition a lavish public exhibition of all the special items, such as the silver armor, assembled for his spectacles.

> Source: Suetonius, *Julius Caesar* 10:[16] During his aedileship, Caesar filled the Comitium, the Forum, its adjacent basilicas, and the Capitol itself with a display of the material which he meant to use in his public shows, building temporary colonnades for the purpose. He exhibited wild-beast hunts and stage-plays; some at his own expense, some in cooperation with his colleague, Marcus Bibulus – but took all the credit in either case.

> Source: Dio Cassius 37.8:[17] Not for this alone did [Caesar] receive praise during his aedileship, but also because he exhibited both the *Ludi Romani* and the *Megalenses* on the most expensive scale and furthermore arranged gladiatorial contests in his father's honor in the most magnificent manner. For although the cost of these entertainments was in part shared jointly with his colleague Marcus Bibulus, and only in part borne by him individually, yet he so far excelled in the funeral contests as to gain for himself the credit for the others too, and was thought to have borne the whole cost himself.

Source: Plutarch, *Caesar* 5.9:[18] [Caesar] spent money recklessly, and many people thought that he was purchasing a moment's brief fame at an enormous price, whereas in reality he was buying the greatest place in the world at inconsiderable expense. We are told, for instance, that before entering upon public office, he was thirteen hundred talents in debt . . . And, when he was aedile, he provided a show of 320 pairs of gladiators fighting in single combat, and what with this and all his other lavish expenditure on theatrical performances, processions and public banquets, he threw into the shade all attempts at winning distinction in this way that had been made by previous holders of the office.

Source: Pliny, *Natural History* 33.53:[19] We too have done things to be deemed mythical by those who come after us. Caesar, the future dictator, was the first person in the office of aedile to use nothing but silver for the appointments of the arena – it was at the funeral games presented in honor of his father; and this was the first occasion on which criminals made to fight with wild animals had all their equipment made of silver.

Gn. Pompeius Magnus, having eluded custom and law to build a permanent venue in Rome for spectacle, gave extravagant games to inaugurate his theater in 55 BCE. The games were not a complete success. Cicero's perception of Pompey's lavish shows demonstrates a certain boredom with lavish spectacle as lavish spectacle, a perception that excessive display did not have the same energy that less expensive shows had. Cicero also expresses a distaste for death by beast as something that appeals to less cultured tastes, even though the most genuine enthusiasm in the letter is for the animal-hunts.

Source: Cicero, *Letters to his Friends* 7.1:[20] (Letter to M. Marius, dated September of 55 BCE) . . . To be sure, the show (if you are interested) was on the most lavish scale; but it would have been little to your taste, to judge by my own. To begin with, certain performers honored the occasion by returning to the boards, from which I thought they had honored their reputation by retiring . . . I need not give you further details – you know the other shows. They did not even have the sprightliness which one mostly finds in ordinary shows – one lost all sense of gaiety in watching the elaborate productions. These I don't doubt you are very well content to have missed. What pleasure is there in getting a Clytemnestra with six hundred mules or a Trojan Horse with three thousand mixing bowls or a variegated display of cavalry and infantry equipment in some battle or other? The public gaped at all this; it would not have amused you at all . . . Or perhaps, having scorned gladiators, you are sorry not to have seen the athletes! Pompey himself admits that they were a waste of time and midday oil! That leaves the *venationes*, two every day for five days, magnificent – nobody says otherwise.

But what pleasure can a cultivated man get out of seeing a weak human being torn to pieces by a powerful animal or a splendid animal transfixed by a hunting spear? Anyhow, if these sights are worth seeing, you have seen them often; and we spectators saw nothing new.

Julius Caesar's enduring popular support was sustained and strengthened throughout his career by a "package" of popular expenditures, including public building and spectacles. When he was granted the special concession of being able to run for a second consulship in absentia, he let it be known that he would produce *munera* and an *epulum*, or public banquet, on behalf of his deceased daughter Julia. Julia had been a popular presence in Rome, wife to Pompey as well as Caesar's only child; this new precedent of honoring women with such presentations points forward to the public prominence of female members of the imperial family during the Principate.

Source: Suetonius, *Julius Caesar* 26:[21] Caesar neglected no expense in winning popularity, both as a private citizen and as a candidate for his second consulship. He began building a new Forum . . . and paid more than a million gold pieces for the site alone. Then he announced a gladiatorial show and a public banquet (*epulum*) in memory of his daughter Julia – an unprecedented event; and to create as much excitement among the commons as possible, had the banquet catered for partly by his own household, partly by the market contractors. He also issued an order that any well-known gladiator who failed to win the approval of the Circus should be forcibly rescued from execution and kept alive.

Costs

All these elaborate preparations for spectacle came at a price. A political career in the late Republic required huge amounts of cash; elites, whose wealth tended not to be in liquid form, went heavily into debt to finance candidacy. The office of aedile demanded considerable financial resources, just for the ordinary games; the additional presentation of *munera* and the increasingly glitzy nature of Roman spectacle made this a heavy burden indeed. By the end of the Republic, the level of expenditure on games by politicians was exorbitant, even ruinous. This was particularly true of the *munera*, which were private, not part of the official calendar and were thus in a special class. Republican notables took it upon themselves to offer gladiatorial games; there was no technical obligation for them to do so. As a result, the cost of giving such spectacles was met by the *editores* alone. This cost could be quite high as noted by Polybius in the mid-second century.

Source: Polybius 31.28:[22] On the occasion of their father's[23] funeral Fabius wished to give a gladiatorial show, but because of the immense cost of such entertainments, he was unable to meet the expense, whereupon Scipio provided half the amount out of his own resources. The total cost of such a show, if it is mounted on such a lavish scale, is not less than thirty talents.[24]

Caesar incurred huge debt to finance his career, but given his remarkable success, he probably considered the money well-spent. Some expressed skepticism about the ramping up of spectacle obligation as part of the price of power. Cicero sees it as a necessary evil, pointing to the long tradition of expenditure by aediles and to the expediency of living up to public expectations.

Source: Cicero, *On Duties* 2.57–58:[25] In our own country, even in the good old times, even the most high-minded citizens were generally expected to produce grandiose displays during the year when they were serving as aediles... [Mamercus'] refusal to seek office as aedile, on grounds of the expense involved, meant that later on he was rejected for the consulship. In other words, since there is a popular demand for these displays, a sensible man is obliged to submit; even if he cannot summon up any enthusiasm for the idea... Another reason why he has to comply is that there are occasions when generosity of this kind towards the public will help him to achieve some more truly significant and useful purposes at a future date.

There were limits, however; Cicero suggests that only an aedile should be expending huge sums on games, that, indeed, the only reason to present spectacles is the political one, having to do with the expectations of one's constituency and their capacity to remember any neglect of such obligations and punish the politician in his later career. Reverent commemoration of the deceased is no longer a sufficient purpose; in the following letter, Milo as "only" an executor is under no obligation to offer games and therefore should not be beggaring himself to put together funeral spectacle.

Source: Cicero, *Letters to His Brother Quintus* 3.8.6:[26] (Rome, late November 54 BCE)... [T. Annius Milo] is preparing games on a most magnificent scale, at a cost, I assure you, that no one has ever exceeded. It is foolish, on two or even three accounts, to give games that were not demanded – he has already given a magnificent show of gladiators; he cannot afford it; he is only an executor, and might have reflected that he is now an executor, not an aedile.

Cicero claims that Milo went through three fortunes in the presentation of spectacles as part of his candidacy for the consulship. In his defense of Milo on charges in the death of Clodius, Cicero pleads that Milo spent so hugely not out of personal ambition but because he wanted to safeguard the Republic from truly dangerous politicians, like the demagogue Clodius. Granted, Cicero is trying to have Milo acquitted of murder charges and so would be presenting Milo's motivation in the most positive and persuasive light. Still, Cicero voices concern in a number of contexts that presentation of games distracts politicians from their "real" service to Rome, and here he suggests that Milo's games have overshadowed his other leadership.

Source: Cicero, *For Milo* 95:[27] Milo reminds us about the plebs and the lowest rabble, which was threatening your [i.e. the Senate's] possessions under the leadership of P. Clodius, and the fact that he worked to safeguard your livelihood not only by turning them with his good example but also by winning them over by spending his three patrimonies; he is not worried that, having pleased the people with his gladiatorial shows, he won't win you over with his distinctive services on behalf of the republic.

In 52 BCE, G. Scribonius Curio gave extremely elaborate games in honor of his father, for which a marvelous mechanized venue was constructed at great expense (see chapter 2). When these events were still in the planning phase, Cicero wrote to Curio about how games were not the best way to go about building political power, with a number of disadvantages arguing against reliance on showmanship to gain support. The games were not the best way to build up a support base. The high cost limits one's options for campaigning, nor do they really demonstrate a candidate's capacity for leadership: they display wealth, not worth. Besides, the money could be put to better purposes, as could the organization and networking required to pull the games together. Cicero suggests that Curio's personal abilities will serve him better politically than wasting his energies and funds on games. Note that it is "the friends" of Curio, i.e. his fellow elites, who are dissuading him from currying popular favor with spectacles, rather than "the people." Nevertheless, Cicero does recognize that nothing pulls people in so much as spectacle.

Source: Cicero, *Letters to His Friends* 2.3:[28] (Letter to Curio dating to the first half of 53) Rupa [acting as Curio's agent] was ready and willing to announce a *munus* in your name, but I and all your friends thought that no step should be taken in your absence by which you would be committed on your return . . . Do realize that you are returning at a juncture in which your gifts of nature, application and fortune will count for more in winning you the highest political prizes than will *munera*. Nobody admires the capacity to give shows, which is a matter of means, not personal qualities; and everybody is sick and tired of them. . . . Be sure that the highest expectations have been formed – all is expected of you that may be expected of the highest qualities and talents. If you are prepared to meet those hopes worthily, and I am confident you are, you will give us, your friends, and all your countrymen, and your country, the greatest of *munera*[29] – and many of them.

Nor is the political purpose for games truly a legitimate one, for Cicero, at least. Cicero is skeptical about the positive value offered not just by games, but by any "event" spending done by Rome's magistrates. This is cheap spending for immediate purposes, nearly bribery, not true beneficence. Here Cicero extols, instead, the "proper" use of wealth to strengthen ties within the ruling class.

Source: Cicero, *On Duties* 2.55–56:[30] In general, there are two sorts of liberal people: some are spendthrifts, some are generous. The spendthrifts are those who pour their cash into feasts and distributions of meat, into shows of gladiators and the equipment of wild-beast shows, and into the kind of spending that will leave behind either no memory of it or only a short one. Generous men, on the other hand, are those who, with their own resources, ransom prisoners from bandits, or underwrite the debts of their friends, or help friends in acquiring or in expanding property.

Some of the less-obvious costs of spectacle, i.e. the expenditure of energy and time, is demonstrated by a series of letters reflecting Caelius Rufus' difficulty in getting enough animals to enhance his aedilician games. He began his efforts well before being elected to office, deputizing friends abroad, like Cicero, to assemble the panthers and other such beasts and ship them to Rome.

Source: Cicero, *Letters to His Friends* 8.2:[31] (Letter from Caelius Rufus, dated early June, 51) . . . I have got one nobleman to contend with [in Caelius' campaign for aedile] and one acting-nobleman – M. Octavius, son of Gnaeus, and G. Hirrus are standing with me. I am telling you this because I know how eagerly you will wait for the result of our elections on Hirrus' account. As soon as you hear I am [aedile] designate, please see to the matter of the panthers.

Source: Cicero *Letters to His Friends* 8.9:[32] (Letter from Caelius Rufus, dated September 2, 51) . . . In almost every letter I have written to you I have mentioned the subject of panthers. It will be little to your credit that Patiscus has sent ten panthers for Curio and you not many times as many [for me]. Curio has given me those same animals and another ten from Africa . . . If you will but keep it in mind and send for beasts from Cibyra and write to Pamphylia likewise (they say the hunting is better there) the trick will be done. I am all the more exercised about this now because I think I shall have to make all my arrangements apart from my colleague. Do be a good fellow and give yourself an order about it. . . . As soon as the creatures are caught, you have the men I sent in connection with Sittius' bond to look after their feeding and transport to Rome.

Source: Cicero, *Letters to His Friends* 8.8:[33] (Letter from Caelius Rufus, dated early October of 51) . . . Curio is behaving handsomely to me and has made me a somewhat onerous present in the shape of the African panthers which were imported for his show. Had he not done that, one might have let the thing go. As it is, I have to give it. So, as I have asked you all along, please see that I have a few beasts from your part of the world.

Source: Cicero *Letters to his Friends* 2.11:[34] (Letter from Cicero to Caelius Rufus, dated April 4, 50) . . . About the panthers, the usual hunters are doing their best on my instructions. But the creatures are in remarkably short supply, and those we have are said to be complaining bitterly because they are the only beings in my province who have to fear designs against their safety. Accordingly, they are reported to have decided to leave this province and go to Caria.

Control

The increasingly competitive nature of politics in the mid to late Republic involved the intensification of individual politicians' efforts to woo new constituents alongside their efforts to limit rivals' ability to do so. Attempts were made by the senate to exert control over the extraordinary games in several ways: by refusing to grant a triumph, by limiting the scale of extraordinary victory games by curtailing funding resources, and by controlling the timing of games (even those considered specifically "private", like *munera*) by excluding them as much as possible from the campaign cycle and the assignment of provincial governorships to recoup financial losses. Efforts were also made to limit access to the prime resource of gladiators; although this had an effect on games-planning, this was its secondary purpose, as gladiators themselves were also becoming a tool of Roman politics.

Games held to fulfill a victory vow were paid for by the general who made the vow, presumably out of the booty acquired during the campaign. M. Fulvius Nobilior set a new precedent by imposing a special tax on the conquered after his campaigns in Greece from 198 to 187 BCE, specifically to pay for the games.

Source: Livy 39.5:[35] [M. Fulvius] went on to tell them that on the day when he took Ambracia he had vowed the Great Games to Jupiter Optimus Maximus, and that for this celebration a hundred pounds of gold had been contributed by the cities; he asked the Senate to direct that this sum should be kept separate, out of the money which he intended to display in his triumphal procession and then to deposit in the treasury. The Senate gave orders that the pontiffs[36] should be consulted whether it was necessary to spend the whole amount [i.e. the whole hundred pounds] on the games. The pontiffs replied that the precise sum to be spent was irrelevant to the religious aspect of the festival; the Senate accordingly left it to Fulvius to decide how much he should spend, provided that he did not go beyond a total of 80,000 sesterces.

The precedent of limiting total expenditure for victory games established for Nobilior was then applied to later triumphant generals: Q. Fulvius Flaccus, consul in 179 BCE, would be compelled to use his own resources, up to the total of 80,000 sesterces, and not collect any *ad hoc* funding from subject peoples or allies. Presumably his personal wealth had been increased somewhat by his campaigns in Spain, even if the territory was not so rich in portable booty as the Greek area.

Source: Livy 40.44:[37] [Q. Fulvius] had vowed, he said, on the day when he had last fought with the Celtiberians, to give games to Jupiter Optimus Maximus and a temple to Fortuna Equestris; for this purpose money had been collected for him by the Spaniards. It was decreed that the games should be held and that two commissioners should be chosen to contract for the temple. As to the cost, the limit was set that a greater sum might not be spent for the games than the amount that had been decreed to Fulvius Nobilior when he gave his games after the Aetolian war, and it was voted too that he should not invite, compel or accept contributions for these or do anything contrary to that decree of the senate which had been passed regarding games in the consulship of L. Aemilius and Gn. Baebius (182 BCE). The senate passed this latter decree because of the lavish expenditures made on games by Ti. Sempronius the aedile, which had been a burden, not only on Italy and the allies of the Latin confederacy, but on outside provinces as well.

These limitations restricted the amounts which could be requisitioned from conquered peoples and the Italians and may have had some effect, for a time, on triumphal expenditure. It did not limit the money spent overall on games, which kept going up as the political potential of entertainment was enhanced. Magistrates spent their own money on the ordinary games they presented, in addition to the allotment from the treasury, to ensure that their *spectacula* would have the desired impact.

A series of legislative efforts were made in the first century to manage the use of spectacle, here, by controlling how they were used in the political cycle, how they featured as political bribery. The *Lex Calpurnia* on electioneering of 67 imposed fines, removal from office and loss of the *ius imaginum*[38] on those convicted of electoral bribery. What, exactly, could be interpreted as electoral bribery was in dispute in 63 BCE, a year when Rome (with Cicero as consul) was also struggling to deal with Catiline's efforts to disrupt elections and overthrow the government. L. Licinius Murena, elected for consul in 62 BCE (after impressive games sponsored as praetor a few years before), was hauled into court and charged with bribery during the campaign: the bribe was not cash but highly valued seats at a gladiatorial spectacle. At state-sponsored shows, Roman elites typically acquired blocks of seating from officials and magistrates, in accordance with the strength of their personal connections to those in charge of the show. In turn, they distributed these passes to their friends and clients, on the basis of ambition or generosity, as Cicero claims. Since gladiatorial combats at this time were still "private" and thus not necessarily following the custom for state-sponsored shows, to whom could these tickets be handed out? Murena had not distributed tickets to his friends and clients, i.e. those with a prior relationship to him who would expect these benefits, but rather to people who may have been the clients of others, whom he may have been trying to woo into supporting his political career. So does this indirect bribery, this opportunistic generosity of Murena's, count as a campaign violation? Cicero says no, that such generosity is an obligation of Rome's ruling class.

> Source: Cicero, *For Murena* 67, 72:[39] You pointed out that the Senate, on my proposal, passed a decree that it should be deemed a violation of the *Lex Calpurnia* if men were paid to meet the candidates, if they were hired to escort them, if seats at gladiatorial games were given out wholesale by tribes, or if lunches were likewise given out wholesale ... "But seating was given out by tribes and invitations to lunch distributed wholesale." Murena abstained entirely from such practices ... and his friends engaged in them only in moderation, and as far as custom allows. Nevertheless, this reminds me how many votes, Servius, these complaints in the senate lost us. For when was there ever a time, in living memory or in the memory of our fathers, when people did not want, whether from self-interested motives or out of simple generosity, to give their friends and fellow-tribesmen seats in the circus or the forum? These are the rewards and benefits that poorer people receive from their fellow tribesmen by time-honored custom.

Earlier in 63, Cicero himself had sponsored legislation specifically against the direct link between *munera* and campaigning: the *Lex Tullia* mandated that politicians could not present gladiatorial shows within two years of running for office. The bribery legislation was publicly scrutinized in the

Roman courtroom in 56 BCE, when Publius Sestius was charged with irregular campaigning tactics and with the use of violence, including the use of gladiators as "muscle," while tribune in 57 BCE. The interrogation of Publius Vatinius by Cicero in his speech defending Sestius includes the denunciation of Vatinius' illegal action of holding *munera* in connection with campaign for public office (Vatinius was running for praetor during 56). Cicero notes an exception to the *Lex Tullia*, if it can be proven, by reference to testamentary wishes, that the *munera* are genuinely offered as funeral celebrations.

Source: Cicero, *For Sestius* 133–135:[40] [Vatinius] despises that law which expressly forbids any one to exhibit shows of gladiators within two years of his having stood, or being about to stand, for any office. And in that, O judges, I cannot sufficiently marvel at his rashness. He acts most openly against the law; he does so and yet is neither able to slip out of the consequences of a trial by his pleasant manner, nor to struggle out of them by his popularity, nor to break down the laws and courts of justice by his wealth and influence. What can induce the fellow to be so intemperate? I imagine it is out of his excessive desire for popularity, that he bought that troupe of gladiators, so beautiful, noble, and magnificent. He knew the inclination of the people, he saw that great clamors and gatherings of the people would ensue. And elated with this expectation, and burning with a desire for glory, he could not restrain himself from bringing forward those gladiators, of whom he himself was the finest specimen. If that were the motive for his violation of the law, and if he were prompted by zeal to please the people on account of the recent kindness of the Roman people to himself, still no one would pardon him; but as the fact is that this band did not consist of men picked out of those who were for sale, but of men bought out of jails, and adorned with gladiatorial names, while he drew lots to see whom he would call Samnites and whom *provocatores*,[41] who could avoid having fears as to what might be the end of such licentiousness and such undisguised contempt for the laws? But he brings forward two arguments in his defence. First of all, "I exhibit," says he, "*bestiarii*, and the law only speaks of gladiators." A very clever idea! Listen now to a statement which is still more ingenious. He says that he has not exhibited gladiators, but one single gladiator; and that he has limited the whole of his aedileship to this one *munus*. A true aedileship truly. One lion, two hundred *bestiarii*. However, let him urge this defence. I wish him to feel confidence in his case; for he is in the habit of appealing to the tribunes of the people, and to use violent means to upset those tribunals in which he has no confidence.

Further legislation is linked to the danger hinted at by Cicero: the potential for violence represented by gladiators themselves and the increasing use of these trained fighters, not in shows, but as a coercive political tool in an increasingly turbulent Republic.

Violence

Gladiatorial *familiae* were highly visible participants in the deterioration of the Roman political system and the disruption of Roman society during the fall of the Republic. Gladiatorial games were extremely popular events which won votes for their candidate *editores*. Candidates thus had to get their hands somehow on troupes or *familiae* of fighters, which could remain in their possession for an extended period of time while the games were being organized. Once the games were over, the surviving combatants could be either sold to another ambitious politician or be kept on as a sort of bodyguard; in practice, these lethal gangs acted as political thugs for Roman political activists growing increasingly violent. The Senate was alarmed, for example, by Caesar's lavish preparations for *munera* in 65 BCE, which included a huge number of professional fighters; the senators responded by restricting the number of gladiators which any private citizen could possess within city limits.

> Source: Suetonius, *Julius Caesar* 10.2:[42] [During his aedileship] Caesar . . . put on a gladiatorial show, but he had collected so immense a troop of combatants that his terrified political opponents rushed a bill through the House, limiting the number of gladiators that anyone might keep in Rome; consequently far fewer pairs fought than had been advertised.

The Senate's fear seems justifiable, given the lingering fear of Spartacus and the alleged involvement of gladiators in the Catilinarian conspiracy in 63 BCE. The situation turned ugly in the 50s, when a number of politicians made overt use of gladiators to further their political interests. Clodius, for example, exploited his brother's *familia* to stage a riot in 57 BCE, in order to prevent a vote on legislation to which he was opposed. The gladiators had been assembled for the aedilician games Clodius anticipated hosting the following year, hoping for success at the elections of January 56. Cicero points to the violation of precedence this represented: instead of using these performers to persuade the public, the public was victimized by the gladiators, as if the people of Rome were the unfortunate losers in a vast *munera*.

> Source: Dio Cassius 39.7:[43] Many disorderly proceedings were the result, chief of which was that during the very taking of the vote on the measure [to recall Cicero from exile] Clodius, knowing that the multitude would be on Cicero's side, took the gladiators that his brother held in readiness for the funeral games of Marcus, his relative, and rushing into the assemblage, wounded many and killed many others. Consequently, the measure was not passed.

Source: Cicero, *For Sestius* 77–78:[44] You remember gentlemen, how the Tiber was filled that day with the bodies of citizens, how the sewers were choked, how blood was mopped up from the Forum with sponges, enough to make everyone think that so great an array and so magnificent a show of gladiators was not provided by any private person, nor by any plebeian, but by a patrician and a praetor.[45] . . . Are you [i.e. Clodius] to send into the Forum before daybreak your raw gladiators, provided for an expected aedileship, with a pack of assassins discharged from prison? Are you to wreak great slaughter? Are you to drive magistrates from the Rostra?

This was not an isolated incident; T. Annius Milo, a rival of Clodius, used tactics very similar to his, leading up to Clodius' eventual death in a bloody skirmish outside Rome.

Source: Dio Cassius 39.8:[46] While contesting this very point [the timing of selection of aedile and quaestor] Milo caused much disturbance, and at last himself collected some gladiators and others like minded with himself and kept continually coming to blows with Clodius, so that bloodshed occurred throughout practically the whole city.

Some Roman aristocrats, Julius Caesar and Cicero's good friend Pomponius Atticus included, invested in gladiatorial *ludi* or training schools as a profitable enterprise; political Romans also could see the advantage in having spectacle resources on hand. Even at the distance mandated by law, it was feared these schools could be a military asset in the event of civil war. This threat is behind contradictory stories about Caesar's gladiatorial school in Capua and the kind of danger it represented in 49 BCE, in the face of Caesar's invasion of Italy. The version preserved in the pro-Caesarean tradition has L. Cornelius Lentulus Crus, one of the consuls of that year and an opponent of Caesar, scrambling frantically to put together some resistance to Caesar and resorting to desperate measures, such as drafting gladiators, to do so. Supposedly, he gave up the plan when he realized what a negative impression this would leave. Cicero's contemporary account of the situation asserts the gladiators themselves presented a danger, apparently planning to take advantage of the civil uproar to escape from custody and, no doubt, run amok.

Source: Caesar, *Civil War* 1.14:[47] It was at Capua that [the opponents of Caesar] first took heart and collected themselves and began a levy among the colonists who had been settled there by the Julian law. The gladiators whom Caesar had in a training school there were brought into the forum by Lentulus, who encouraged them with the hope of freedom, gave them horses, and ordered them to follow him; later, because this action was universally condemned, on the advice of his friends he distributed them among the households of the Campanian Assembly so that they could be kept under guard.

Source: Cicero, *Letter to Atticus* 7.14:[48] (January 25, 49) . . . Pompey has expressed a wish for me to go to Capua and help with the levy, in which the response among the Campanian settlers is less than enthusiastic. Caesar's gladiators at Capua, about whom I earlier sent you a false report based on Torquatus' letter, have been very sensibly distributed by Pompey among the population, two per household. There were 1,000 shields in the *ludus* and they were said to be going to break out. Certainly a valuable precaution in the public interest.

Shows as political assembly

As games became more regularized and the popular will became a more important feature of political persuasion, the shows offered the opportunity for the audience to express popular feeling on important matters. Cicero argues for the spectacle venue as a legitimate and representative assembly of the Roman electorate, alongside more overtly political gatherings, such as elections and the *contiones*; he contrasts this with informal public meetings called by populist demagogues, such as Clodius, outside a formal and traditional venue. His speech for Sestius contains extended analysis of how one can discern the will of the people from their reactions in the audience at spectacles. Cicero's analysis in this speech has been influenced by his own experiences in 58 BCE, when political rivalry resulted in Cicero's exile from Rome and substantial loss of property, as well as public humiliation imposed on Cicero by the sentence. His suspicion of *contiones* and *comitiae* is proabably based on their condemnation of him, and the role played by his opponent P. Clodius in crafting this outcome.

Source: Cicero, *For Sestius* 106:[49] For in three places the opinions and sympathies of the Roman people concerning public matters can be demonstrated; in a public meeting, at the elections, and in the communal attendance at games and gladiatorial shows.

How it is that the people air their views at spectacles is then explained by Cicero. Applause or hissing may seem, to a modern reader, to be fairly generalized means of declaring a political stance; one should keep in mind the political system of the Roman Republic, in which the general body of the citizenry did not personally participate in policy debates. Cicero lauds the "sincerity" of this kind of popular expression as well as its wisdom in selecting righteous targets for their clapping.

Source: Cicero, *For Sestius* 115:[50] Let us now come to the shows . . . expressions of public opinion at *Comitiae* and *Contiones* are sometimes the voice of truth, but sometimes they are falsified and corrupt: at theatrical and gladiatorial shows it is said to be common for some feeble and scanty applause to be started by a hired and unprincipled claque, and yet, when that happens, it is easy to see how and by whom it is started and what the honest part of the audience does.

Cicero acknowledges that claques could, through rehearsed chants, manufacture a false "will of the people", but suggests that this can be easily detected and disregarded by Rome's leaders and by the "honest" citizens. True popular opinion was spontaneous and universal and directed its energies toward the "best men," by which Cicero generally means the conservative elites. One of Cicero's letters to Atticus from 59 discusses the multiple expressions of the people's views specifically on the so-called First Triumvirate. There was uproarious laughter at ridicule of Pompey, the silence of mute disapproval for Caesar (who is actually present) and cheers for Curio the younger, which annoys Caesar. Pompey and Caesar take the opposition expressed at the shows very seriously and even contemplate legislative reprisals.

Source: Cicero, *Letter to Atticus* 2.19:[51] (July of 59) Pompey, the man I loved, has, to my infinite sorrow, ruined his own reputation. They[52] hold no one by affection, and I fear they will be forced to use terror . . . The feeling of the people was shown as clearly as possible in the theatre and at the shows. For at the gladiators both master and supporters were overwhelmed with hisses. At the *Ludi Apollinares* the actor Diphilus made a pert allusion to Pompey, in the words: "By our misfortunes thou art Great." He was encored countless times. When he delivered the line, "The time will come when thou wilt deeply mourn / That self-same valor," the whole theatre broke out into applause, and so on with the rest. For the verses do seem exactly as though they were written by some enemy of Pompey's to hit the time. "If neither laws nor customs can control," etc., caused great sensation and loud shouts. Caesar entered as the applause died away, followed by the younger Curio. The latter received an ovation such as used to be given to Pompey when the constitution was still intact. Caesar was much annoyed. A message is said to have been sent flying off to Pompey at Capua. They are offended with the equestrians, who rose to their feet and cheered Curio and are at war with everybody. They are threatening the *Lex Roscia* and even the grain law.

Cicero's sensitivity to nuances of applause and jeers stretched to include an appreciation for timing and the ability to unpack gesture and expression, as well as, no doubt, audible emoting, to indicate political support of specific issues as well as condemnation of, for example, the agenda of his political opponent Clodius.

> Source: Cicero, *For Sestius* 117:[53]: What feelings the Roman People showed they entertained at that time was made plain in both ways [i.e. at both the explicitly political venue of the senate hearing and at the shows]. First, when the decree of the Senate had been heard, unanimous applause was given to the measure itself, and to the Senate, before they came in; next, to the senators, when they returned one by one from the Senate to see the shows. But when the consul[54] himself, who gave the entertainment, took his seat, people stood up with outstretched hands, giving thanks, and weeping for joy openly showed their goodwill and sympathy for myself. But when Clodius arrived, that raging fiend, at the height of his frenzy, the Roman People could scarcely restrain themselves, men could scarcely help wreaking their hatred upon his foul and abominable person; cries, menacing gestures, loud curses came in a flood from all. But why do I speak of the spirit and courage of the Roman People, when at last after long servitude they had a glimpse of freedom, in their attitude towards a man whom even the actors did not spare to his face as he sat in the audience, though he was then a candidate for an aedileship!

Although Cicero himself had been the glad recipient of popular support, in his speech for Sestius he declares that the most-favored target of such approval had been Sestius, the defendant. The fact that this alleged declaration of enormous support had taken place at *munera* hosted by Scipio Nasica may have been something of a disappointment to Scipio Nasica, who as presenter of the spectacle might have hoped to be the primary object of the crowd's gratitude and affection.

> Source: Cicero, *For Sestius* 124–125:[55] But the strongest expression of the judgment of the whole Roman People was plainly given by an audience at gladiatorial games. They were a show given by Scipio, one worthy both of the giver and of Quintus Metellus in whose honor it was held.[56] And it was that kind of show which is attended by crowds of all classes in great numbers, and which has a special charm for the masses. Into that crowd of spectators came Publius Sestius, then tribune of the plebs . . . and showed himself to the People, not that he was eager for applause, but he wished that our enemies themselves might recognize the goodwill of the whole Roman People . . . At once from all the spectators' seats right down from the Capitol, and from all the barriers of the Forum, there were heard such shouts of applause, that it was said that the whole Roman People had never shown greater nor more manifest unanimity in any cause . . . I for my part think that there has never been a greater crowd than at that gladiatorial show, neither at any *contio* nor indeed at any *comitia*. What then

did this countless throng of men, this unanimous expression of the feeling of the entire Roman People . . . what did it declare except that the welfare and honor of the best citizens was dear to the whole Roman People?

Alongside the advantage to be gained from presenting spectacle, advantage to be built on in the exchange, verbal or not, between the *editor* and the spectators, there was also a real risk of evoking a negative reaction from the target audience. This could be prompted by a "failure" of the spectacle; Pompey's elephant show of 55 BCE became a notorious example of beneficence gone bad.

Source: Cicero, *Letter to his Friends* 7.1:[57] . . . The last day was for the elephants. The groundlings showed much astonishment thereat, but no enjoyment. There was even an impulse of compassion, a feeling that the beasts had something human about them.

Source: Pliny, *Natural History* 8.20–21:[58] In Pompey's second consulship [in 55 BCE], when the temple of Venus Victrix was dedicated, twenty elephants (some say seventeen) fought in the Circus against Gaetulians armed with throwing-spears. One elephant put up a fantastic fight and, although its feet were badly wounded, crawled on its knees against the attacking bands. It snatched away their shields and hurled them into the air . . . All the elephants, en masse, tried to break out through the iron railings that enclosed them, much to the discomfiture of the spectators . . . But when Pompey's elephants had given up hope of escape, they played on the sympathy of the crowd, entreating them with indescribable gestures. They moaned, as if wailing, and caused the spectators such distress that, forgetting Pompey and his lavish display specially devised to honor them, they rose in a body, in tears, and heaped dire curses on Pompey, the effects of which he soon suffered.

Fear of generating a bad response exerted some power over Roman politicians, shaping their public presence by changing their plans for day-to-day activity. Indeed, Piso had refused to go to the dedication games for the Theater of Pompey in 55 BCE; Cicero claims that this was due to his fear of rejection of the crowd, that their cat-calls might turn to body-blows.

Source: Cicero, *Against Piso* 64–65:[59] Come on, the senate hates you . . . The Roman equestrians cannot bear the sight of you . . . The Roman people wishes your destruction . . . All Italy execrates you . . . Test this excessive and universal hatred if you dare. The most carefully prepared and magnificent games within the memory of man are now at hand, games not only like none ever shown before, but such that we cannot even imagine how any like them ever could be exhibited in future. Trust yourself to the people ... Are you afraid of [their] hisses? ... Are you afraid that there will be no acclamations raised in your honor? Surely it does not become a philosopher even to consider such a thing as that. You are afraid that violent hands may be laid on you. For pain is an evil, as you assert. The opinion which men entertain of you, disgrace, infamy, baseness – these are all empty words, mere trifles. But about this I have no question. He will never dare to come near the games.

Appian depicts the efforts to sway popular opinion in 44 BCE, in the months following the death of Caesar when domination of the Roman government swiftly passed from one set of leaders to another. At this moment, the interests of Antony seem to align with those of Caesar's assassins, who have been forced out of Rome. Here, games become the means of persuasion and the venue for an articulation of the will of the people, heavily prompted by the organizers. Cash payoffs to the audience by Octavian, cloaked as his performance of filial duty, stymie the efforts.

Source: Appian, *Civil War* 3.23–24:[60] The games were now approaching, which Gaius Antonius, the brother of Antony, was about to give on behalf of Brutus, the praetor, as he attended also to the other duties of the praetorship which fell upon him in the absence of Brutus. Lavish expense was incurred in the preparations for these games, in the hope that the people, gratified by the spectacle, would recall Brutus and Cassius. Octavian, on the other hand, trying to win the mob over to his own side, distributed the money [to pay out the legacy granted by Caesar to the Roman people in his will] derived from the sale of his property among the head men of the voting tribes by turns, to be divided by them among the first comers ... [the people] showed their feelings clearly while Brutus' games were in progress, lavish as these were. Although a certain number, who had been hired for the purpose, shouted that Brutus and Cassius should be recalled, and the rest of the spectators were thus caught up in a feeling of pity for them, crowds ran in and stopped the games until the spectators stopped the demand for the recall.

Cicero was an eye-witness to this competition for the support of the spectators at games in 44. In his denunciation of Antony, he emphasizes the chants on behalf of Brutus as the "true" expression of the people's will.

Source: Cicero, *Philippics* 1.36:[61] Think of the clamor raised by countless citizens at gladiatorial shows, think of all the versified popular slogans, think of those endless acclamations in front of the statue of Pompeius ... Did you attach no importance to the applause at the *Ludi Apollinares*? – rather I should call it the testimony and judgment of the entire Roman people. What an honor for the men who were prevented by armed violence from being present in person – though they were present in the hearts and emotions of the people of Rome! ... Brutus was the man for whom the cheering and the prize were intended. He could not himself attend the games that were displayed in his name, but the Romans who witnessed that sumptuous show paid their tribute to him in his absence and sought to comfort the sadness which they felt because their liberator was not with them by incessant cheers and shouts of sympathy.

Imperial Spectacle

The Republican tradition of using public games as an enhancement of political achievement was extended and elaborated during the empire, when the number of days allocated to each of the *ludi* was inflated in commemoration of accomplishments of the emperor and his family; archaic festivals, newly resurrected and revised, were brought "up-to-date" with the addition of *ludi* to the old-fashioned rituals. The nature of politics was radically changed under the Principate, however. Augustus' establishment of the imperial monarchy meant that all leadership was subordinated to that of the emperor; individual senators would no longer compete to dominate Roman politics, so the typical Republican motivation for presenting spectacles, i.e. the wooing of the electorate, was no longer present. The meaning and purpose of the games was adjusted to fit the emperor's agenda.

Augustus centralized the institution of the games, to a great extent, and made significant provisions in the infrastructure of support. Under Augustus, the first permanent amphitheater was built in Rome and imperial *ludi* were established, to supply the needs of the games. Augustus also regularized access to the spectacles, particularly for the elite, by mandating that spectators be seated by status. Venues for *munera* began to spread across the empire to key locations, particularly administrative centers and military zones, nexuses of contact between Roman authority and the subjects of empire. The emperor took control of spectacle of all kinds. Outside Rome, the local officials acted as the agents of the center, not only in providing the arena facilities, but also in sponsoring the events as local *editores*. As the representatives of Augustus and of the Roman power structure, they had much to gain from the assertion of control and the validation of the hierarchy.

Even so, during the empire *munera* and *venationes* were presented on an extraordinary basis, for the most part. Although the Roman people were guaranteed a certain minimum of such blood spectacles as part of the regular calendar, the potential persuasive impact of these games made it desirable that the emperor alone control the presentation of particularly lavish, and politically charged, *munera*. In this, as in other matters, Augustus set the standard by providing for *munera* to be presented as part of the "ordinary" games with certain limitations: these events, sanctioned formally by the Senate, were restricted in size and expenditure.

Ordinary spectacle

In 22 BCE, the praetors were put in charge of the ordinary or official imperial *munera*. These took place in December, with more days devoted to gladiatorial spectacle being gradually added over the years; by the fourth century ten days were given over to ordinary *munera*.[62] They were to receive a certain amount of public funding for these spectacles, which could be topped up by the individual magistrate, but on a limited basis: each could spend no more than any of his peers. They were limited as well to sixty pairs, maximum, of fighters. The nature of these limitations points to the fact that Augustus wanted to decrease the utility of these events in the competition for elite prestige. To put a more positive spin on his agenda, Augustus wanted to eliminate the waste of resources and manipulation of vulgar emotions entailed in the politicization of the games, decried by Cicero and others as the corruption of Republican politics. He recognized that the shows were important, but minimized the negative effects of the late Republican games by limiting the political impact they could have. By giving control to the praetors, instead of the aediles as in Republican tradition, Augustus cut back on how much games could serve as career builders for budding politicians.[63] These limits were continued under Tiberius.

Source: Dio Cassius 54.2:[64] He committed the charge of all the festivals to the praetors, commanding that an appropriation should be given them from the public treasury, and also forbidding any one of them to spend more than another from his own means on these festivals, or to give a gladiatorial combat unless the senate decreed it, or, in fact, oftener than twice in each year or with more than one hundred and twenty men.

Source: Dio Cassius 54.17:[65] . . . later [Augustus] raised [the senatorial rating] to one million sesterces . . . And because of this he allowed the praetors who so desired to spend on the public festivals three times the amount granted them from the treasury.

Caligula eased up on the imperial control of the *munera* and other spectacles, although the analysis of his motives provided by Dio Cassius does not indicate this was done to foster uninhibited campaigning by senatorials nor to encourage public generosity among a wider range of potential benefactors. Dio reads this action as part of a pattern of hostility toward the elites expressed by Caligula, hostility that often turned to actual bloodshed. This, in turn, fits the pattern of condemnation of tyrants, alienated from the elites by their bad behavior, abuse of power and reliance on popular support that bespeaks their insecurity in ruling. In this instance, Caligula is trying to entrap and bankrupt Rome's ruling class.

> Source: Dio Cassius 59.13–14:[66] [In 39 CE] Gaius now became consul again . . . he held the office for only thirty days . . . during these and the following days many of the foremost men perished in fulfillment of sentences of condemnation . . . and many others of less prominence [died] in gladiatorial combats . . . At the same time that he was perpetrating these murders, apparently because he was in urgent need of funds, he devised another scheme for getting money, as follows. He would sell the survivors in the gladiatorial combats at an excessive valuation to the consuls, praetors and others, not only to willing purchasers, but also to others who were compelled very much against their will to give such exhibitions at the Circensian games, and in particular he sold them to the men specially chosen by lot to have charge of such contests (For he ordered that two praetors should be chosen by lot to have charge of the gladiatorial games, just as had formerly been the custom); and he himself would sit on the auctioneer's platform and keep raising the bids. Many also came from outside to put in rival bids, the more so as he allowed any who so wished to employ a greater number of gladiators than the law permitted and because he frequently visited them himself. So the people bought them for large sums, some because they really wanted them, others with the idea of gratifying Gaius, and the majority, consisting of those who had a reputation for wealth, from a desire to take advantage of this excuse to spend some of their substance and thus by becoming poorer save their lives.[67]

Claudius, in an effort to demonstratively cut back on the spectacular excesses of Caligula, placed limitations on honors given the imperial family and formalized the games and rituals affiliated with the Imperial Cult. His ban on *munera* was meant to make the point that his regime was to be austere and well within the traditions of Rome that had been so flouted by Caligula. Later, Claudius gave responsibility for the ordinary *munera* to the quaestors, the lowest of the magistracies in Rome. Sponsorship of the *munera* thus became a sort of tithe on those who were elevated into the senatorial class by being elected to this office. Tacitus interprets this as bribery, putting an extremely nostalgic spin on Republican practice as emblematic of virtuous and clean competition.

Source: Dio Cassius 60.5:[68] [Claudius] ordered the praetors not to give the customary gladiatorial exhibitions and also commanded that if anyone else gave them in any place whatsoever, it should at least not be recorded or reported that they were being given for the emperor's preservation.

Source: Tacitus, *Annals* 11.22:[69] During the same consulship (47 CE), Publius Dolabella proposed that a spectacle of gladiators should be annually exhibited at the cost of those who obtained the quaestorship. In our ancestors' days this honor had been a reward of virtue, and every citizen, with good qualities to support him, was allowed to compete for office . . . the quaestorship was obtained, without expense, by merit in the candidates or by the good nature of the electors, till at Dolabella's suggestion it was, so to speak, put up to sale.

Nero reversed Claudius' decision as one of the first actions of his reign; the context in which it appears links the quaestorian games to corruption under Claudius, to abuse of imperial judicial power and over-stepping of the boundaries of the emperor's authority. Supposedly, Nero extended the ban to the provinces, although there is no clear indication that this ban was ever enacted. Tacitus reads this as a move against corruption on the part of Nero, embedded in the "good years", i.e. the first few years of his rule when he allegedly was under the influence of responsible advisors and thus pursued a prudent and high-minded policy.

Source: Tacitus, *Annals* 13.5:[70] [At Nero's accession] several arrangements were made on the Senate's authority. No one was to receive a fee or a present for pleading a cause; the quaestors-elect were not to be under the necessity of exhibiting gladiatorial shows.

Source: Tacitus, *Annals* 13.31:[71] The emperor [in 57 CE] by an edict forbade any magistrate or procurator in the government of a province to exhibit a show of gladiators, or of wild beasts, or indeed any other public entertainment; for hitherto our subjects had been as much oppressed by such bribery as by actual extortion, while governors sought to screen by corruption the guilty deeds of arbitrary caprice.

It should be understood that the membership of the ruling class changed during the shift from Republic to Principate; the civil wars had decimated the elite on the battlefield and in proscriptions. Augustus' restoration of the Republic involved the recruitment of great numbers of Italian and, eventually, provincial, elite to fill the senatorial and equestrian ranks. These were people with no personal experience of the upper levels of Republican politics; they also had a certain obligation to the emperor, their patron, with regard to their new status. This kind of upward mobility becomes typical for the time of the emperors. Juvenal is unimpressed by Rome's nouveau elite, whom he characterizes as dishonest contractors. Their allegedly deceitful approach to exchange has warped the relationship of power in the games.

Source: Juvenal, *Satires* 3.29–40:[72] So farewell Rome, I leave you to sanitary engineers and municipal architects, fellows who by swearing black is white find it easy to land contracts for a new temple, swamp-drainage, harbor-works, river-clearance, undertaking, the lot – then pocket the profit and fraudulently file their petition in bankruptcy. These creatures used to be horn-players, stumping the provinces in road-shows, their puffed-out cheeks a familiar sight; but now they stage gladiatorial games, and at the mob's thumbs-down will butcher a loser for popularity's sake, and then move on to lease public privies. But why draw the line at that? These are such men as Fortune, by way of a joke, will sometimes raise from the gutter and make Top People.

Juvenal is also responsible for the most notorious assessment of the imperial games.

Source: Juvenal, *Satires* 10.77–81: There was a time when the People bestowed every honor – the governance of provinces, civic leadership, military command – but now they hold themselves back, now two things only do they ardently desire: bread and games.

The statement is often interpreted as an indication of Roman imperial decadence, of the disempowerment of the public which was lured away from political engagement by government food subsidies and sensational entertainment. The continuing relationship between *editor* and audience, emperor and plebs, is more complex and powerful than this suggests, as it is played out in the arena.

The emperor and the arena

Augustus, the first of Rome's emperors, recognized the good public relations value of bloody spectacular entertainment and proudly published for posterity the shows he'd presented; the permanent record on display meant that the impact of the games would transcend the time and place they were actually held. But the sheer scale of his games would ensure their endurance in the collective memory of the Roman people. Augustus' spectacles were the largest ever seen, far more splendid than anything offered by the politicians of the Late Republic.

> Source: Augustus, *Res Gestae* 22: Three times I gave gladiatorial games in my own name and five times in the names of my sons and grandsons; at these displays about ten thousand men fought . . . I gave the people twenty-six *venationes* of African animals in either the circus, the forum or the amphitheater; about thirty-five hundred animals were killed in these spectacles.

On the basis of the numbers given by the emperor, the imperial *munera* averaged 1,250 combatants, ten times the size of the praetors' games, and each of the *venationes* offered 135 animals. The cost of simply staffing the arena with sufficient personnel must have been staggering.

The occasions for the imperial spectacles varied a great deal. Most of them were given to celebrate victories and to commemorate the anniversaries of events of particular significance to Rome, typically identified as achievements of imperial family members or their birthdays or funerals. One of the earliest public actions of Octavian, long before he became monarch, was the establishment of games for Julius Caesar, his adopted father; the story circulated that the sighting of a new star at these games in 44 BCE heralded the arrival of a new god in the heavens. The cult of the deified Julius developed over time and an elaborate set of spectacles commemorated the completion of his temple on the Forum in 29 BCE.

> Source: Dio Cassius 51.22:[73] At the consecration of the shrine to Julius there were all kinds of contests . . . Wild beasts and tame animals were slain in vast numbers, among them a rhinoceros and a hippopotamus, beasts then seen for the first time in Rome. . . . Dacians and Suebi fought in groups against one another . . . The whole spectacle lasted many days, as one would expect, and there was no interruption, even though Caesar fell ill, but it was carried on in his absence under the direction of others.

In 2 BCE, the sons of Agrippa, Augustus' deceased right-hand man and son-in-law, celebrated the dedication of the Forum of Augustus and the Temple of Mars Ultor; likely one of the five important spectacles noted by Augustus in his *Res Gestae*, this was an important demonstration of dynastic leadership because of the focus on the next generation of Julio-Claudians.

> Source: Dio Cassius 55.10:[74] Augustus dedicated this temple of Mars, although he had granted to Gaius and Lucius once for all the right to consecrate all such buildings . . . and they did, in fact, have the management of the Circensian

games on this occasion, while their brother Agrippa [Postumus] took part along with the boys of the first families in the equestrian event called "Troy." Two hundred and sixty lions were slaughtered in the Circus. There was a gladiatorial combat in the Saepta, and a naval battle between the "Persians" and the "Athenians" was given on the spot where even today some relics of it are still pointed out.

The precedents established under Augustus were followed by generations of emperors after him. The largest spectacles known for Rome were presented by the emperor Trajan, who celebrated victory in his second war against the Dacians. Dio's brief account does not do justice to the scale of the event.

Source: Dio Cassius 68.15:[75] Upon Trajan's return to Rome . . . he gave spectacles on one hundred and twenty-three days, in the course of which some eleven thousand animals, both wild and tame, were slain, and ten thousand gladiators fought.

Septimius Severus combined a number of significant imperial commemorations at his games of 202 CE, when he bestowed spectacular gifts on the people in recognition of his holding of the imperial power.

Source: Dio Cassius 77.1:[76] On the occasion of his tenth anniversary of his coming to power, Severus presented to the entire populace that received the grain dole and to the soldiers of the Praetorian Guard gold pieces equal in number to the years of his reign. . . . no emperor had ever before given so much to the whole population at once; the total amount spent for the purpose was two hundred million sesterces . . . [processions and banquets followed] At this time there occurred too all sorts of spectacles in honor of Severus' return, the completion of his first ten years of power, and his victories. At these spectacles sixty wild boars . . . fought together at a signal, and among many other wild beasts that were slain were an elephant and a corocotta . . . The entire arena of the amphitheater had been constructed to resemble a boat in shape, with a capacity for holding or releasing four hundred beasts at once; and, as it suddenly fell apart, bears, lionesses, panthers, lions, ostriches, wild asses, and bisons . . . came rushing out so that seven hundred beasts total, both wild and domesticated, all at once were seen running about and were slaughtered.

The political necessity of the games is acknowledged by Fronto, tutor to the future emperor Marcus Aurelius, in an analysis that nuances the cynicism of Juvenal. Here, he considers that the presentation of spectacle elevates the positive value of the government beyond the practical and the essential to position the State as a source of pleasure, pleasure that has the capacity to unify Romans across the dividing lines of class and culture.

Source: Fronto, *Preamble to History* 17:[77] ... for the arts of peace scarcely anyone has equaled Trajan in popularity with the people ... based on the loftiest principles of political wisdom, that the Emperor did not neglect even actors and the other performers of the stage, the circus, or the amphitheater, knowing as he did that the Roman people are held fast by two things above all, the grain-dole and the shows, that the success of a government depends on games as much as more serious things ... by the spectacles the whole population is conciliated.

The emperor and political spectacle

Roman politics was transformed by the long period of civil war at the end of the Republic. The Principate that followed greatly minimized the formal opportunities for the average male citizen to participate in politics; popular assemblies were rarely held during the reign of Augustus and phased out completely under Tiberius. Under the emperors, then, venues for political expression for "the people" as a group were few. Rather than viewing this change as the result of cynical manipulation by the powerful few, countered but feebly by a jaded and lethargic electorate, we can see the spectacles as the best forum for direct interaction between ruler and ruled. On issues of pressing importance to the people, they were regularly given immediate access to the emperor, who could take instantaneous action.

It was politically expedient for the emperor to attend spectacles and, furthermore, to demonstrate active interest and at least moderate enthusiasm for the events. It was thus important for the emperor to be seen, to be a visible focus at the spectacles as the directing force behind the presentation of all such displays of Roman power and wealth. Pliny hails such occasions as opportunities for the emperor (Trajan in this case) to improve his public image, by sharing the enjoyments of Romans of all stations.

Source: Pliny, *Panegyric* 51:[78] Elsewhere the vast facade of the circus rivals the beauty of the temples, a fitting place for a nation which has conquered the world, a sight to be seen on its own account as well as for the spectacles there to be displayed: to be seen indeed for its beauty, and still more for the way in which prince and people alike are seated on the same level. From one end to the other is a uniform plan, a continuous line, and Caesar as spectator shares the public seats as he does the spectacle. Thus your subjects will be able to look on you in their turn; they will be permitted to see not just the Emperor's box, but their emperor himself, seated among his people – the people to whom you have given an additional five thousand seats.

Claudius' spectator image was decidedly plebeian, with little pretense at imperial dignity. This need not have been a spontaneous presentation on his part. Claudius' physical limitations and the unusual circumstances of his elevation to imperial power may have proven a barrier between him and other elites, pushing him toward the development of a "popular" image at the public games, in which he explicitly yielded power to his true "masters", the people of Rome.

Source: Suetonius, *Claudius* 21:[79] He gave many gladiatorial shows and in many places . . . Now there was no form of entertainment at which he was more familiar and free, even thrusting out his left hand[80], as the commons did, and counting aloud on his fingers the gold pieces which were paid to the victors; and always and repeatedly he would address the audience, and invite and urge them to merriment, calling them "*domini*" (masters) from time to time, and interspersing feeble and far-fetched jokes.

Claques, like those noted during the late Republic, continued under the emperors, working often in cooperation with a given emperor's interests. Nero became notorious for his performance on the public stage, pushing the public persona required for an emperor to an extreme that conservative Roman values, with their repugnance for performers as a class, found disgraceful. Perhaps because he anticipated a negative reaction, Nero assembled at the same time a claque, called the Augustani, specifically to lead the crowd in rousing praise of the emperor's tremendous performance abilities. In return, these high-status Augustani could anticipate benefits from the emperor.

Source: Tacitus, *Annals* 14.15:[81] There were also present, to complete the show, a guard of soldiers with centurions and tribunes, and Burrus, who grieved and yet applauded. Then it was that Roman equestrians were first enrolled under the title of Augustani, men in their prime and remarkable for their strength, some, from a natural frivolity, others from the hope of promotion. Day and night they kept up a thunder of applause, and applied to the emperor's person and voice the epithets of deities. Thus they lived in fame and honor, as if on the strength of their merits.

As Nero's performance tendencies grew stronger, the emperor's claque was enhanced by drafting new members on an *ad hoc* basis, as need demanded. This proved something of a burden, Tacitus claims, for those who were serendipitously in town on other business, who, exhausted and afraid, were coerced into joining Nero's highly supportive audience. To falter in this support was dangerous, hence Tacitus' allusion to informers' inspection of spectators' faces, looking for signs of boredom or contempt.

Source: Tacitus, *Annals* 16.5:[82] All, however, who were present from remote towns and still retained the Italy of strict morals and primitive ways; all too who had come on embassies or on private business from distant provinces, where they had been unused to such wantonness, were unable to endure the spectacle or sustain the degrading fatigue, which wearied their unpracticed hands, while they disturbed those who knew their part, and were often struck by soldiers, stationed in the seats, to see that not a moment of time passed with less vigorous applause or in the silence of indifference. It was a known fact that several equestrians, in struggling through the narrow approaches and the pressure of the crowd, were trampled to death, and that others while keeping their seats night and day were seized with some fatal malady. For it was a still worse danger to be absent from the show, as many openly and many more secretly made it their business to scrutinize names and faces, and to note the delight or the disgust of the company.

Commodus also took the lead in claque work at his shows, as relayed by Dio Cassius, who, along with the other senators at the time, was himself pressed into participating in the verbalized rhythmic approval of the emperor's feats in the arena.

Source: Dio Cassius 73.20: When he [the emperor Commodus] fought, we senators always went together with the equites, although Claudius Pompeianus the elder never happened to appear . . . preferring to have his throat cut for this rather than to look at the emperor, son of Marcus [Aurelius] doing such things. For among other things that we did, we would shout out whatever we were commanded, and especially these words continually: "You are lord and you are first, of all men most fortunate! Victor you are, and victor you shall be; from everlasting, Amazonian, you are victor!"

There is evidence, however, for the spectators' expressing their will in forceful and even hostile outbursts. The audience at the ancient spectacle made use of a certain freedom granted them in these venues, to articulate not only approval or disapproval of the *princeps* himself, but also to make known their needs and desires on a range of issues. This freedom is recognized by the ancient authors, referred to by them as *theatralis licentia*, "permission of the theater." Not only were spectators empowered to voice their needs at the games, emperors were obliged to respond to these requests, demands, comments. The nature of the imperial response was viewed as a demonstration of character and leadership. It became standard behavior to petition the emperor at the games, a context more likely to generate an immediate response than other options. At court, any given petition would be prioritized in competition with many others, assigned merit in accordance with the importance of the petitioner or the request, as determined by the emperor on his timetable. At the shows, however, thousands of spectators served as witnesses to the petition and the emperor's response had to factor in the potential impact on his public image. It also became more difficult for the emperor to present his reasons for denial, should he decide to reject the petition, and yet important to do so to maintain a positive public image.

Titus was an extremely popular (albeit short-lived) emperor; in this particular instance, his declaration that all requests would be granted and that he relied on the public will to determine the progress of the event would, in itself, have a very positive response, whether or not he could realistically hold to his promise.

Source: Suetonius, *Titus* 8:[83] [Titus] had a rule never to dismiss any petitioner without leaving him some hope that his request would be favorably considered ... Titus maintained that no one ought to go away disappointed from an audience with the emperor ... He took such pains to humor his subjects that, on one occasion, before a gladiatorial show, he promised to forgo his own preferences and let the audience choose what they liked best; and kept his word by refusing no request and encouraging everyone to tell him what each wanted.

In Pliny's long and enthusiastic speech in praise of the emperor, Trajan is presented as the ultimate petitionee, who anticipates and grants the unspoken wishes of the people and yet still urges them to submit even more requests. Specific criticism of Trajan's unsatisfactory predecessor is also given in the context of his behavior at spectacles.

Source: Pliny, *Panegyric* 33:[84] What generosity went to provide this spectacle! And what impartiality the Emperor showed, unmoved as he was by personal feelings or else above them. Requests were granted, unspoken wishes were anticipated, and he did not hesitate to press us urgently to make fresh demands; yet still there was something new to surpass our dreams. How freely too the spectators could express their enthusiasm and show their preferences without fear! No one risked the old charge of impiety if he disliked a particular gladiator: no spectator found himself turned spectacle, dragged off by the hook to satisfy grim pleasures, or else cast to the flames! [Domitian] was a madman, blind to the true meaning of his position, who used the arena for collecting charges of high treason, who felt himself despised and condemned if we failed to revere his gladiators, taking any criticism of them as criticism of himself and interpreting them as violations of his godhead and divinity, he who deemed himself the equal of the gods yet treated his gladiators as equals.

Tiberius' general lack of ease in this kind of interaction meant that his public image was not a positive one, despite the overall success of his administration. Tiberius responded to spectacle protests even when he was not in the capital city, although he replied by scolding the Senate rather than the spectacle audience. His strategy fell somewhat flat; Tiberius' lack of direct response to the protesters is not interpreted as his use of traditional channels in support of their interests but, rather, as further indication of his distance from the people, his "arrogance." Tiberius eventually stopped financing and even attending games, allegedly to avoid being put in a position where his responses to petitions would be constrained.

> Source: Tacitus, *Annals* 6.13:[85] In the same year [33 CE] the high price of grain nearly caused riots. In the theater, for several days, sweeping demands were shouted with a freedom of language rarely displayed to emperors. Upset, Tiberius reproved the officials and senate for not using their authority to restrain popular demonstrations. He enumerated the provinces from which he was importing grain – more extensively than Augustus. So the senate passed a resolution of old-fashioned strictness censuring the public. The consuls too issued an equally severe edict. Tiberius was silent. However, this was not taken for modesty as he hoped, but for arrogance.

Fronto, Marcus Aurelius' tutor, had given him specific advice about the value for the emperor in attending to the crowd. The way that Fronto treats this is interesting: he expects that Marcus is familiar with approved conduct for the emperor at the games and should learn from that paradigm how to treat audiences at non-spectacle venues. The normative political interaction, then, is that of the *princeps* and the spectators.

> Source: Fronto, *To the Caesar Marcus* 1.8:[86] Be prepared, when you speak before an assembly of men, to study their taste, not, of course, everywhere and by every means, yet occasionally and to some extent. And when you do so, remind yourself that you are but doing the same as you do when, at the people's request, you honor or enfranchise those who have slain beasts manfully in the arena; even though they are murderers or condemned for some crime, you release them at the people's request. Everywhere then the people dominate and prevail.

Emperors who ignored or abused this relationship were, almost by definition, "bad" emperors. The reign of Caligula offers a number of exemplary incidents of how not to behave at spectacles.[87] The following description by Dio Cassius of one such indicates the expectations of "normal" audience behavior: the display of visible gratitude for the emperor's generosity, the anticipated applause for the emperor's favorite performers, and the ability to engage in political criticism, even if only at the level of gesture. Caligula's "bad" response was to abuse the "bad" audience.

Source: Dio Cassius 59.13:[88] In fact, there was nothing but slaughter, for the emperor no longer showed any favors even to the populace, but opposed absolutely everything they wished, and consequently the people on their part resisted all his desires. The talk and behavior that might be expected at such a juncture, with an angry ruler on one side, and a hostile people on the other, were plainly in evidence. The contest between them, however, was not an equal one; for the people could do nothing but talk and show something of their feelings by their gestures, whereas Gaius would destroy his opponents, dragging many away even while they were witnessing the games and arresting many more after they had left the theaters. The chief causes of his anger were, first, that they did not show enthusiasm in attending the spectacles . . . and again, that they did not always applaud the performers that pleased him and sometimes even showed honor to those whom he disliked. . . . once he said, threatening the whole people: "Would that you had but a single neck."

The assassination of Gaius was alleged to be inspired, to some extent, by resentment of his spectacular abuse of the Roman people. Josephus, a near-contemporary of Caligula, asserts that all and sundry lived in terror of Gaius' fatal whimsy, which was especially likely to burst out when the audience made demands at the games. Cassius Chaerea and Cornelius Sabinus, members of the Praetorian Guard, would have been responsible for carrying out Caligula's orders; their resentment at this "barbarity" is a key factor in their successful conspiracy.

Source: Josephus, *Jewish Antiquities* 19.24–27:[89] Now at this time came the Circensian games; this spectacle was eagerly desired by the people of Rome, for they come with great alacrity into the circus at such times, and petition their emperors, in great multitudes, for what they need; the emperors usually did not deny them their requests, but readily and gratefully granted them. Accordingly, they most importunately desired that Gaius would now ease off on their tribute and reduce the harshness of the taxes imposed upon them; but he would not hear their petition; and when their clamors increased, he sent soldiers, some in one direction and some another, and ordered them to seize those that made the clamors and without any delay bring them out and put them to death. These were Gaius's commands, and those who were commanded carried them out; and the number of those who were killed on this occasion was very great. Now the people saw this, and bore it so far, that they left off clamoring, because they saw with their own eyes that this petition to have their payments reduced brought immediate death upon them. These things made Chaerea more resolute to go on with his plot, in order to put an end to this barbarity of Gaius against men.

Emperors could have discouraged the *theatralis licentia*; even if resisted at first, continuous and energetic suppression of this kind of expression would eventually have had effect. Emperors could also routinely have followed the lead of Tiberius and stop attending shows. They did not do so. Emperors kept accepting petitions at shows well into the Byzantine period. They only did so, one assumes, because the perceived benefit to them outweighed the risk.

The unwanted criticism periodically mentioned by the ancient authors represented an unusual event and thus was reported as atypical behavior for crowd and for emperor. Normally, emperors expected applause and acclaim at the shows, an upwelling of gratitude not just for the games but for the impetus behind the presentation of games, be it the extraordinary achievement of victory, recognition of significant events in the life of a beloved and benevolent ruler, or the steady continual efforts to maintain the peace and prosperity of the empire. The setting was redolent with reminders of similar achievements in the past, such as the statues carried in the *pompa* and the monuments erected in and near the theater, the amphitheater, and the circus.

Hostile reactions could also serve as a safety valve; with the grievance articulated, a response from an emperor, even a minimal one, would diminish the tension in a given situation. Indirectly, this is demonstrated by the examples of Caligula and Domitian, whose efforts to silence the crowd are linked with their eventual assassinations. Dissent forced underground became much more dangerous.

In the aftermath of the death of Commodus, the relieved and angry people expressed their hatred of the former emperor in acclamations, like those habitually used by spectators at the games. The preserved chants are the "negative" ones, indicating disapproval (to say the least) and the recommendation that the target be dragged to execution and that the body be denied proper burial, a severe treatment appropriate for an enemy of the state. Mixed in are versions of the "positive" chants, like those that Dio and other spectators had been forced to perform at the games, here given new meaning in the context of the emperor's assassination.

Source: Historia Augusta, *Commodus* 18–19:[90] Let the parricide's honors be dragged away! Let the parricide be dragged away! Let the enemy of the fatherland, the parricide, the gladiator, be mangled in the charnel house! . . . He that killed the Senate, let him be dragged with the hook! He that killed the innocent, let him be dragged with the hook! Enemy! Parricide! Truly! Truly! He that did not spare his own blood, let him be dragged with the hook! He that was about to kill you, let him be dragged with the hook! . . . Good fortune to the victory of the Roman people, good fortune to the trustiness of the soldiers, good fortune to the trustiness of the praetorians, good fortune to the praetorian cohorts! . . . Let the remembrance of the parricide, the gladiator, be wiped out! Let the statues of the parricide, the gladiator, be dragged away! Let the remembrance of the foul gladiator be wiped out!

Gladiators outside Rome

Munera and other spectacles were regularly presented as part of the municipal package; magistrates were responsible for organizing and financially supporting this activity alongside the upkeep of roads and maintenance of public cult. Shows were an obligation of public office, as mandated in the municipal charters by which the central government regularized provincial practice in accordance with Roman expectations. Gladiatorial events were offered by local magistrates to celebrate traditional deities and the deified emperor; spectacles commemorated the dedication of public buildings and fulfilled vows for the health of the emperor and the victory of Rome.

The *Lex Ursonensis* is the charter for the colony of Urso in Baetica (modern-day Portugal), dating to the time of Julius Caesar. It offers details about the ordinary spectacles that could be anticipated by the residents. Note especially the fairly low level of expenditure on these events, in comparison with practice in the city of Rome during the Republic.

> Source: *Lex Ursonensis* 71:[91] Whoever shall be aediles, during their magistracy they are to organize a *munus* or *ludi scaenici* for Jupiter, Juno and Minerva, during three days, for the greater part of the day, as far as shall be possible, and during one day (games) in the circus or (gladiators) in the Forum for Venus, and each one of them is to spend on that spectacle and on that show not less than 2,000 sesterces from his own money and it is to be lawful to take from public funds 1,000 sesterces for each aedile.

These funding limits were meant to keep municipal budgets in line with imperial priorities: magistrates were not to bankrupt themselves on games when their personal financial resources were required to maintain the infrastructure of empire.

Pompeii offers a range of material documenting spectacular practice outside Rome. The volcanic debris provided protection for ephemeral evidence lost at other sites, such as graffiti and painted notices for games. The evidence indicates how important the shows were in assessing leadership during the imperial period. Funerary inscriptions, for example, which serve as the final accounting of a man's political career, are weighted heavily toward the description of resources pulled together to present spectacle.

> Source: *Corpus Inscriptionum Latinarum*, hereafter *CIL* 10.1084d: Aulus Clodius Flaccus, son of Aulus, Menenia tribe[92], elected duumvir three times, once as quinquennial magistrate, elected military tribune by the people. During his first duumvirate, he offered the *ludi Apollinares* including a procession in the forum, bulls, bullfighters and their helpers, three pairs of *pontarii* fighters, group boxers and Greek-style boxers, all plays and musical pantomimes with Pylades. And he

paid ten thousand sesterces to the public treasury in return for holding the duumvirate. During his second duumvirate, as quinquennial magistrate, he provided the *ludi Apollinares* including a procession in the forum, bulls, bullfighters and their helpers and group boxers. On the next day, on his own, in the amphitheater he provided 30 pairs of athletes, five pairs of gladiators and with his colleague in office he provided 35 pairs of gladiators and a wild animal hunt, bulls, bullfighters, boars, bears, and other kinds of *venationes*. In his third duumvirate, he provided, with his colleague, games with a first-ranked troupe with musical accompaniment.

Here documented on the family tomb is the impressive spectacle history of Aulus Clodius Flaccus, son of Aulus Clodius Flaccus, who was three times elected duumvir, the senior magistrate in a Roman town, and served one of those terms as a prestigious quinquennial magistrate, an office filled every five years as the top rung of the political ladder. Flaccus is one of a group of prominent Pompeiian magistrates during the reign of Augustus, whose affiliations with the regime were an important factor in their public success. The games presented by Flaccus took place during his terms in office, two of them for the festival of Apollo, a deity of particular significance to the emperor. Flaccus is careful to distinguish different kinds of generosity, such as the cash payment into the local treasury that was expected of municipal officials in the empire, in addition to other services they were required to subsidize financially. He also makes clear what events he personally sponsored in the amphitheater and which were jointly sponsored by himself and his fellow-magistrate. The types of animals noted here, the bulls, bears and boars, are not as exotic as those found in the capital city and may represent a more "typical" *venatio* for the Roman world.

Source: *CIL* 4.9979: A wild animal hunt and twenty pairs of gladiators, presented by Marcus Tullius, will fight at Pompeii the day before the *nones* of November and seven days before the *ides* of November.

Source: *CIL* 4.9980: A wild animal hunt and twenty pairs of gladiators, presented by Marcus Tullius, will fight at Pompeii the day before the *nones* of November, the *nones* of November, and the eighth and seventh day before the *ides* of November.

Source: *CIL* 4.9981a: A wild animal hunt and twenty pairs of gladiators, presented by Marcus Tullius, will fight at Pompeii the day before the *nones* of November, the *nones* of November, and the eighth and seventh day before the *ides* of November.

These are three painted notices of a set of games scheduled for November 4–7. The descriptions are spare and do not suggest that the events took place as part of Marcus Tullius' magisterial duties, which is unusual. This has led some scholars to suspect that these may represent the opening salvo of Marcus Tullius' political career, which was indeed a very successful one. Like Flaccus, Tullius held the duumvirate three times, once as quinquennial magistrate, and was military tribune, an equestrian rank specific to the Augustan period. Although Suetonius claimed the military tribunate was awarded to local leaders by the townsfolk, scholars note that supporters of the Augustan administration are the recipients of this honor at Pompeii, which suggests that the choices for this award were not made on strictly local grounds. Marcus Tullius built the Temple of August Fortune on a lot in Pompeii that he'd purchased with his own money, thus joining his resources with a surge of construction that parallels (and may have been inspired by) the extensive building program sponsored by Augustus in Rome. This public structure was an explicit link to the regime of Augustus, completed probably in 3 CE, a time when the future of the imperial family was in a state of flux; the temple serves as a show of support for the emperor. Tullius' November games were effective in helping to establish a public persona in line with the emperor's vision of a renewed Roman world. The fact that these painted notices were left in place long after the games were held indicates the lasting influence Marcus Tullius had on Pompeii, despite the absence of children who became practical heirs to his public prominence.

Source: *CIL* 4.3884: Brought to you by Decimus Lucretius Satrius Valens, permanent priest of Nero Caesar, son of Augustus, twenty pairs of gladiators. And presented by Decimus Lucretius, son of Valens, ten pairs of gladiators. They'll fight at Pompeii from the sixth day before the *ides* of April, through the day before.[93] There will be a standard *venatio* and awnings.

Source: *CIL* 4.7995: Brought to you by Decimus Lucretius Satrius Valens, permanent priest of Nero Caesar, son of Augustus, twenty pairs of gladiators. And presented by Decimus Lucretius, son of Valens, ten pairs of gladiators. From the fifth day before the *kalends* of April.[94] There will be a *venatio* and awnings.

These notices of two sets of games follow a somewhat different pattern from that of Marcus Tullius. The name of the *editor* is very much foregrounded here, suggesting both that enhancing the public reputation of the giver was the point of the notice and the games, and that the name would already be recognizable to a potential audience, who would be drawn to games offered by someone with a track record. D. Lucretius Satrius Valens is one of the most-documented Pompeiians, adopted as an adult by a prominent politician of the preceding generation. His son, with whom he's affiliated here, like him changed names after adoption and was regularly associated with him in public actions and, in return, was the recipient of inscribed acclamations recording popular gratitude for their efforts. The family would be associated with Nero's regime; Satrius Valens' priestly title indicates that he took on this role in the Imperial Cult before Nero became emperor, when he was merely the *filius Augusti*, (adopted) son of the emperor Claudius. The games here, as elsewhere in the Roman world, are presented as part of the Imperial Cult, a more explicitly political aspect of Roman religion. Formal expressions of reverence and devotion toward the ruling family grant an elevated, numinous quality to what is primarily political power. Individual Pompeiians, like Lucretius Satrius Valens, took the initiative to declare their support for the elder of Claudius' two potential heirs; Nero, as it turned out, had a powerful network of such advocates in place at the time Claudius died, a key factor in his smooth succession to the role of *princeps*. Valens backed the right imperial horse.

Source: *CIL* 4.7991: Presented by Gnaeus Alleius Nigidius Maius, as quinquennial magistrate, without the use of public funds, twenty pairs of gladiators and their *suppositicii* will fight at Pompeii.

Source: *CIL* 4.1179: Presented by Gnaeus Alleius Nigidius Maius, as quinquennial magistrate, thirty pairs of gladiators and their *suppositicii* will fight at Pompeii on the eighth, seventh and sixth day before the *kalends* of December. Ellius[95] will be there and a *venatio* will be held.

Source: *CIL* 4.7990: To Gnaeus Alleius Maius, first among the presenters of *munera*, happily [we hail you].

Source: *CIL* 4.7993: In dedication of the work of the painted panels funded by Gnaeus Alleius Nigidius Maius, at Pompeii, on the *ides* of June, there will be a procession, a *venatio*, athletes and awnings.

Source: *CIL* 4.1177b: To Maius, first of the colony, happily [we hail you].

Source: *CIL* 4.1180: On behalf of the health of the Emperor Vespasian Caesar Augustus and his children, on the occasion of the dedication of the altar, pairs of gladiators, presented by Gnaeus Alleius Maius, *flamen* of Caesar Augustus, will fight at Pompeii without any delay on the fourth day before the *nones* of July. There will be a *venatio*, sprinkles and an awning.

Gnaeus Alleius Nigidius Maius, born to the Nigidii and adopted as an Alleius, served as quinquennial duumvir in 55 CE and presented *munera* as part of his official responsibilities; popular acclamations preserved as graffiti indicate that his efforts were well received. This is the last known set of gladiatorial combats prior to the riot in 59, after which *munera* were banned by senatorial decree for ten years at Pompeii (see chapter 3). During this decade, announcements were made for games but not with combats of pairs: athletes seem to have taken the place of gladiators. Alleius Nigidius Maius was also involved in repairs of the amphitheater made necessary by the earthquake in February of 62 CE, funding, for his part, the addition of paintings on the podium of the amphitheater. These panels featured gladiatorial combats, possibly even recreations of actual matches, a visual substitute for what was still forbidden in Pompeii and a reminder of past glories to be resurrected some day.[96] Games held to commemorate the completion of the renovation project still were absent gladiators, focusing instead on the athletes and the *venatio*, nevertheless, another salute in graffiti form indicates appreciation for Maius' continuing leadership, in the colony as in spectacle. Later in his career, Alleius Nigidius Maius served as priest of the Imperial Cult for Vespasian and dedicated an altar in this capacity. The act was commemorated with a set of *munera*, as might be expected for the Imperial Cult. Claiming this was done "without any delay" is unusual and may indicate the urgency felt by locals after their long dry spell during the ban on gladiators. The ten years imposed by the Senate would have been completed in 69, the year in which Vespasian claimed the imperial power.[97]

This letter from the Younger Pliny to his friend, Valerius Maximus, gives us evidence for how spectacles functioned in towns outside the capital city and indicates the kind of relationship of "obligation" constructed between the *editor* and the potential audience at the games, who apparently could "request" that an individual sponsor funeral games with gladiators at great expense and with a certain risk involved, here with the delayed panther order. Note also that, here in Verona, *munera* offered in honor of a deceased woman occasion no comment; apparently Julius Caesar's innovation on behalf of his daughter Julia has become a commonplace some 150 years later.

Source: Pliny, *Letters* 6.34:[98] You did well to put on a show of gladiators for our people of Verona, who have long shown their affection and admiration for you and have voted you many honors. Verona was also the home town of the excellent wife you loved so dearly, whose memory you owe some public building or show, and this kind of spectacle is particularly suitable for a funeral tribute. Moreover, the request came from so many people that a refusal would have been judged churlish rather than strong-minded on your part. You have also done admirably in giving the show so readily and on such a lavish scale, for this indicates a true spirit of generosity. I am sorry the African panthers you had bought in such quantity did not turn up on the appointed day, but you deserve the credit though the weather prevented their arriving in time; it was not your fault that you could not show them.

Suetonius relates how in the time of Tiberius, the "request" that a private individual present *munera* for a deceased loved one could have a certain coercive element. Tiberius took decisive action to deter this abuse of spectacle and to maintain the prerogatives of the *editor* in this top-down relationship of power.

Source: Suetonius, *Tiberius* 37:[99] Trouble occurred in Pollentia, a Ligurian town at the northern foot of the Apennines, where the townsfolk would not let the corpse of a leading centurion be removed from the forum until his heirs had agreed to meet their importunate demands for a free gladiatorial show. Tiberius detached one cohort from Rome, and another from the kingdom of Cottius, to converge on Pollentia, after disguising their destination. They had orders to enter the town simultaneously by opposite gates, suddenly display their weapons, blow trumpets and consign most of the inhabitants and magistrates to life-imprisonment.

Significant legislation was sponsored by the emperor Marcus Aurelius in 177, again in an effort to maintain the power of the presenter of games as an agent of empire. Catalyzed by the skyrocketing cost of games and its corrosive effect on the financial stability of the elite classes, the central government took action to limit the financial burden spectacle placed on local magistrates. The preserved law on limiting the prices for gladiators includes a portion of the senatorial discussion of the problem, as well as a system for setting price ceilings. The inscription dramatizes the rationale for this measure in an anecdote on the financial woes of a priest of the Imperial Cult, one of the major categories of *editores* in the Roman world.

Source: *CIL* 2.6278:[100] (lines 16–18) There was one who upon being appointed priest had given up his fortune for lost, had named a council to help him in an appeal addressed to the Emperors. But in that very gathering, he himself, before and after consulting his friends, exclaimed, "What do I want with an appeal now? Their most sacred Majesties the Emperors have released the whole burden which crushed my patrimony. Now I desire and look forward to being a priest, and as for the duty of putting on a spectacle, of which we once were solemnly asking to be relieved, I welcome it."

The specific limitations are based on the total expenditure the magistrate or priest planned for the games, the lowest of which greatly exceeds the costs specified for the colony at Urso two centuries earlier. The law lays out package prices as well, spreading the cost over gladiators grouped by "grade", which probably reflects skill level and veteran status (see chapter 4).

Source: *CIL* 2.6278: (lines 29–37)[101] [the law mandates] that to those, however, who produce spectacles at an expenditure between 30,000 and 60,000 HS[102], gladiators be furnished in equal number in three classes: maximum price for the first class be 5,000 HS, for the second class 4,000 HS, for the third class 3,000 HS. That when it is from 60,000 to 100,000 HS, the company of gladiators be divided into three classes: maximum price of a gladiator of the first class be 8,000 HS, middle class 6,000, lowest 5,000. Next, that when it is from 100,000 to 150,000 HS, there be five grades: for a man of the first grade the price be 12,000 HS, second 10,000, third 8,000, fourth 6,000, last 5,000. Next in order, finally, that when it is from 150,000 to 200,000 HS or any sum which may be over and above this, the price of the gladiator of the lowest grade be 6,000 HS, of the next higher 7,000, of the third by backward count 9,000, fourth 12,000 up to 15,000 which is the amount fixed for the gladiator of the highest and last grade. That at every spectacle of all the categories into which they have been classified the *lanista* provide as half of the whole group a number of men who are not expected to perform singly, and that of these, who are known as *gregarii*, one who may be rated "superior among *gregarii*" fight in a team under a standard for 2,000 HS and that no one from this group fight for less than 1,000.

A third-century mosaic from a private home in Smirat in Tunisia (figure 1.1) documents how the financial commitment by the *editor* helps to establish a positive relationship between the holders of imperial power and the subjects of the empire. Both image and text clarify how this is done. Along the long sides of the mosaic are a series of duels between men and leopards, with the names of each performer, human and feline, given. The viewer's attention is drawn to the center by a name repeated in the vocative case: the mosaic hails Magerius, the sponsor of the game, just as the audience would have done at the games themselves, just as the ancient reader of the mosaic would

Figure 1.1   Magerius mosaic. Gilles Mermet/Art Resource, NY

echo the salute. Inside the vocative brackets are two divinities appropriate to the arena but also suitable to the message conveyed in the representation. On the left is a winged female in hunting boots, who may be Nemesis/Fortuna, a powerful divinity of the amphitheaters; she was the goddess who saw to the appropriate outcome in each combat and also safeguarded the financial risk of the sponsor of the games. On the right is a youthful god, wearing a cloak and sandals and carrying a caduceus. This is prabably Mercury, the god of commerce, who in the arena would be known as Hermes Psychopomp, who leads the souls of dead performers through the gates of death down to the underworld. The divinities gesture toward the remaining two figures, drawing the eye of the viewer further inward. Next to Nemesis, an unnamed, well-dressed youth faces out toward the audience, carrying a tray loaded down with bags, each labeled 1,000 *denarii*, representing a portion of what Magerius spent on the games. To the right of the moneyholder is the transcription of the dialogue between Magerius as *editor* and the audience.

Source: Magerius mosaic: "Magerius!" "Magerius!" Through the herald was said: "My Lords, since the Telegenii[103] have earned your favor, give to them 500 *denarii* for each leopard." It was acclaimed: "By your example may those to come learn the *munus* and may those past hear. Who has ever offered such games? When have such games been offered? By the example of the quaestors, you will present the *munus*. At your own expense you will present the *munus* on that day." Magerius gives. "This is what it means to be wealthy. This is what it means to be powerful . . . From your *munus* they are let go with these sacks."

Magerius' epigram about the meaning of wealth and power is a strong statement that captures the meaning of the arena in Roman society. Magerius, who likely put on the show as part of holding a high magistracy, spent his money well and engaged the audience appropriately. His capacity to command the resources of empire demonstrated simultaneously his cultural sophistication, his organizational skills and his understanding how best to use the power over life and death. The members of the community vigorously recognize his favor and recognize his effort as a model for past and future interactions of imperial authority. This is why Magerius is the figure being crowned by Mercury, officially hailed as the true victor of the games.

2

The Venue

As with the games themselves, the arena was symbolic of an idealized Rome. Augustus mandated seating by sociopolitical status: the higher up you were in the Roman power structure, the closer you were to the action. Just as the organization of the amphitheaters projected an ideal hierarchy, the structure of the Circus Maximus was touted as a manifestation of cosmic order.

The arena was not just in Rome; Augustus and other emperors deliberately fostered its spread to areas chosen to enhance the effect of the message. Amphitheatrical structures, for example, were established in major centers of Roman world, especially in the west, where there were some 252 amphitheaters.[1] The amphitheater served as a permanent reminder not only of the power of the empire, but of the danger in challenging Rome's supremacy. Amphitheaters were set up in centers of the Imperial Cult, beginning at Lugdunum, which from 12 BCE housed regular ritualized expressions of loyalty to the emperor. The arena went to legionary headquarters as well, to incorporate the immediate defenders of the empire in the celebration of Roman hierarchy.

We rely heavily on archaeological information for our understanding of spectacular venues in the ancient Roman world. The surviving textual sources devote little attention to analyzing the architectural settings for shows. Incidental references give us a bit of the color and the little attentions to detail that sponsors of spectacular venues arranged. There are a few indications of the legal status of these structures, or, rather, the legal controls placed on their builders that guided how the venues could be used, in the interests of audience security and of maintenance of political order. Exploring the development of formal spectacle structures tells us a bit about the expectations that shaped them, from the use of cemeteries for funeral games, to the rise of urbanization and the planning of the Circus Maximus, to the negotiation of public space in the *fora* of Rome, to the standardization of specific building types to enhance the impact of the games. The long-term reluctance to build a permanent theater or amphitheater in Rome can be tied to the importance of shows in political competition in the late Republic; even in the early Principate, emperors found it expedient to limit this kind of construction, at least in the capital city. Outside Rome, the first century saw the building of many amphitheaters in the Roman world, to accommodate the spread of spectacle supported by the imperial government. The Flavian Amphitheater was the most sophisticated expression of this architectural form and was a major accomplishment in crowd management and spectacle.

Republican Arenas

The original venue for funeral games was probably the cemetery, located typically outside the city walls where contests may have been held in any open area near the grave. This seems to have been the custom for the Etruscan and the Campanian spectacles that may have served as original models for the Roman institution. Those attending the obsequies would have stood around a cleared space, some possibly seated on the ground or on folded or improvised seats. The backdrop for the events would have been the landscape and vegetation of the extra-urban environment, with the addition of built tombs and monuments framing the action.

Source: Ausonius Griphus 36–7: The sons of Junius sent the three first combats of Thracians in three sets to the underworld at the tomb of their father.

Source: Tertullian, *On the Spectacles* 12: when they had trained them in the weapons which they then used and they were as well disciplined as they could make them, inasmuch as they were taught to die, then on the day set aside for the dead, they killed them at the tombs.

Source: Servius, *On the Aeneid* 10.519: Indeed, it was the custom to kill captives at the graves of powerful men; because this, in later days, seemed cruel, it was decided to have gladiators fight before the grave, gladiators who were called "Bustuarii" for the tombs (*busti*).

Prior to the imperial period, gladiatorial games in Rome were held in the area set aside for public congress: the forum. According to Valerius Maximus, the first public *munera* took place in the old cattle market near the Tiber, the Forum Boarium. Some advantages of the location include its ability to handle blood spillage, given its ordinary function as a meat market, as well as the presence of an old Temple of Hercules, often claimed as a deity of particular importance to the combats.

Source: Valerius Maximus 2.4.7: For gladiatorial games were first given at Rome in the Forum Boarium during the consulship of Appius Claudius and Marcus Fulvius (264 BCE). Marcus and Decimus, the sons of Brutus Pera, gave them as funeral games to honor the memory of their father's ashes.

In 216 BCE, the year of the second known set of gladiatorial combats in Rome, the *munera* settled in to their regular Republican location, the Forum Romanum. The Forum was more spacious than the Forum Boarium and laid claim to more prestige as the heart of Roman political, cultural, and religious life. Romans exported the custom of *munera* to their colonies in Italy and abroad, which influenced the shape of Roman fora outside of Rome proper. Vitruvius explains the details of forum design specific to the holding of games: the allowance of space for visibility and the rectangular forum shape.

Source: Vitruvius 5.1.1–2: But in the cities of Italy, the construction plan is not the same (as in Greek-style *fora*), in that the custom of holding gladiatorial *munera* in the forum has been handed down from our ancestors. Therefore around the spectacles, the colonnades should be given wider intercolumniations . . . have balconies on the upper floor arranged so as to be convenient . . . The magnitude of the forum should be appropriate for a large gathering of people, lest the space be too small for use or, because of a lack of people, the forum seem huge. But the dimensions should be such that when the length is divided into three parts, two are assigned to the width. For thus the plan will be oblong and the arrangement suitable to the holding of spectacles.

The general configuration of the Forum Romanum was established by 170 BCE as a roughly rectangular area, bounded by basilicas with colonnaded porches, which would be used as seating areas during the presentation of shows. The forum's central area had tribunals at either short end that also would serve as seating; the curved form of the tribunals made the space look a bit like a small stadium area. There is some evidence that certain landmarks were claimed by individuals and families as desirable viewing space in an area limited in size and likely to be crowded for spectacles. Access to this privilege was granted for a variety of causes, from a sort of "right of way" guaranteed in a sale of property to a public honor bestowed by the Republic.

Source: Pseudasconius, *On Cicero's "On divination"* 50: Maenius, when he sold his house to Cato and Flaccus, the censors [of 185 BCE], so that they could build a basilica there, claimed the right to one column for himself, where he and his descendants could view the gladiatorial combats, which were even then held in the forum.

Source: Cicero, *Philippics* 9.7: Since such a man died while a legate for the Republic, it is the Senate's decision that a bronze statue on foot be erected for Servius Sulpicius on the Rostra, and around that statue there be a space of five feet on all sides reserved for gladiatorial games for his children and descendants, because he has met death in service for the Republic.

As a performance space, the forum had certain limitations, including a diminished seating capacity; even if sponsors erected temporary bleachers, the presence of monumental public buildings restricted the height and capacity of these structures. Granted, the audience could (and did) make use of balconies in private residences to view the shows. The presence of buildings and memorials also could block visibility for some spectators, as acknowledged by Vitruvius in his recommendations for forum design. Even so, the dimensions of most fora made it hard for people at one end of the improvised arena to catch the action at the other end. There was much competition for good seats, a situation capitalized on, apparently, by some sponsors. Improving visibility for one's political constituency became a strong declaration of loyalties for Gaius Gracchus, who was tribune of the plebs 123–122 BCE with a broad agenda of social and political reform.

Source: Plutarch, *Gaius Gracchus* 12.3–4:[2] It so happened that at this moment he had also given offense to one of his fellow-tribunes for the following reason. A gladiatorial display had been arranged for the people to watch in the Forum, and most of the magistrates had had seats built around the arena, which they intended to rent to the spectators. Gaius insisted that these should be taken down so that the poor could watch the show without payment. But since his orders were ignored, he waited until the night before the event and then took all the workmen whom he had under his orders for public contracts and dismantled the seats, so that by the morning he was able to show the people a completely empty space. The people thought him a man for this, but his fellow-tribunes were furious and regarded it as a piece of interference of the most presumptuous and violent kind. In fact, it was generally believed that this action cost him his election to the tribunate for the third time, because although he won a majority of the votes, his colleagues falsified the returns and the declaration of the result.

The difficulty of guaranteeing spectator safety also restricted the use of wild animals to small numbers of relatively docile and diminutive types for Forum shows, if they were present at all. A demonstration of this was seen at Pompeii (chapter 1), when Aulus Clodius offered bulls as part of the *Ludi Apollinares* presented in the Forum during his first magistracy. In his second magistracy, the relative security of the amphitheater space enabled him to expand the show to include boars, bears and other kinds of animals. Without this kind of built protection, sponsors might choose to severely limit the movement of animals at a public show, in order to guarantee the public's safety. Oppian refers to a *venatio* in which the large feline was contained in a cage, viewing the *venator* through "the edge of sharp iron"; despite the zesty description by Oppian, such a spectacle has relatively less excitement, being more akin to shooting the proverbial fish in a barrel.

Source: Oppian, *Fishing* 2.350–356:[3] As when a man skilled in the work of slaying wild beasts, when the people are gathered in the house-encircled marketplace, awaits the leopard, maddened by the cracking of the whip and with long-edged spear stands athwart her path; she, though she beholds the edge of sharp iron, mantles in swelling fury and receives in her throat, as it were in a spear-stand, the brazen lance.

The perceived drawbacks of the forum space persuaded many towns and cities in the Roman world to expend financial and human resources on the construction of a formal arena. The vast majority of Roman amphitheaters are in the western empire, where eventually there would be some 252 of these spectacle structures. But not, for a long time, in Rome.

During the Republic and into the early Principate, there was resistance in Rome to the construction of permanent buildings to house Rome's increasingly opulent shows. This resistance can be placed alongside the other efforts to control ostentatious displays by Rome's fiercely competitive ruling class. The political tension underlying these disputes, however, focused on providing permanent and formal seating for a large number of Romans, when discussing the problem of building. Tacitus, as a means of registering disapproval of a new set of games inaugurated by the emperor Nero, resurrected the heated discussion over the establishment of a formal venue for such games generations before, and how this constituted a threat to Rome on the basis that luxury and the laziness of sitting were damaging to the people's morals and traditional austerity. These claims were countered by an appeal to imperial power and financial pragmatism.

Source: Tacitus, *Annals* 14.20–21:[4] There were some who declared that even Gnaeus Pompeius was censured by the older men of the day for having set up a fixed and permanent theater.[5] "Formerly," they said, "the games were usually exhibited with hastily erected tiers of benches and a temporary stage, and the people stood to witness them, that they might not, by having the chance of sitting down, spend a succession of entire days in idleness" . . . Many people liked this very license, but they screened it under respectable names. "Our ancestors," they said, "were not averse to the attractions of shows on a scale suited to the wealth of their day, and so they introduced actors from the Etruscans and horse-races from Thurii. When we had possessed ourselves of Greece and Asia, games were exhibited with greater elaboration . . . even economy had been consulted, when a permanent edifice was erected for a theater, in preference to a structure raised and fitted up yearly at vast expense. Nor would the magistrates, as hitherto, exhaust their substance . . . when once the State undertakes the expenditure."

Temporary structures in Rome

To get around this resistance to permanent spectacle buildings, most *editores* of shows put together temporary arrangements. At first these were probably fairly simple: bleachers, a cleared and leveled performance area, rudimentary fencing for blood events. Over time, however, the temporary structures became opportunities for lavish expenditure; the fact that they were ephemeral only enhanced the depth of the public generosity involved.

Gaius Scribonius Curio constructed an unusual theater for his spectacles of 52 BCE, a double theater capable of rotating to form the two halves of an amphitheater; the spectators could even remain in their seats while the rotation was in progress, or so the story goes. Scholars today are not in agreement as to whether ancient engineering was capable of crafting a mechanism to support such a structure. Pliny's description of it also carries a definite critical tone that seems to focus on Curio's irresponsible exposure of his audience to such danger, and the audience's thrill-seeking attitude in riding Curio's amphitheater. Pliny compares the risk to a national disaster (the battle of Cannae) and clearly links the whole spectacle to the dangerous politics of the late Republic and Curio's demagoguery in particular.

Source: Pliny, *Natural History* 36.15.117–120:[6] Curio, therefore, had to exercise his ingenuity and devise something else. It is worth taking the trouble to learn what he conceived and be glad of our modern moral code and, reversing the usual terminology, to call ourselves "older and better." Curio built two vast wooden theaters side by side, each balanced on a revolving pivot. Before midday, a performance of a play was staged in both; the theaters faced in opposite directions so that the actors should not drown each other's lines. Then suddenly the theaters revolved (it is agreed that after the first few days this happened while some of the audience actually remained in their seats), and their corners came together to form an amphitheater. Here Curio staged fights between gladiators – although the Roman people found themselves in even greater danger than the gladiators, as Curio spun them round. It is difficult to know what should amaze us more, the inventor or the invention, or the sheer audacity of the conception. Most amazing of all is the madness of a people rash enough to sit in such treacherous and unstable seats! What contempt for human life this shows! How can we justify our complaints about Cannae! What a disaster this could have been! Here the whole Roman people, as if put on board two ships, were supported by a pair of pivots and watched themselves fighting for their lives and likely to perish at any moment should the mechanism be put out of gear! And the aim of all this was merely to win favor for the speeches Curio intended to make as tribune: he wanted to be able to continue to sway the undecided voters. On the speaker's platform he would stop at nothing in addressing those whom he had persuaded to participate in this dangerous activity.

Caesar made some effort to enhance the Forum as a venue for spectacles. Subterranean tunnels with openings to the pavement floor were added, apparently to allow for some minimal special effects, such as sudden entrances of performers or props or scenery.

Source: Dio Cassius 43.22:[7] [Caesar] built a kind of hunting-theater of wood, which was called an amphitheater[8] from the fact that it had seats all around without any stage. In honor of this[9] and of his daughter he exhibited combats of wild beasts and gladiators; but anyone who cared to record their number would find his task a burden without being able, in all probability, to present the truth.

Even the spectators at the dictator's quadruple triumph were treated lavishly: Caesar erected an enormous silk awning along an important chunk of the parade route. While moderns might interpret such shades, even silk ones, as more practical provisions, offering minimum relief from the sun's glare, Romans could and did regard the awnings as special effects, altering one's perceptions of the world. Lucretius was a contemporary of Julius Caesar; his description of the effect is lyrical.

Source: Lucretius, *On the Nature of Things* 4.75–83:[10] . . . awnings, yellow, scarlet and maroon, stretched flapping and billowing on poles and rafters over spacious theaters. The crowded pit below and the stage with all its scenery are made to glow and flow with the colours of the canopy. The more completely the theater is hemmed in by surrounding walls, the more its interior, sheltered from the daylight, is irradiated by this flood of colour.

Even after the Theater of Pompey had broken the barrier on stone spectacle venues, sponsors still chose to build temporary facilities. The advantages were still there: sponsors could still impress spectators and the general public by constructing something completely new and highly decorative for a specific set of games. In 57 CE, Nero built a notoriously lavish, huge wooden arena in the same general vicinity of the Campus Martius, northwest of the Pantheon. Calpurnius' description of Nero's amphitheater fills in the details in a tone of near wonderment, emphasizing the glittering costliness of the fabric used as well as the mastery of nature through special effects.

Source: Calpurnius, *Eclogues* 7.23–24:[11] I saw a theater[12] that rose skyward on interwoven beams and almost looked down on the summit of the Capitoline. Passing up the steps and slopes of gentle incline, we came to the seats, where in dingy cloaks the baser sort viewed the show close to the women's benches. For the uncovered parts, exposed beneath the open sky, were thronged by equestrians or white-robed tribunes. Just as the valley here expands into a wide circuit and, winding at the side, with sloping forest background all around, stretches its concave curve . . . the sweep of the amphitheater encircles the level ground, and the oval in the middle is bound by twin piles of building. Why should I now relate to you things which I myself could scarcely see in all their many details? So dazzling was the glitter everywhere . . . "Certainly, we rate all cheap we saw in former years and shabby every show we once watched." Look, the begemmed *balteus*[13] and the gilded portico vie in brilliance; . . . Bright too is the gleam from the nets of gold wire which project into the arena hung on solid tusks, tusks of equal size; and . . . every tusk was longer than our plough . . . Oh, how we quaked, whenever we saw the arena part asunder and its soil upturned and beasts plunge out from the chasm cleft in the earth; yet often from those same caverns the golden leaves and branches of wild strawberry sprang amid a sudden fountain spray (of saffron).

Amphitheaters

Nero's arena utilizes the design for spectacle structure that came into being more than a century earlier; the amphitheater as a building type was developed south of Rome, in Campania. The amphitheater at Pompeii is among the oldest such structures in stone, dating to 70 BCE. All the basic features of the classic amphitheater type are in place: the arena, elliptical in plan, surrounded by a podium wall, to separate the bloody action from the spectators, whose seats, supported by a series of barrel vaults, surrounded the performance area on all sides of the ellipse (see figure 2.1). Tucked into the southeast corner of the city, Pompeii's amphitheater also makes use of the city wall as part of the support fabric for the building. Its easy access to two city gates, the Porta Nocera and the Porta Sarno, was convenient for the movement of animals

Figure 2.1 Pompeii, interior of amphitheater

and other special equipment into the facility. It is remarkable, too, in that the dedicatory inscription survives. The sponsors of the new building were public officials of the new colony at Pompeii, established by the soon-to-be-dictator Sulla after the Italian war. Pompeii had been on the anti-Roman side in that conflict, and the placement of a colony in this old Graeco-Italian town served both as punishment and as a guarantee of future security. The singling out of the colonists here as the recipients of this gift likewise points to the political exclusion of the former, still-untrustworthy, residents of this town.

> Source: *CIL* 10.852: Gaius Quinctius Valgus, son of Gaius, and Marcus Porcius, son of Marcus, the quinquennial duumvirs of the colony, because of the honor of holding public office, saw to the construction of the spectacle building with their own money and gave reserved seating to the colonists in perpetuity.

The first permanent amphitheater in Rome was built in 27 BCE by Statilius Taurus, a friend and solid supporter of Augustus in the struggle against Antony. This seems to have been a smallish structure, possibly run by the Statilii as a semi-private facility. Even so, the political value of this structure is indicated by the honor granted in acknowledgment of this public service.

Source: Dio Cassius 51.23: In the fourth consulship of (Augustus) Caesar, Statilius Taurus constructed a stone hunting theater in the Campus Martius at his own expense and celebrated its completion with gladiatorial combats. Because of this he was allowed by the people to choose one of the praetors every year.

The Statilian Amphitheater was not much used, however, and *munera* continued to be held in the Forum and, from around 9 BCE, in the Saepta Julia, a large and relatively open public square located on the Campus Martius. The Statilian Amphitheater may have been too small, or lacked the prestige of the Forum, or was otherwise not amenable to the lavish productions sponsored by the emperor.

Disaster and control

The catastrophic collapse of a "temporary" amphitheater during the reign of Tiberius is documented by both Tacitus and Dio Cassius. Tacitus blames the disaster on shoddy construction but also connects it with the social status of the builder and his inappropriate motives for offering such a spectacle, i.e. in order to profit from it. The legislation that resulted to prevent future accidents likewise set a class stipulation on such initiatives. The huge number of casualties (50,000) resulting from this collapse points to a truly (even unbelievably) enormous temporary structure; the Flavian Amphitheater, not yet in existence at this time, would have a maximum seating capacity of around 50,000. Note also how the authors do manage to blame Tiberius for the disaster, indirectly at least, because his parsimony had deprived the people of "their" games.

Source: Tacitus, *Annals* 4.62–63:[14] In the year of the consulship of Marcus Licinius and Lucius Calpurnius[15], the losses of a great war were matched by an unexpected disaster, no sooner begun than ended. One Atilius, of the freedman class, having undertaken to build an amphitheater at Fidenae for the exhibition of a show of gladiators, failed to lay a solid foundation and to frame the wooden superstructure with beams of sufficient strength; for he had neither an abundance of wealth, nor zeal for public popularity, but he had simply sought the work for sordid gain. Thither flocked all who loved such sights and who during the reign of Tiberius had been wholly debarred from such amusements; men and women of every age crowding to the place because it was near Rome. And so the calamity was all the more fatal. The building was densely crowded; then came a violent shock, as it fell inwards or spread outwards, precipitating and burying an immense multitude which was intently gazing on the show or standing round. . . . For the future it was provided by a decree of the Senate that no one was to exhibit a show of gladiators, whose fortune fell short of four hundred thousand sesterces[16], and that no amphitheater was to be erected except on a foundation, the solidity of which had been examined. Atilius was banished.

Source: Dio Cassius 58.1a:[17] [Tiberius] wasted the lives of men both in the public service and for his private whim. For example, he decided to banish the hunting spectacles from the city; and when in consequence some persons attempted to exhibit them outside, they perished in the ruins of their own theaters, which had been constructed of boards.

As noted, the senatorial decree stemming from the Fidenae disaster stipulated that only the wealthy elite were to build amphitheaters. Aemilius Macer, a third-century jurist, discusses other limitations placed on new construction, particularly spectacle buildings. This legislation recognizes the power of public generosity in providing public architecture and the potential danger represented by certain kinds of buildings. It was in the emperor's best interests to maintain close control of the public figures who might put up such popular structures, an interest inscribed in Roman law.

Source: *Digest* 50.10.3: From Macer's second book on Official Duties: New construction privately funded may be built without authorization from the *princeps*, except when it leads to rivalry with another city or offers the opportunity for sedition or is a circus, theater, or amphitheater. But it is proclaimed by law that new construction built with public funds may not go up without imperial authorization. Nor may any name be inscribed on any public work, excepting only the emperor and the person who paid for the construction.

The Colosseum[18]

The Flavian Amphitheater was the crowning example of the building type. Shining with marble that faced the brick-and-concrete fabric of the building, the Amphitheater made use of the latest advances in crowd control and materials technology, becoming a model of design for arenas empire-wide. It had the largest seating capacity in the Roman world, hosting a maximum number of spectators estimated at 50,000 to 80,000.[19] More importantly, it became a tremendous public relations statement for the Flavian dynasty, which succeeded the Julio-Claudian imperial family after more than a year of civil war in 69 CE.

The Flavians selected this area of the city for a series of public buildings, devoted to the pleasure and well-being of the Roman people. This was in deliberate contrast to Nero, who had converted this area to his own personal use, constructing a palace with sophisticated architectural refinements, placed among carefully landscaped gardens with statuary, fountains, even a lake, all created to enhance his personal happiness. One particularly lavish dining room incorporated a rotating ceiling studded with stars; the emperor diverted the universe towards his personal pleasures. The Flavians, particularly Vespasian, presented themselves as both simpler and more civic-minded than Nero, using their less-than-blue-blooded ancestry to their advantage to strengthen their connection to the population of Rome. Nero's lake was drained; the greatest amphitheater in the Roman world was built in its place. Where before the cosmos served the emperor, now the emperor deployed the massive resources of the Roman world to serve the pleasure of the people. The contrast between the Flavians and Nero is celebrated by Martial, eyewitness to the amphitheater's construction, while the tremendous achievement of Titus, especially, is touted centuries after the event by the late imperial author Cassiodorus.

Source: Martial, *Spectacles* 2:[20] Where the starry colossus[21] sees the constellations at close range and lofty scaffolding rises in the middle of the road, once gleamed the odious halls of a cruel monarch, and in all of Rome there stood a single house. Where rises before our eyes the august pile of the Amphitheater, was once Nero's lake. Where we admire the warm baths, a speedy gift, a haughty tract of land had robbed the poor of their dwellings. Where the Claudian colonnade unfolds its wide-spread shade, was the outermost part of the palace's end. Rome has been restored to herself, and under your rule, Caesar, the pleasances that belonged to a master now belong to the people.

Source: Cassiodorus, *Variae* 5.42:[22] [The Colosseum] was conceived by the power of imperial Titus, spending a river of gold, to display the chief of cities. And since a viewing place is called in Greek a theatre, which is a hemisphere, when two are, as it were, joined into one, it must rightly be termed an amphitheatre. Its arena is shaped like an egg: thus there is a fit space for runners, and the spectators may see the more easily, since its vast circle has gathered them all in.

A relief requisitioned by members of the Haterii family, who were involved in construction in the capital city, shows the exterior of the Colosseum as it appeared during the rule of Titus (see figure 2.2). The three levels of the arcade then present (Domitian added another level of seating) are visible, with the upper two levels decorated by heroic statues and eagles, symbols of imperial power. On the bottom level, one can glimpse a stairway leading into the interior, a feature of the building meriting much celebration. The system of access into the Flavian Amphitheater was tremendously sophisticated and enabled relatively speedy and safe movement in the structure. Each arched entranceway was numbered; each spectator held a ceramic *tessera* that gave the number of the exterior entrance, as well as that of the *maenianum* (a horizontal section of seating), the *cuneus* (a wedge-shaped subdivision of

Figure 2.2 Tomb of Haterii relief. Scala/Art Resource, NY

Figure 2.3 Colosseum vaulting   **Figure 2.4** Colosseum arena

the *maenianum*), the *ordo* (or row) and the *locus* (the seat). Once the spectator entered the building, a series of passages, stairs, and ramps directed him toward the specific area of his seat, easing up on crowding tremendously. At the top of the relief, a compressed view of the interior can be seen, at this time probably a wooden wall; there is no indication, as yet, of the awnings that would eventually be maneuvered to maximize the shade for the crowd in the Colosseum.

The Flavian Amphitheater in its current state of preservation tells us much about the fabric of the building, the concrete, masonry and brickwork and the intersecting barrel vaults capable of supporting the weight of the structure and the weight of thousands of spectators (see figure 2.3). The visitor today

Figure 2.5 Puteoli, arena of amphitheater

may be most impressed by the interior of the Colosseum, confronting the exposed substructures underneath what would have been the arena floor in antiquity (see figure 2.4). There would originally have been trap doors through which animals, *bestiarii* and props would have sprung forth into the performance space; these trap doors are still in situ in the amphitheater at Puteoli, which was built not long after the Colosseum (see figure 2.5). Selective choreography of movement, to distract the audience's attention from a given trap door, would have enhanced the surprise element, giving the impression that a fierce beast had suddenly materialized from nowhere. Originally invisible to the spectator were the substructures; these are probably the most elaborate surviving facilities from the Roman world and represent the pinnacle of a process of development. The substructures are organized around passages on line with the major axis of the amphitheater. Stairs to the imperial box lead from a smaller passage along the minor axis, allowing the *editor* to get to his seat promptly after the opening procession for the games, while the performers took their places in the substructures to prepare for their entrances. Storage rooms opened onto the passage and the annular gallery encircling the substructures, providing much-needed space for props, containment for animals and prisoners, and waiting areas for performers.

Military amphitheaters

Many arenas were built in militarized areas, such as the Rhine–Danube frontier, and in association with legionary headquarters. Others acknowledge the agency of military and ex-military personnel in their construction. Military amphitheaters were probably multifunctional, serving as a venue for drill and weapons practice as well as a morale-boosting facility for spectacle per-formances. The imperial mandate was also served by military amphitheaters: the lessons about Roman power, about conquest and control, taught by spectacles would be considered appropriate for those on the limits of Roman authority. The pleasure involved in such shows would likewise ease the process of assimilation to Roman practices.

Roman legionaries were a tremendous labor resource. The soldiers were trained in construction as key to Roman strategy; Roman troops built highly sophisticated camps whenever they were on the march, camps that provided a secure fall-back position, should such be necessary, or that could be easily converted into more permanent headquarters. These construction skills were frequently deployed on Imperial projects, especially those of strategic value, such as roads, aqueducts, and amphitheaters. Direct evidence of this activity can be found in inscriptions from the amphitheater at Caerleon, documenting labor crews drawn from the legions at work.

Source: *Roman Inscriptions of Britain*, hereafter *RIB*, 339: The century of Rufinius Primus, from the third cohort, built this.

Source: *RIB* 343: The century of Flavius Julinus, from the tenth cohort, built this.

Source: *RIB* 345: The century of Fulvius Macer built this.

Inscriptions from Tomen-y-Mur document activity of military work crews in competition with each other, as to which group could finish more construction in specific period of time. These are associated with a more informal arena.

Source: *RIB* 422: The century of Mansuetus built 39 feet.

Special features

Security was a consideration for the spectacles. Although the gladiatorial armature did not, for the most part, include missile weapons that might damage unwary spectators, the *venationes* did present a real hazard, especially when they featured large, possibly leaping, felines. The podium wall that was a requisite part of any amphitheater varied in height from two to four meters or so, which falls within the jumping capacity of big cats. Evidence for additional safety features can be found associated with many *podia*: a fence with a net or grill between the posts was fixed atop the wall at, for example, Carthage, to safeguard the audience from leaping beasts. In the Flavian Amphitheater, this protective netting may have been placed a few meters inside the podium wall, allowing for a passageway between the fence and wall that could be patrolled by guards, to prevent the escape of animals as well as convicts, if need be. Nero's temporary amphitheater combined some kind of fence and netting with the ingenious device of rollers mounted on the horizontal, which would not allow the claws of a leaping feline to find purchase (and might also present the amusing, if dangerous, vision of a frantically-scrambling cat).

Source: Calpurnius, *Eclogues* 7.50–56:[23] And just where the edge of the arena reveals the spectacles next to the marble podium wall, wondrous ivory is inlaid on connected rods and unites into a cylinder which, gliding smoothly on well-shaped axle, could by a sudden turn throw off any claws set upon it and shake off the beasts.

Privately owned *ludi* and *familiae* were barred from the capital during the empire; their proven utility in violently competitive politics was too much of a risk to imperial interests. Aside from the threat of civic disruption posed by private *ludi*, the economics of the issue were undesirable. The emperor controlled the giving of extraordinary *munera*; he could hardly be dependent on an outside source of supply. The imperial *ludi* were formed under the auspices of the emperor as part of the expanded bureaucracy, each to be run by an imperial procurator.

Circuses

The Circus Maximus was the most important venue for chariot racing in the Roman world, with a building history that stretched back into the earliest

Figure 2.6 Circus Maximus: view from Palatine

days of urban development in Rome. Early chariot racing in Rome was probably done on improvised tracks; any flat length of land would serve the purpose. Spectators could be accommodated on a nearby hillside or perhaps wooden bleachers. This is in line with relatively simple arrangements made for horse racing in the Greek world; the hippodrome seems typically to have been an improvised setting with little monumentality. The elongated depression between the Palatine and the Aventine Hills is the *Vallis Murcia*, the "Murcian Valley," the home of the Circus Maximus (see figure 2.6). Its convenient size and location next to slopes, for seating, meant that it saw use as a venue for events since the earliest days of Rome. Although Rome's founder, Romulus, was credited with the first circus games here, actual construction in this location, in the form of enclosing the track, establishing turning posts, building shrines, was remembered as part of the urban development in the late regal period. Over the course of the Republican period, few innovations were made to the area: sculptural decoration to the barrier and rudimentary lap-counting devices were added. The real monumentalization of the structure came with the end of the Republic and the rise of the Principate. The circus as a formal building type was thus developed by the Romans over time, with innovations devised for the Circus Maximus providing a model for other such structures in the empire.

The Tarquin dynasty, in Roman tradition, was notorious among the early kings for its troubling "tyrannical" efforts to create a political standing outside the Roman aristocracy. Much money was expended on remaking the urban landscape with massive projects, which would, ideally, carry the stamp of the Tarquins for generations to come. The Circus Maximus was part of that; an added advantage was the fact that repeated shows in this venue would present a continuous reminder of King Tarquinius Priscus' leadership and generosity. Livy's account of its formal construction notes Tarquin's efforts to outshine all other Roman leaders, asserting that his political talents and successes were likewise unprecedented. His description of the seating organization differs from that in Dionysius of Halicarnassus; the latter's presentation also casts the audience in a political light, but not one so overtly class based.

Source: Livy 1.35:[24] [After Tarquin's first victorious campaign] he celebrated public games on a scale more elaborate and opulent than any of his predecessors. It was on this occasion that our Circus Maximus was originally planned. On the ground marked out for it, special places were assigned to Senators and equestrians to erect their stands in – or "decks" – as they were called. These stands were supported on props and raised twelve feet from the ground. Horses and boxers, mostly from Etruria, provided the entertainment.

Source: Dionysius of Halicarnassus 3.68:[25] Tarquinius also built the Circus Maximus, which lies between the Aventine and Palatine Hills, and was the first to erect seats around it on scaffolding, the wooden stands being supported by beams, for till then the spectators had stood. And dividing the places among the thirty *curiae*[26], he assigned to each *curia* a particular section, so that every spectator was seated in his proper place.

Julius Caesar spearheaded a grand reconstruction of the Circus Maximus, straightening the long sides of the course and adding tiered seating at the curved end. He is also credited with the construction of the twelve covered starting pens or *carceres* at the straight end of the Circus; this allowed the races to have a more formal beginning with all the horses being released at once. It also added to the excitement of the race by creating the impression that the horses exploded simultaneously from the starting gates. These improvements were undertaken for the huge triumphal celebrations of 46 BCE, for which Caesar had also constructed a stadium, a *naumachia* facility for the holding of naval performances, a "hunting theater," and subterranean facilities at the Roman Forum, meant to enhance the special effects of the *munera* regularly held there (see chapter 1). As with all of Caesar's projects, viewers were supposed to be awestruck by the magnificence, the huge size, the opulent materials, all transmitting the message of Caesar's own generosity, success, and tremendous leadership. Suetonius' description highlights the flexibility of the Circus as a performance area, able to accommodate the visibility needs of a variety of events.

> Source: Suetonius, *Julius Caesar* 39:[27] A broad ditch had been dug around the race-course[28], now extended at either end of the Circus, and the contestants were young noblemen who drove four-horse and two-horse chariots or rode pairs of horses, jumping from back to back . . . Wild-beast hunts took place five days running, and the entertainment ended with a battle between two armies, each consisting of 500 infantry, twenty elephants, and thirty cavalry. To let the camps be pitched facing each other, Caesar removed the central barrier of the Circus, around which the chariots ran.

Augustus added the *pulvinar*, the platform supporting the imperial box, to the Circus Maximus. To some extent, this was a monumentalization of one of the formal honors received by Julius Caesar as dictator, and although its construction is in line with the performance of hierarchy that Augustus consolidates for spectacle audiences, the emperor himself also was known to ostentatiously avoid the exaltation of the imperial box by sitting with friends in the circus stands (see chapter 1). Still, the visibility of the box and the aggrandizement of the Circus overall, combined with the presence on the Palatine Hill of Augustus' residence and the Temple of Apollo, drew a powerful link between the emperor and spectacle in Rome.

> Source: Augustus, *Res Gestae* 19: I built the Curia [Julia] and the Chalcidium attached to it, and the Temple of Apollo and its porticoes on the Palatine Hill, the Temple of the Deified Julius, the Lupercal, the portico at the Circus Flaminius, which I let be called the Porticus Octavia after the name of he who had built an earlier portico on the same spot, the imperial box at the Circus Maximus, the Temple of Jove Feretrius and Jove Tonans on the Capitoline Hill, the Temple of Quirinus.

Dionysius's description of the Circus Maximus dates to his time of residence in that city, under the rule of Augustus. The Circus has by that point assumed its fully monumental form, with multi-level seating supported by both the hillsides and vaulting. The exterior facade of the structure resembled the highly decorative scheme of Roman theaters and amphitheaters, i.e. a series of columned archways that allowed for spectator access and movement. The reconstruction in the modern model of Imperial Rome gives an impression of what this must have looked like in antiquity (see figure 2.7).

Figure 2.7 Model of Rome with Colosseum, Circus. Scala/Art Resource, NY

Source: Dionysius of Halicarnassus 3.68:[29] [The Circus Maximus] was also destined to become in time one of the most beautiful and most admirable structures in Rome. For the circus is three *stades* and a half in length and four *plethra* in breadth.[30] Round about it on the two longer sides and one of the shorter sides a canal (*euripus*) has been dug, ten feet in depth and width to receive water. Behind the canal are erected porticos three stories high, of which the lowest story has stone seats, gradually rising, as in the theatres, one above the other, and the two upper stories wooden seats. The two longer porticos are united into one and joined together by means of the shorter one, which is crescent-shaped, so that all three form a single portico like an amphitheatre, eight *stades* in circuit and capable of holding 150,000 persons. The other of the shorter sides is left uncovered and contains vaulted starting-places for the horses, which are all opened by means of a single rope. On the outside of the Circus there is another portico of one story which has shops in it and habitations over them. In this portico there are entrances and ascents for the spectators at every shop, so that the countless thousands of people may enter and depart without inconvenience.

Figure 2.8 Relief with Circus Maximus. Scala/Art Resource, NY

Trajan expanded the seating capacity of the Circus Maximus and was celebrated for this act of generosity, as seen earlier (in chapter 1) in Pliny's *Panegyric* to that emperor and as demonstrated by an inscription set up by representatives of the voting tribes in which all Roman citizens were enrolled. Here again, then, the connection is made between the spectacles and the citizenry, with the implication that the circus served the interaction between ruler and ruled.

Source: *CIL* 6.955: To the Emperor Nerva Trajan Augustus Germanicus Dacicus, son of the deified Nerva . . . holder of the tribunician power for the seventh time[31]. Set up by the thirty-five tribes because their advantages have been increased by an addition to their seats, due to the generosity of the best of emperors.

A relief from Ostia, dating to the reign of Trajan, depicts the Circus Maximus in action (figure 2.8). The piece was a funerary monument, honoring one or both of the couple standing on the left of the figural frame. The featured action depicts a racing *quadriga*, moving across the foreground away from the couple. The chariot is paced by an outrider and a *sparsor* in front of the horses sprinkles water to keep the dust down. The eye is drawn, however, to the detailed reconstruction of the barrier's key features, the rounded cones of the *metae* at either end, an obelisk on the left of middle, a pair of female statues, possibly Victoria figures, atop columns, and the dolphin lap-counters. Behind the barrier, back to the viewer, waits a helmeted figure with a victory palm, ready to declare the victor. On the far right are the *carceres*, turned sideways and shallowly carved, to give the impression of perspective. The double doors of each starting gate are separated from the next by pilasters with *herms* set before them. The relief may have originally honored someone affiliated with the races, possibly one of the faction leaders, possibly a magistrate/producer of a fine set of *ludi circenses*. The fact that only one driver is depicted may suggest a close connection to the male deceased; perhaps everyone in the relief belonged to the same color (see chapter 6).

Features of the Circus Maximus

A circus was an enormous stadium; like the stadium, it needed a track that was spacious enough for the racing events and yet maximized visibility for the spectators. The resulting performance area was an elongated horseshoe shape, accommodating most of the seating on the long sides. Since horses were racing in the circus (as opposed to humans in the stadium), the size was much greater, with the largest circuses stretching some 550 meters or so in length.[32] The *carceres* or starting boxes were on the short straight end, each closed off by a set of wooden doors all held in place by a single torsion mechanism. Once the presider let fall the *mappa* or cloth signal, circus personnel pulled a cord that released the controlling bolt for the *ostia* or gates of each box, making them suddenly and simultaneously spring open. The shining marble of the *carceres* combined with the anticipation of the race and the fast start to heighten the emotional intensity of the experience.

The arena was divided lengthwise by the central barrier of the track, typically referred to as the *spina* in modern scholarship, but usually called the *euripus* in antiquity.[33] In the Circus Maximus, the barrier was an 8-meter-wide wall, on which accumulated a number of special features. This was where the eggs and dolphins were, platforms with monumental frames that held lap-counters sculpted in these distinctive shapes, one egg or dolphin for each of the seven laps of a standard race. Eggs, raised on individual spikes, had been used for this purpose since the early second century BCE; as the lead chariot finished each lap, an egg would be lowered to mark the progress of the race. Dolphins were of course known by the Romans as a racing animal, due to their behavior around ships at sea. They were also associated with the god Neptune, patron of horses. The addition of dolphins in 33 BCE would also serve indirectly as a victory monument, as the recently-defeated Sextus Pompey, one of Octavian's major rivals, had made much use of such sea symbolism.

Source: Dio Cassius 49.43:[34] And seeing that in the circus men made mistakes about the number of laps completed, [Agrippa] set up the dolphins and egg-shaped objects, so that by their aid the number of times the course had been circled might be clearly shown.

The central barrier was ornamented with an Egyptian obelisk, removed to this location from Heliopolis during Augustus' reign; as with a number of Egyptian artifacts imported at this time, this served to remind people of that exotic new addition to the empire of the Romans, as well as the victory over its last ruler.[35] This message of Egyptian victory and domination was reiterated by the inscription Augustus added to the base of the obelisk.

Source: *CIL* 6.701: Emperor Caesar Augustus, son of the god,[36] chief priest, after Egypt had been returned to the power of the Roman people, gave this gift to the sun-god.

The obelisk in the Circus Maximus became a landmark and a model feature for circus design. While its general connection to the cult of the sun, both in Egypt and in Rome, was recognized, the specific meaning of the original inscription by Seti I was not. Pliny understood the obelisk as a document of the ancient Egyptians' famous wisdom.

Source: Pliny, *Natural History* 36.71:[37] The obelisk set up by the late Emperor Augustus in the Circus Maximus was quarried for King Psemetnepserphreus[38] who was king at the time that Pythagoras was in Egypt; it is 85 feet high, excluding its base which is an integral part of the obelisk. The monolith in the Campus Martius[39] is about ten feet shorter; it was quarried for Sesothis. According to learned Egyptians, both carry hieroglyphs that give an account of natural science.

White lines, painted on the track in designated spaces, organized the chariot races. Lines that led from the starting gates or *carceres* toward the first turn laid out lanes to keep the chariots separated from each other at the outset of the race. Cassiodorus describes a line that goes all the way across the performance space, crossing the track on both sides of the central barrier.

Source: Cassiodorus, *Variae* 3.51:[40] Not far from the gates, a white line has been drawn, straight as a ruler, to either parapet: when the *quadrigae* set out, their contest begins from that point, lest, while they try to smash each other in their excessive speed, the people should lose the pleasure of its spectacle.

The implications of Cassiodorus' statement are a source of some dispute. His reference to the beginning of the "contest" has been taken as an allusion to the "break" line, a line across the track at the first *metae*, from which point the chariots could start jockeying to get to the faster inside position. The matching line on the other side of the barrier is more of a puzzle. Some have identified this as the finish line, to be crossed by the lead chariot after

Figure 2.9 Gallo-Roman mosaic of circus race. Erich Lessing/Art Resource, NY

Figure 2.10 Circus beaker with race and acclamations

the seven laps. Others place the finish line on the same side of the barrier as the break line, close to the farther turning point, a reconstruction that fits some visual renderings of races from antiquity, such as a Gallo-Roman mosaic from Lyons (figure 2.9).

This piece depicts eight *quadrigae* racing in a circus from a modified bird's-eye viewpoint. On the left are the wooden *carceres*, with three presiding magistrates in a shaded box above the central entryway into the track. The central barrier of the circus is quite clearly a series of basins; *metae*, eggs, dolphins, and a low obelisk decorate the feature, with the four eggs in a lowered position suggesting that the race is a bit more than half over. A serious accident has occurred on the left, directly after the turn (always the most dangerous part of the race), and bits of wreckage are scattered over the track. The artist has indicated two white lines, the break line and the finish line, presumably, in the foreground, on the same side of the racecourse.

A glass beaker from the first century CE, found in Colchester, depicts a race between four teams in three registers of blown relief work (figure 2.10). The top range is inscribed with cheers of the spectators, rooting for their favorites.

Source: *RIB* 2419:[41] Go Hierax! Go Olympus! Go Antilocus! Hail Cresces!

The lower two ranges are punctuated by a representation of the *metae* or turning posts that extends over both levels. The lowest register has the four *quadrigae* of the racers, rendered in their essentials. The middle range shows the monuments and features of the barrier, a few in some detail. The eggs and dolphins, for example, are clearly marked, with the spikes of the seven eggs clearly visible.

Shrines were embedded in the earliest circuses in Rome, as the legendary first races were dedicated to the god Consus. By the time of Tertullian, the barrier was crowded with religious ornamentation; Tertullian views this as part of the inherent evil of spectacle, corrupted by the presence of the (demonic, to his way of thinking) Graeco-Roman pantheon.

Source: Tertullian, *On the Spectacles* 8.3–6:[42] Every ornament of the circus is a temple by itself. The eggs are regarded as sacred to Castor and Pollux by people who do not feel ashamed to believe the story of their origin from the egg made fertile by the swan, Jupiter. The dolphins spout water in honor of Neptune; the columns bear aloft images of Sessia, so called from "*sementatio*" ("sowing"); of Messia, so called as deity of "*messis*" ("reaping"); and of Tutulina, so called as 'tutelary spirit' of the crops. In front of these are seen three altars for the triple gods: the Great, the Potent, the Prevailing. They think these deities are Samothracean. The huge obelisk, as Hermateles maintains, has been set up in honor of the Sun. Its inscription which, like its origin, is Egyptian, contains a superstition. The gathering of the demons would be dull without their Great Mother, so she presides there over the ditch. Consus, as we have mentioned, keeps in hiding underground at the Murcian Goals (*metas Murcias*).

Circus as cosmos

For some Romans, the Circus was a manifestation of the cosmos. The reasons behind this are embedded in the links between religion and architecture, going beyond the specific meanings attributed by ancient authors to the features of chariot races and circuses. The rituals of city founding, for example, were a means of drawing the heavens down into the landscape, infusing the urban environment with the power and protection of the divine. The specific connections between spectacle and imperial power made by prominent emperors likewise contained these links between divine order and the experiential reality of the Roman games: the emperor was the agent of the gods, and all he created was blessed and sanctified.

Source: Cassiodorus, *Variae* 3.51:[43] But Augustus, the lord of the world, raised a work equal to his power, and laid out a construction [the Circus Maximus] in the Murcian valley that is a marvel even to the Romans. A vast mass, firmly girded in by hills, encloses a space which contains images of the universe. Hence, they placed twelve gates for the twelve signs of the zodiac. These are opened suddenly and together, by ropes let down from small herms . . . The *biga* was invented as an imitation of the moon, the *quadriga* of the sun. The outriders' horses, on which the circus attendants announce the heats to be run, imitate the speed of the morning star, the sun's fore-runner . . . The whole race is run with seven goals, an image of the week's recurring seven days. The goals themselves, like the zodiacal divisions, have three peaks, around which the swift *quadrigae* wheel like the sun. They signify the limits of east and west. The central *euripus* gives an image of the glassy sea; hence, marine dolphins there pour in the waters. Moreover, lofty obelisks are raised to the heights of heaven; yes, and the taller is dedicated to the sun, the lower to the moon, while the mysteries of the ancients are marked on them by Chaldaean signs, as though by letters . . . Nor is it by chance that the rule of the contest is for a decision in twenty-four heats, as the hours of day and night are assuredly summed up in this number.

Naumachiae

Recreations of famous naval battles were presented in association with a number of major extravaganzas, including the quadruple triumph of Julius Caesar in 46 BCE and the dedication of the Temple of Mars Ultor by Augustus in 2 BCE. Building a facility to house them was a challenge: there had to be some sort of water-proof container, large and deep enough to host sufficient ships and men to hold the audience's interests, and yet also of a size that allowed visibility for the audience, whose seating would also need to be provided. Specialized structures that offered all these features were called *naumachiae*, using the Latin word that means "sea battles."

The *Naumachia* of Julius Caesar seems to have been the first formal facility for water battles built in Rome. Part of the lavish accommodations prepared for Caesar's quadruple triumph in 46 BCE, the *naumachia Caesaris* was an artificial basin that could accommodate a sizeable naval battle, with thousands of participants, both rowers and marines. Appian documents the enormous size of this spectacle, which would of course require an equally large venue to allow space for maneuvering.

Source: Appian, *The Civil Wars* 2.102:[44] [in Caesar's quadruple triumphal celebration] There was . . . a naval engagement of 4,000 oarsmen, where 1,000 fighting men contended on each side.

Source: Suetonius, *Julius Caesar* 39:[45] The naval battle was fought on an artificial lake dug in the Lesser Codeta,[46] between Tyrian and Egyptian ships, with two, three, or four banks of oars, and heavily manned. Such huge numbers of visitors flocked to these shows from all directions that many of them had to sleep in tents pitched along the streets or roads, or on roof tops; and often the pressure of the crowd crushed people to death. The victims included two senators.

This may not have been intended as a permanent facility: Caesar soon had other plans for the space.

Source: Suetonius, *Julius Caesar* 44:[47] His first projects [following his completion of civil war fighting] were a temple of Mars, the biggest in the world, to build which he would have had to fill up and pave the lake where the naval sham-fight had been staged.

Although Caesar never progressed with the Temple of Mars project, his artificial lake was indeed filled in. The size of the *naumachia* might have been a problem for Caesar anyway; such an expanse of water, unless continuously in use, presented a risk of disease. During the years following Caesar's assassination, military expenditure channeled the funds of Rome's leaders away from lavish construction. In 43 BCE, the *naumachia Caesaris* was filled in.

Left with a gap in the spectacular venue, Augustus provided an even more lavish facility for sea battles than Caesar's: located in the Campus Martius, this artificial lake was large enough to contain an island. Augustus noted the measurements in his *Res Gestae*: this would be an area larger than the combined performance space of the Circus Maximus and the Circus Flaminius.

Source: Augustus, *Res Gestae* 23: I presented a *naumachia* to the people across the Tiber where the grove of the Caesars is located, having had an area 1,800 feet long and 1,200 feet wide dug out for the purpose. In this spectacle thirty ships with rostra, either triremes or biremes, fought, along with a large number of smaller ships. There were about 3,000 combatants on these ships, in addition to the rowers.

Determining the location of each event is sometimes a bit tricky; the Circus Flaminius described by Dio as the site of Augustus' crocodile hunt was not an enclosed space. How was the water contained?

Source: Dio Cassius 55.10:[48] [In 2 BCE] There was a gladiatorial combat in the Saepta, and a naval battle between the "Persians" and the "Athenians" was given on the spot where even today some relics of it are still pointed out . . . Afterwards, water was let into the Circus Flaminius and thirty-six crocodiles were slaughtered there.

The question becomes more controversial still when considering the Flavian Amphitheater. The accounts of the dedicatory games to celebrate the opening of this facility in 80 BCE refer to a number of water events, including synchronized swimming by "Nereids," a water *venatio* with specially water-trained bulls and horses, as well as several recreations of Greek naval battles (see chapter 3). But were these water spectacles housed in the Colosseum? And if so, how?

Source: Dio Cassius 66.25:[49] For Titus suddenly filled this same theatre with water and brought in horses and bulls and some other domesticated animals that had been taught to behave in the liquid element just as on land. He also brought in people on ships, who engaged in a sea-fight there.

Source: Suetonius, *Titus* 7:[50] At the dedication of his Amphitheater and the Baths, which had been hastily built beside it, Titus provided a most lavish gladiatorial show; he also staged a sea-fight on the old artificial lake, and when the water had been let out, used the basin for further gladiatorial contests and a *venatio*.

Source: Martial, *Spectacles* 27:[51] If you are here from a distant land, a late spectator for whom this was the first day of the sacred show, let not the naval warfare deceive you with its ships, and the water like to a sea: here but lately was land. You don't believe it? Watch while the waters weary Mars. But a short while hence you will be saying: "Here but lately was sea."

Source: Suetonius, *Domitian* 4:[52] Domitian presented many extravagant entertainments in the Colosseum and the Circus. Besides the usual two-horse chariot races he staged a couple of battles, one for infantry, the other for cavalry; a sea-fight in the amphitheater.

Dio specifically says that the Colosseum was flooded; Suetonius' narrative is contradictory, with the Augustan basin as the venue in one emperor's biography and the Flavian Amphitheater itself in another. Martial's more poetic account refers to sudden changes between land and sea in the spectacle; the rapid flooding and draining of the performance space implied by this is in accord with Suetonius' description in the Titus biography. Whether, and how, the Flavian Amphitheater was flooded remains a topic for debate. The event took place before Domitian added the arena substructures: was there a *hypogaeum* or water basin underneath the arena floor in the original phase of the Colosseum? How deep was this basin? Could it have accommodated large numbers of men on relatively shallow-drafted boats? Could it have been drained (and if so, how?), or perhaps permit the arena floor to be returned to its place while water was still present? Minimal material evidence for water-tight design in the performance area has created doubt for other scholars, who place the major water shows in the *naumachia Augusti*, the usual venue in the first century. Perhaps, they suggest, a shallow and brief flooding of the arena created the impression of a sea and allowed for some splashy events. More serious demands would be placed on a facility hosting naval battles, amply provided by the vastly-larger basin of the official *naumachia*.

Stratification and Seating

As early as the second century, organizers of spectacle were concerned that prime seating be reserved for Rome's elite. Despite the fact that shows were perceived as populist, as a primary method of attracting the favor of the Romans at large, the strong tradition of marking and preserving social status by visible means was carried over into the venues for spectacle. Livy traces official enforcement for this privilege to the early second century, the period when games became a prominent feature of Roman public life.

Source: Livy 34.54:[53] At the *Ludi Romani* [for 194 BCE] the senate for the first time looked on segregated from the common people, and this caused gossip, as every novelty usually does, some thinking that this distinction, which should have been granted long before, was at last bestowed upon a most honorable body; others taking the view that whatever was added to the majesty of the senate was subtracted from the dignity of the commons, and that all such discriminations, which tended to draw the orders apart, were dangerous to impartial concord and liberty . . . This was a novel and arrogant caprice, never desired nor practiced by the senate of any other people. It is reported that in the end even Africanus had repented that in his consulship he had suggested the innovation.

Despite Africanus' regrets, the practice continued. Less controversial than seating by rank was seating set aside for those who had performed significant public service. Recipients of the civic crown, the highest military honor, granted for the saving of the life of a fellow citizen, were entitled to special seating at the games, and repeated acknowledgment of that honor by applause.

Source: Pliny, *Natural History* 16.6:[54] When a man has received this wreath, it is his privilege to wear it for the rest of his life. When he makes his appearance at the celebration of the games, it is customary for the Senate even to rise from their seats, and he has the right of taking his seat next to the senators. Exemption, too, from all civic duties is conferred upon him as well as his father and his father's father.

Augustus' major program of social reform was touted as the revival of Roman tradition and the resurrection of Roman values, after the chaos of the civil war. Part of the package was the restoration of the Roman hierarchy, now purified of decadence, and rededication to the rebuilding of Roman piety and prestige. Restricted seating in the spectacles was demanded by the *lex Julia theatralis*, a highly visible sign of Augustan restoration of Roman order.

Source: Suetonius, *Augustus* 44:[55] [Augustus] issued special regulations to prevent the disorderly and haphazard system by which spectators secured seats for these shows; having been outraged by the insult to a senator who, on entering the crowded theater at Puteoli, was not offered a seat by a single member of the audience. The consequent Senatorial decree provided that at every public performance, wherever held, the front *ordo* of stalls must be reserved for senators. At Rome . . . other rules of his included the separation of soldiers from civilians; the assignment of special seats to married commoners, to boys not yet come of age, and close by, to their tutors; and a ban on the wearing of dark cloaks, except in the back rows. Also, whereas men and women had hitherto always sat together, Augustus confined women to the back rows even at gladiatorial shows: the only ones exempt from this rule being the Vestal Virgins, for whom separate accommodation was provided, facing the praetor's tribunal.

The display of proper clothing, in accordance with class and traditional practice, seems to have been observed in Flavian Rome as well, as suggested by Martial, who notes that a dark cloak is out of place at the shows, where spectators dazzle just as the performers do. Given the weather, the *munera* here could be the ordinary gladiatorial combats in December.

Source: Martial, *Epigrams* 4.2:[56] Horatius was watching the show just now in a black cloak, the only one in the entire assembly, while the plebs and the lesser order and the greatest[57] sat dressed in white together with our revered leader. Suddenly snow fell from the whole sky. Horatius watches in a white cloak.

Figure 2.11   Colosseum, preserved seating

Domitian is credited with renewed enforcement of the *Lex Roscia*, a law originally passed during the Republic that reserved the fourteen front rows for equestrians; remnants of this section, faced with marble, are preserved in the Colosseum (see figure 2.11). That this constituted a change is indicated by Martial, who also notes the presence of ushers to check for qualifications of claimants, which might include the proper stripe on the toga or the proper ring to symbolize elite status.

Source: Martial, *Epigrams* 5.14:[58] Nanneius, who always used to sit in the front row in the days when squatting was allowed, was roused and moved camp twice and thrice. Finally he sat down behind Gaius and Lucius, right between the seats, almost making a third. From that position he peered out with a hood over his head and watched the show with one eye in no seemly style. Dislodged from there too, the wretch moves to the aisle and half-supported by the end of a bench, where he is ill-received, he pretends to the equestrians with one knee that he is sitting and to Leitus[59] with the other that he is standing.

Aside from numerous poems that document the violation of the law in spectators' attempts to sit closer than their genuine status allowed them, Martial also asserts that contemporary elites had abandoned the austere moral rectitude espoused by Augustus, a morality particularly to be shown by the elites as justification of their privilege.

Source: Martial, *Epigrams* 5.41:[60] Although you are more emasculate than a flabby eunuch, and softer than the concubine of Celaenae,[61] whose name the gilded priest of the Mother howls, you talk of theaters and rows and edicts and purple stripes and Ides and clasps and property qualifications, and point at poor men with your manicured hand. Whether you have the right to sit on the equestrian benches I shall consider Didymus; you have none to sit on the husbands'.

3

A Day at the Games

The *munus legitimum* or standardized show established by Augustus had three main parts. *Venationes*, the wild animal fights, took place in the morning. At mid-day were the executions. In the afternoon, viewers enjoyed the highlight of the spectacle, the gladiatorial combats. Much effort was expended to add variety to these events, to surprise, delight, or shock the audience, with much success by all accounts. Spectators would come for the entire day or just a portion, depending on their tastes and other responsibilities. But watching the performers (or victims) was just one part of the lure of the spectacle; the games offered a wide range of opportunities for those in the stands to meet new and attractive people, to engage in conversation, to enjoy free handouts of food or prizes, and to protest or approve recent actions of the emperor or the state. For some, the games themselves were a sideshow for the main attraction, which was the formal gathering of the Roman people. For others, the Roman crowd was something to be avoided at all costs.

Preparation and *Pompa*

How was a spectacle set up? The preparation began some time in advance. The *editor*, if he did not own his own *ludus* or gladiatorial school (and most did not), contacted a *lanista*, one of the professionals in charge of *ludi*; in Rome and a number of regions of the empire, he could tap into the extensive resources of an imperial *ludus*, under the control of the emperor. The *editor* would negotiate the number of gladiators, the skill level and the payment. This process might not be an amiable one: the text of Marcus Aurelius' law on the prices of gladiators (see chapter 1) suggests that *lanistae* engaged in price gouging.

Source: *CIL* 2.6278:[1] the *lanistae* should also be warned against a low desire to profiteer and be warned that they no longer have a free hand in supplying the half which the group of *gregarii* constitute . . . in order that the *lanistae* may be compelled to observe this rule as carefully as possible, competence must be assigned to provincial governors and their legates, or to quaestors, or to legates in command of legions.

The *editor* would then start the advertising process, through word of mouth and by hiring professional scribes to paint announcements of the upcoming shows, like those that survive from Pompeii (see chapter 1). The main information about the *munera* would be given on these announcements: the reason for the show, the name of the *editor*, the number of pairs of combatants and the additional features and amenities, such as *venationes*, music, executions, and accommodations for the audience. Day and location of the show were noted as well.[2] Shortly before the day of the *munera*, a program with the details of the show would be prepared for distribution to the spectators. Names of gladiators, their success records, and the order in which they were to appear would appear on the *libellus* or program. This kind of information would heighten the anticipation of the audience; it might also allow gamblers to calculate the odds on any given match. A painted version of such a program was found at Pompeii; after the show, the results of the matches were added to the record of the listed gladiators. The graffito survives in fragmentary form, but indicates the attention paid to career achievements of individual gladiators.

Source: *CIL* 4.2508: First gladiatorial show of Marcus Mesonius on the sixth day before the *nones* of May [May 2]. Thraex vs. Murmillo: -nator of the Neronian *ludus*, twice victor, against Tigris of the Julian *ludus*, once victor; -ci-s of the Neronian *ludus*, three times victor and dismissed once standing, against Speculator, victor in 69 combats. . . . Hoplomachus vs. Murmillo: -eacius of the Julian *ludus*, dismissed standing, against M- of the Julian *ludus*, victor in 55 combats . . . Gladiatorial show on the fifth, fourth, third and day before the *ides* and the *ides* of May [May 11–14]. Dimachaerus vs. Hoplomachus: I-ciens of the Neronian *ludus*, victor in twenty combats, granted *missio*, against Nobilior of the Julian *ludus*, victor in two combats, winner. Thraex vs. Murmillo: Lucius Sempronius, granted *missio*, against Platanus of the Julian *ludus*, winner. Thraex vs. Murmillo: Pugnax of the Neronian *ludus*, victor in three combats, winner. Murranus of the Neronian *ludus*, victor in three combats, died. Hoplomachus vs. Thraex: Cycnus of the Julian *ludus*, victor in nine combats, winner. Atticus of the Julian *ludus*, victor in 14 combats, granted *missio*. Thraex vs. Murmillo: Herma of the Julian *ludus*, victor in four combats, winner. Quintus Petillius, granted *missio*. Chariot Fighters: Publius Ostorius, victor in 51 combats, granted *missio*. Scylax of the Julian *ludus*, victor in 26 combats, winner. Thraex vs.

Murmillo: Nodu- of the Julian *ludus*, victor in seven combats, winner. Lucius Petronius, victor in 14 combats, granted *missio*. Thraex vs. Murmillo: Lucius Fabius, victor in nine combats, died. Astus of the Julian *ludus*, victor in 14 combats, winner.

The night before the *munera*, the performers were given a banquet, a feast that was apparently open to the public for observation. Mosaic representations of this banquet (see figure 3.1) much resemble depictions of the symposium,

Figure 3.1   Mosaic from El Djem, of gladiatorial banquet. Gilles Mermet/Art Resource, NY

Figure 3.2 Grave relief of *munera* from Pompeii. Museo Archaeologico di Napoli

the idealized dinner party of elite Greek males in which discussion of philosophy and politics was interspersed with drinking games and entertainment. The gladiators' banquet was a site of moral value for Roman observers, as is indicated by Plutarch's approving commentary on how participants made prudent use of this time; no doubt it also allowed the oddsmakers another opportunity to assess potential outcomes.

> Source: Plutarch, *Moral Essays* 1099B:[3] Even among the gladiators I see those who are not entirely bestial but Greeks, who, when preparing to enter the arena, even though costly food items are set before them, find greater pleasure at that moment in recommending their wives to the care of their friends and in setting free their slaves, than in gratifying the appetite.

The spectacle itself began with the *pompa*, a procession that included political and religious elements as well as the performers at the games. A tomb relief uncovered at Pompeii is a rare representation of this particular part of the show, preliminary to the main event (see figure 3.2).

First to appear are the lictors, who announce the coming of the magistrate *editor* and carry the symbols of his office. On the Pompeiian relief they bear the *fasces*, the bundle of rods and axes that symbolized *imperium*, the lethal capacity of Roman imperial authority. They are dressed in the toga, the traditional garment of active Roman citizenship. The lictors are followed by the *tubicines*, the trumpeters whose fanfare called the attention of the spectators, and then by men carrying a platform on their shoulders. This platform was typically a means of transporting the images of the gods and the deified emperors that were a standard part of the *pompa*. Tertullian's description of the procession emphasizes this religious aspect; his argument is that the spectacles are tainted by demonic idolatry, although the features of the *pompa* are based on usual practice for festival ritual. Bear in mind that all spectacle began as elaborate celebrations of the divine powers.

Source: Tertullian, *On the Spectacles* 7.2–3:[4] The *"pompa"* procession – which comes first, proves in itself to whom it belongs, with the long line of idols, the unbroken train of images, the cars and chariots and conveyances for carrying them, the portable thrones and garlands and the attributes of the gods. Moreover, how many sacred rites are observed, how many sacrifices offered at the beginning, in the course, and at the end of the procession, how many religious corporations, furthermore, how many priesthoods, how many bodies of magistrates are called upon to march in it – each is known to the inhabitants of that city where all the demons have gathered and taken up their abode.

On the Pompeiian relief, the next figures carry a writing tablet and a palm branch, to record the victories and to honor the victors. After them is a person identified as the *editor*, surrounded by his entourage who carry the deluxe armor of the gladiators. More musicians follow, and then horses. In an actual procession, the horses would probably be followed by the human performers, the gladiators and *bestiarii*. Cinematic representations typically place the so-called "salute of the gladiators" here.

Little evidence for the use of the gladiators' salute can be found; far more exists from nineteenth-century novelists and poets who were captivated by the cheerful fatalism they perceived in the formal greeting. The only source for the ritual dates to the reign of Claudius and the elaborate *naumachia* he presented prior to the draining of the Fucine Lake. The narrative context, however, implies that it was not part of the regular procedure, but rather something improvised for the occasion that did not achieve its desired effect, i.e. a pardon from the emperor for the convict performers.

Source: Dio Cassius 60.33:[5] Those who were to take part in the sea-fight were condemned criminals . . . First they assembled in a single body and all together addressed Claudius in this fashion: "Hail Emperor! We who are about to die salute you." And when this in no way worked to save them and they were ordered to fight just the same, they simply sailed through their opponents' lines, injuring each other as little as possible. This continued until they were forced to destroy one another.

The events would begin with an announcement of what was to come, the same kind of information found on the *libellus*, with names and records of the performers. Under optimal conditions, the *praeco* or herald could make himself audible to most of the spectators. Large inscribed placards circulating in the audience would reiterate the information; placards could also be used for special announcements by the *editor*.

Venationes

The morning event for the *munus legitimum* would be the *venationes*, the animal shows. Here animals would fight other animals or *venatores* would combat them. In the earliest Republican spectacles, animals would sometimes simply be exhibited in the arena, without the excitement and blood of the hunt; this practice may have continued under the emperors as well. Calpurnius' poetic narrator, a naive visitor from the countryside, was most impressed by the beasts on display during a set of lavish spectacles hosted by the emperor Nero.

Source: Calpurnius, *Eclogues* 7.24:[6] Beasts of every kind I saw; here I saw snow-white hares and horned boars, here I saw the elk, rare even in the forests which produce it. Bulls too I saw, either those of heightened nape, with an unsightly hump rising from the shoulder-blades, or those with shaggy mane tossed across the neck, with rugged beard covering the chin, and quivering bristles upon their stiff dewlaps. Nor was it my lot only to see monsters of the forest; sea calves also I beheld with bears pitted against them and the unshapely herd called by the name of horses, bred in that river whose waters, with spring-like renewal, irrigate the crops upon its banks.[7]

During the imperial period, *venatores* seem to have been very lightly armed, using lances or spears against the animals and protected only by *fasciae* or padded wraps on legs or torso. Some *venatores*, such as the *taurocentae* or bull-fighters, fought from horseback; those facing boars, bears and great cats did so on foot. *Missio* was possible for the *venator*; if he had performed well, he could be released for the day even if he had not killed the animal. This would also preserve a costly animal for future combats.

Meridiani

The *ludi meridiani*, the mid-day executions, followed the animal shows. The number and scale of executions, or indeed, whether they were presented at all, depended on the supply of condemned criminals. Rome and provincial capitals, as centers for Roman judicial activity, would have had more regular access to the *damnati*. Mosaics have fairly straightforward representations of the enactment of these executions. A mosaic from Zliten has several criminals, lashed upright to a kind of chariot or small wagon, being wheeled out to face their carnivorous doom; in one case, arena personnel wield a whip to urge the lion to his victim.

Figure 3.3 Sollertiana Domus mosaic of execution. Gilles Mermet/Art Resource, NY

Another mosaic from North Africa comes from the Sollertiana Domus, a villa in El Djem (figure 3.3). The mosaic, as preserved, features the arena during the *meridiani*, with leopards and bears wandering across the blood-stained sands. In the center is an empty stage, probably a special prop for a gladiatorial event; in the corners several condemned men, arms bound behind them, hair shaggy and disarrayed, are being killed by leopards. The mosaic shows the execution in progress in fairly graphic detail; in the southeast corner, the *damnatus* struggles back against the *bestiarius* pushing him from behind as the snarling leopard springs toward his bare chest. In the northeast vignette, the *damnatus* is being supported by the captor under the weight of the leopard, which clings to the condemned man's chest and thigh as it bites his face. Blood streaming from his wounds gives a narrative context for the other pools of blood marking the arena. This mosaic, in particular, also suggests the vulnerability of the *bestiarii* managing the execution, in very close proximity to animals being made to kill.

Not all *damnati* were killed by animals. Gladiators also served to fulfill Roman justice, as described by some Christian martyr acts; at other times, the condemned were forced to carry out executions on each other, as documented by Seneca for the mid-first century CE.

Source: Seneca, *Letters*, 7:[8] I happened to go to one of these shows at the time of the lunch-hour interlude, expecting there to be some light and witty entertainment then, some respite for the purpose of affording people's eyes a rest from human blood. Far from it. All the earlier contests were charity in comparison. The nonsense is dispensed with now: what we have now is murder pure and simple. The combatants have nothing to protect them; their whole bodies are exposed to the blows; every thrust they launch gets home . . . There are no helmets and no shields repelling the weapons. What is the point of armor? Or of skill? All that sort of thing just makes the death slower in coming . . . The spectators insist that each on killing his man shall be thrown against another to be killed in his turn; and the eventual victor is reserved by them for some other form of butchery; the only exit for the contestants is death. Fire and steel keep the slaughter going. And all this happens while the arena is virtually empty.

Rome and the provincial capitals would have the resources to mount lavish demonstrations of Rome's coercive power, which by the end of the first century had become much less straightforward, staged, instead, as spectacle. Not infrequently, executions were crafted as mythic narratives or framed as a sort of dramatic retribution. In both cases, the punishment exacted was manipulated to hit one or more high points, in which the emotional impact of death and mutilation fulfilled a narrative function. These have been called "fatal charades" and are described with some relish in a number of ancient texts.

Here Strabo describes an execution he witnessed himself, in which the condemned, a Sicilian bandit, met his doom in a setting meant to recall the location of his criminal activity as well as his criminal nickname. The dramatic deconstruction of the scenery could also be read by the audience as a volcanic eruption, appropriate for Mt. Aetna.

Source: Strabo *Geography* 6.2:[9] And recently, in my own time, a certain Selurus, called "son of Aetna," was sent up to Rome because he had put himself at the head of an army and for a long time had overrun the regions round about Aetna with frequent raids. I saw him torn to pieces by wild beasts at an appointed combat of gladiators in the Forum, for he was placed on a lofty scaffold, as though on Aetna, and the scaffold was made suddenly to break up and collapse, and he himself was carried down with it into cages of wild beasts, fragile cages that had been prepared beneath the scaffold for that purpose.

In another deadly vignette, the audience is transported from a sensational peak to the depth of shock and horror by the contrast between the rich fabrics of the dancers' costumes and the execution, punctuated by the unexpected explosion of those desirable fabrics. Plutarch, as a moralizing biographer, does not find this kind of entertainment terribly sophisticated, probably because of the easy manipulation of the audience's emotional reaction.

> Source: Plutarch, *Moral Essays* 554b:[10] But there are some people, no different from little children, who see criminals in the arena, dressed often in tunics of golden fabric with purple mantles, wearing crowns and doing the Pyrrhic dance, and, struck with awe and astonishment, the spectators suppose that they are supremely happy, until the moment when, before their eyes, the criminals are stabbed and flogged, and that gaudy and sumptuous garb bursts into flames.

A number of these "mythic" executions were carried out at Titus' inauguration of the Flavian Amphitheater. As memorialized by the poet Martial, the mythic setting for each not only amazed the spectators, it reminded them of particular aspects of the power wielded by the emperor. Titus makes legends real, he punishes crimes of legendary scale, he recreates nature itself.

> Source: Martial, *Spectacles* 9:[11] As Prometheus, bound on Scythian crag, fed the tireless bird with his too abundant breast, so did Laureolus, hanging on no sham cross, give his naked flesh to a Caledonian boar. His lacerated limbs lived on, dripping gore, and in all his body, body there was none. Finally he met with the punishment he deserved; the guilty wretch had plunged a sword into his father's throat or his master's, or in his madness had robbed a temple of its secret gold, or laid a cruel torch to Rome. The criminal had outdone the misdeeds of ancient story; in him, what had been a play became an execution.

> Source: Martial, *Spectacles* 24:[12] Whatever Rhodope is said to have watched on Orpheus' stage, the arena, Caesar, displayed to you. Rocks crept and a wondrous forest ran, such as the grove of the Hesperides is believed to have been. Every kind of wild beast was present, mingling with the tame, and many a bird hovered above the bard. But himself lay torn by an ungrateful bear. This thing alone was done contrary to the legend.

The following selection from a short novel features a form of torture or execution for female criminals, i.e. rape by a quadruped. This kind of spectacle also appeared in the games of Titus, there given the mythic frame of the story of Dicte. Here the novel's perspective is that of a young man who, as a result of various misadventures, has been magically transformed into an ass and made to undergo a number of unfortunate experiences, only to end up part of a spectacle, the designated perpetrator of the punishment through bestial sexuality. The sexually charged nature of Roman shows, particularly the mime and pantomime performances that monopolized Roman theaters, find a parallel in this kind of spectacle. As this is a comic novel, the execution is presented as a parody of romantic seduction, with luxurious bedding and food and drink to restore the energies of the "lovers."

Source: Ps. Lucian, *The Ass* 52–53:[13] Delighted with the spectacle, [the master of the ass] conceived the desire of exhibiting me doing this in public and told [the keeper] to keep it a secret, "so that," he said, "on the day of the show we may introduce him in the amphitheater with a condemned woman, and he will mount her before the eyes of everyone." Then they brought in to me a woman condemned to be killed by the animals and told her to make advances to me and fondle me. Then finally when the day came for my master to show his munificence, they decided to take me to the amphitheater. When I entered, I found a huge couch made of Indian tortoise-shell and inlaid with gold. On this they made me lie and the woman lie on it by my side. Then they put us on a trolley, wheeled us into the arena and deposited us in the middle. The people raised a loud shout and all clapped their hands to applaud me; a table was placed at one side with many of the dainties which gourmets have at dinner. Handsome wine boys stood beside us, serving us wine in golden goblets. My keeper stood behind me and told me to eat. But I was not only ashamed to be reclining in the amphitheater but also afraid that a bear or lion would leap on me.

One of the more famous stories attached to the corpus of Aesopic folktales is that of Androclus (or Androcles) and the Lion. Set in the early empire, the narrative tells of the surprising outcome of an execution. The surprise here, however, is not in the cleverly appropriate means of dealing death, but the unexpected reprieve for the condemned and the pleased acknowledgment by the crowd (and the emperor) that both animal and *damnatus* were agents in their release.

Source: Aulus Gellius, *Attic Nights* 5.14: [quoting account of Apion] "In the Circus Maximus," he said, "a lavish animal combat was being given for the people. I was a spectator at this event, since I happened to be in Rome. Many fierce wild animals were there, vast numbers of beasts, all rare of shape or ferocity. But beyond all the others the huge size of the lions caused wonder and one lion beyond all the rest. This one lion turned the thoughts and eyes of all on him because of the vigor and size of his body and because of his terrifying loud roar, and because of the muscles and mane rippling on his neck. A slave of a man of consular rank was brought on among many others, handed over to fight the animals. This slave's name was Androclus. When that lion saw this man from afar, suddenly he stood as if astonished and then tentatively and quietly, as if he was examining him closely, he approached the man. Then in the custom and manner of fawning dogs, he gently and courteously wagged his tail and rubbed against the man's body and softly licked with his tongue the legs and hands of the man, who was almost dead with fear by now. The man Androclus recovered his senses, which he had lost during those caresses of such a ferocious wild animal and gradually focused his eyes to look at the lion. Then, as though mutual recognition had been made, you would have seen man and lion happy and rejoicing." The greatest clamor of the people was raised by such an amazing thing, he said, and Androclus was summoned by Caesar and asked the cause, why so excessively fierce a lion would be merciful only to him. Then Androclus told the story of this wondrous and surprising matter. "When my master was imperial proconsul in the province of Africa, I was driven to run away by his harsh daily beatings . . . Then in the blazing heat of the mid-day sun, I happened upon a remote and secret cave into which I entered and hid myself. Not long after, this lion came to the same cave, with one foot lamed and bloody, emitting groans and pitiful moans because of the wound's pain." And he said at first he was terrified at the sight of the coming lion and his spirit frightened. "But after the lion came in," he said, ". . . he saw me hiding in the distance, and meek and mild he approached and seemed to show me his lifted paw and held it out as if seeking help. Then," Androclus said, "I pulled out a huge stalk stuck to the bottom of his foot and I squeezed out poison that had made its way into the deep wound and I carefully drained it and wiped away the gore, now without great fear. Relieved by my efforts, the lion lay down and fell asleep with its paw still in my hands and from that day for three whole years the lion and I lived in that same cave and in the same way . . . But when I became weary of that wild life, when the lion had gone hunting, I left the cave and traveled the road for about three days when I was sighted and taken by soldiers and removed from Africa to my owner in Rome. He immediately saw to it that I was condemned of a capital crime and handed over *ad bestias*. But I realize that this lion also, after I left, was then taken and now returns the thanks for my help and medical care." Apion recounts that Androclus said these things and after all these were written down on a tablet and circulated and announced to the people and then Androclus, at the request of all, was set free and his punishment suspended and the lion given to him by the vote of the people.

Munera

The high points of the spectacle were the *munera*, the gladiatorial combats. Gladiators were usually paired off to fight, with combatants determined by type of armature and by skill level, to keep the audience engaged in the spectacle by·maximizing the suspense and drama of the duel. Gladiators themselves were thought to have internalized the needs of the audience, to such an extent that they wanted "equal" matches in which the outcome was uncertain.

Source: Seneca, *On Providence* 3.4: The gladiator judges it ignominious to be set against an inferior, as he knows it is without glory to defeat one who can be defeated without danger.

The armatures

The earliest gladiators were probably prisoners of war, who used weapons and fighting techniques learned as soldiers in a foreign army. As the gladiatorial institution developed, weapons and techniques were standardized in a number of categories or armatures. Some of these carried names of national groups, such as Samnite, *Thraex* or Thracian and *Gallus* or Gaul, which in origin may have been styles of weaponry and combat brought to Rome by war prisoners. Others are categorized by a particular weapon, such as the *retiarius* or "net-man," or a peculiar feature of his armor: the *murmillo* was a heavy-armed gladiator with a decorative fish or *murmillo* on his substantial helmet. Some were named for their main technique or behavior: the *secutor* "follows" or chases his opponent.

The armatures fall into two main groups: the light-armed and the heavy-armed. Matches were set up between, not within, these two main groups, to give distinctive advantages (and disadvantages) to each combatant. While heavy armor offered better protection, it weighed down the gladiator, made him slower, made him tire more easily. Light armor allowed greater speed and agility, but the greater vulnerability of the armature was a real risk if the gladiator was cornered and his mobility cut off. The different tactics and skills required of the different armatures made the combats more exciting for the spectators. No doubt it was exciting enough for the combatants too.

Some items or equipment were standard for the majority of armatures. The gladiator typically wore a loincloth or *subligaculum*, attached around his waist with a *balteus* or belt. The *fasciae* were leather or cloth padded bands, wrapped around the legs for protection and support. Many types of armature included the *manica* or arm protector, made of padded leather or cloth, often covered with overlapping metal plates. Most gladiators wore helmets and carried shields, although these varied from armature to armature. Helmets also had the effect of depersonalizing the wearer, making it more difficult to empathize with the faceless combatant. This basic equipment gave the gladiator at least partial protection of certain crucial areas, i.e. the head, the arms, and the legs. The purpose here was to minimize the risk of a combatant being disabled quickly by an indirect hit. The torso was unprotected, however, and visibly vulnerable to the opponent and the audience.

The ancient authors that survive do not analyze the armatures in great detail; indeed, most references to the different kinds of gladiators are incidental, cursory at best. Scholars attempt to identify the various types using the abundance of visual representations from antiquity. The overlap between different types, changes in names and in popularity over time, and the occasionally cryptic labels for different armatures make it difficult, however, to correlate representations and names with absolute certainty.

The Samnite armature, possibly derived from the weapons of the Samnites, Rome's enemy in three wars of the fourth and third centuries BCE, is frequently mentioned during the Republic but fades away in the Principate. The weaponry and technique continued in use, by other heavy-armed types such as the *secutor* and the *murmillo*.

The *murmillo* designation comes from the Greek word for a certain kind of salt-water fish.[14] A fish crest may have usually decorated his visored helmet. The *murmillo's* right arm, the sword arm, was protected by the *manica*. Short greaves covered the lower parts of his legs. The rest of his body was protected by the oblong body-shield he carried, covering him from nose to shin when he crouched in the combat-ready position. The offensive weapon used by the *murmillo* was the *gladius*, the short thrusting sword common to the Roman infantry.

The *thraex* or *thrax* may have derived originally from the weapons of the Thracian people; Thracian POWs were taken by Sulla from the army of Mithridates, King of Pontus, in the 80s BCE. The *thraex* carried a small rectangular shield that protected at most the torso. Longer greaves covered his legs to mid-thigh to help compensate for the limited shield. The *thraex* used a *sica*, a type of short saber that was curved or even bent, as a thrusting weapon. A representation of a match involving a *thraex* was found at Bologna (figure 3.4); the long greaves and rectangular shield of the *thraex* at the right are clearly visible, as is a slight curve in the sword he holds over his head. The *thraex* is often represented fighting the *murmillo* or the *hoplomachus* (see figure 3.5). In the Bologna relief, however, he seems to await the outcome of a combat between two *essedarii* with oval shields, now no longer on their signature British-style chariots.

Hoplomachus in Greek means "shield-fighter"; the *hoplomachus* gladiator carried a short, round shield, a lance and a long dagger, all weapons that may have derived from those of the Greek infantry. The defensive equipment was similar to that of the *thraex*, with visored helmet, *manica* on the right, *fasciae* and long greaves to protect the length of the leg.

The most distinctive armature was that of the *retiarius*, who fought with a *rete* or weighted net as his main offensive weapon; this was backed by a trident with sharpened prongs and a long dagger, clutched, apparently, in the same hand that held the trident. With no helmet, no greaves and no shield, the *retiarius* was very lightly supplied with defensive equipment. His *manica* was on the left arm, often supplemented by a *galerus* or *spongia*, a raised metal guard that protected the shoulder and, to some extent, the head and neck.[15] The technique here was to entangle one's opponent in the net, disarming or immobilizing him before moving in to wield the trident. Using both hands, the *retiarius* marshaled considerable force against a helmet or

Figure 3.4   Thraex relief from Bologna. Alinari/Art Resource, NY

Figure 3.5   Relief from Scaurus' tomb at Pompeii

Figure 3.6 Mosaic of Astyanax vs. Kalendio combat from Madrid

greaves; in close contact, however, the trident could at best parry the blows of a sword. It was best for the *retiarius* to fight from a distance.

A mosaic now in the National Archaeological Museum in Madrid depicts different phases of the combat of a specific *retiarius*, Kalendio, in two registers (figure 3.6). The lower, earlier stage shows Astyanax, a *secutor*, fighting Kalendio, whose back is turned toward the viewer. Clearly visible, therefore, is Kalendio's *galerus* or neck-and-shoulder guard, which continues the limited protection offered by the *manica* on his left arm. Although Kalendio has thrown his net over Astyanax, the *secutor* seems unfazed by this and continues fighting. In the later stage of the combat, the viewer sees the crucial moment, where Kalendio is down, wounded (as evidenced by the puddles of blood on the sands) and raising his dagger in submission. Two arena personnel raise their hands and direct their attention toward the *editor*, outside the frame of the picture, whose decision would determine the fate of Kalendio. The inscription above this later scene has the null sign, symbolizing death, following the name of Kalendio, which suggests that the *editor* did not opt for *missio* in his case.

The *secutor* armature was a variation on the *murmillo* type. The main difference was in the *secutor's* helmet, which flowed smoothly down from the top of the head to the shoulders, instead of incorporating a visor to

Figure 3.7 Mosaic of combats from Verona. Cameraphoto Arte, Venice/Art Resource, NY

protect the face. Two round eyeholes allowed limited visibility. The peculiar shape of this helmet gave the *secutor* better protection against the *retiarius'* trident, as the prongs tended to be deflected by the smooth surface. It also made the *secutor's* head look a bit like that of a fish. The closed helmet would, however, limit the *secutor's* air supply, intensifying the long-term burden of the heavy armor. One of several gladiatorial mosaics from Verona, dating to the later second/early third century CE, depicts the moment of decision for a *retiarius*, forced to his knees by his *secutor* opponent (see figure 3.7, left). The distinctive helmet of the *secutor*, smoothly covering the head and face to the shoulders, with two round holes for visibility, is carefully picked out by the mosaicist.

Equites, as the name implies, fought on horseback (see figure 3.5, left), although visual representations of this type show them facing off on foot. Presumably the *eques* tried to unseat his opponent, so the crucial, deciding moments typically depicted visually would happen on the ground. *Equites* wore a visored helmet, often decorated with a pair of feathers on the sides, and carried a small, round shield. They may have started their fights with a lance, switching to the sword after they dismounted. They were usually depicted wearing tunics instead of the *subligacula*. They are also shown fighting each other, instead of being matched against an "opposite" armature; a mounted gladiator would have too much of an advantage over one on foot and the Romans wanted these matches to be genuine contests.

The combats

Gladiators were paired off to fight, with combatants determined by type of armature and by skill level, to keep the audience engaged in the spectacle by

Figure 3.8 Graffito from Pompeii with Attilius and Felix

maximizing the suspense and drama of the duel. A prelude to the matches
might be a battle with blunted weapons, like those used for training in the
ludus. The *probatio armorum* would follow, the test to make sure the weapons
were sharp. Then the combat started.

The tomb of Umbricius Scaurus near the Porta Herculanea of Pompeii (see
figure 3.5) displayed originally a number of friezes depicting various events
from a spectacle probably presented by N. Festius Ampliatus, whose name is
painted above the relief; the names and records of the individual gladiators
were also painted in. Bebryx and Nobilior, two *equites*, are in combat on the
left of the upper register: note their distinctive cloaks and round shields. The
next pair is a *murmillo*, with a long rectangular shield, and a *thraex*, with
shorter shield and long greaves; note the artist's care in depicting the bands
of the *fasciae* wrapped around the thighs of the *thraex*. Then the climactic
moment of a combat between a *hoplomachus* (left) and a *murmillo*; the *murmillo*
has been wounded by his opponent and, on one knee, lifts a finger to ask the
editor for *missio*. The next pair is two *essedarii*, one of whose wounded thigh
has caused him to collapse. The next pair, *retiarii* with tridents brandished in
the air, were probably not set against each other. *Murmillo* and *thraex* finish
off this register; the lower register is likewise two pairs of *murmillo/thraex* duels.

Impromptu sketches enliven the graffiti documenting the first combats of
a gladiator in Pompeii: M. Attilius, who by his long shield was a *murmillo*,
was matched against an established veteran in his first bout. As Fortuna (or
Nemesis) would have it, he defeated his opponent, who left the arena alive.
Attilius' next match is also depicted in sketch-and-graffiti form: another win
for Attilius and another opponent, disarmed and unhelmeted, granted *missio*
(see figure 3.8).

Source: *CIL* 4.10238: Marcus Attilius, *tiro*, won. Hilarus of the Neronian *ludus*,
14 matches, 13 victories, dismissed standing.

Source: *CIL* 4.10236: Marcus Attilius, one match, one victory, won. Lucius Raecius Felix, 12 matches, 12 victories, dismissed standing.

Rules of combat did exist for gladiatorial bouts, although little detail about what they were has survived. The *summa rudis* served as the chief referee, depicted at times with an assistant alongside him, both clad in tunics that distinguish them from the actual combatants. Failure of weaponry that resulted from manufacture or mischance, rather than, say, the outcome of damage during the fighting, may have warranted a pause in the combat to correct the problem. A very long bout could be paused by the referee, to give the combatants a break. Some have suggested that the middle range of the tomb relief from Pompeii (figure 3.2) shows such a pause in the action, when the gladiator is drinking liquid and getting a rub-down from arena personnel. The *summa rudis* would also enforce the pause when a downed gladiator asked for *missio*, as shown in the Verona mosaic (figure 3.7). Here, the *summa rudis* takes action in both scenes, for the kneeling *retiarius* on the left as well as the *murmillo* on the right; the latter has been severely wounded and lies prone on the sands, blood pooling under his body. The arena officiant raises hands and eyes to the editor outside the frame, suggesting that the loser is not yet dead and a decision is needed to authorize the final blow.

Tied matches were rare; gladiators were supposed to fight to a conclusion. Sometimes the vanquished opponent was killed in combat or received a mortal wound. Preferably, they fought until one was forced to submit by being disarmed or immobilized. The loser lowered any remaining weapons and raised one finger in submission. The *summa rudis* would intercede and direct the final decision toward the *editor*, the "real" controller of the *munera*. Meanwhile, the audience would be rendering their opinions: a call of "*Missum!*" or the waving of a cloth would be a recommendation for *missio* for the loser, while turned thumbs or the shriek of "*Iugula!*" advocated death on the sands. Advised by the spectators, the *editor* could demand a death blow for the defeated gladiator or could allow both fighters, in acknowledgment of their effort and skill, to leave standing. This kind of interaction is shown on the Symmachius mosaic (figure 3.9), complete with a replication of the chanting of the audience.

The mosaic is divided into two registers, the bottom scene preceding, chronologically, the one above. In the lower, earlier scene, two dismounted *equites*, recognizable by their tunics, round shields and plumed visored helmets, face off against each other, swords raised. They are flanked by two officials, the *summa rudis* on the right carrying a staff. The gaze of the viewer is directed inward by the gaze of the participants. The objects of the focus, the gladiators, are labeled above: Habilis is the combatant to the right and Maternus to the left. Next to Maternus' name is the null symbol, Ø, indicating the death of Maternus and foreshadowing the action on the register above.

Figure 3.9 Symmachius mosaic from Madrid. Museo Arqueologico Nacional

An inscription crowns the bottom scene and summarizes the critical action of the combat: "While they were fighting, Symmachius thrust the sword." The agent of death, Symmachius, is not one of the gladiators represented. Who, then, is responsible for the death? In the scene above, Habilis, left of center, leans over Maternus, now shown bleeding and prone on the sands of the arena. On the far left stands the *summa rudis*; his body turned away from the pair, toward the unseen *editor*, who is to decide whether Maternus is to be killed or to be granted *missio*. Written above the official is "I kill [him]"; the crowd responds with "We see this," here articulating their primary function of "seeing" and receiving the message of the arena. The audience then addresses the *editor*: "Symmachius, you fortunate man!" As *editor*, he is the one who wielded the sword, he is the one who killed Maternus. He is the final arbitrator of life and death. He is acclaimed as "fortunate" in so doing;

his spectacle was a good one, he made the right decision as the agent of Roman authority and he earned the respect and gratitude of the community.

Good Spectacles vs. Bad Spectacles

Roman audiences apparently had developed tastes as to what constituted a good show, not just in terms of what kinds of armature, what kinds of events, what kinds of amenities would give them satisfaction and pleasure, but what kind of behavior they expected from a good *editor*. The prospective audience in Puteoli, in attendance at the banquet given by Trimalchio in the novel *Satyricon*, has definite opinions about an upcoming set of games offered by Titus Mammaea, a local politician seeking the votes of spectators. The passage contains useful tidbits for how shows worked, as well as how the quality of the competition affected the relationship between the *editor* and the recipients of his generosity.

Source: Petronius, *Satyricon* 45:[16] And another thing, we'll be having a holiday with a three-day show that's the best ever – and not just a hack troupe of gladiators but freedmen for the most part. My old friend Titus has a big heart and a hot head. Maybe this, maybe that, but something at all events. I'm a close friend of his and he's no way wishy-washy. He'll give us cold steel, no quarter and the slaughterhouse right in the middle where all the stand can see it. And he's got the wherewithal – he was left thirty million sesterces when his poor father died. Even if he spent four hundred thousand, his pocket won't feel it and he'll go down in history. He's got some real desperadoes already, and a woman who fights in a chariot, and Glyco's steward who was caught having fun with his mistress. You'll see quite a quarrel in the crowd between jealous husbands and lover-boys. But that two-bit Glyco threw his steward to the beasts, which is just giving himself away. How is it the slave's fault when he's forced into it? It's that old pisspot who really deserved to be tossed by a bull. But if you can't beat the ass you beat the saddle.

But I can almost smell the dinner Mammaea is going to give us – two *denarii* apiece for me and the family.[17] If he really does it, he'll make off with all Norbanus's votes, I tell you he'll win at a canter. After all, what good has Norbanus done us? He put on some two-for-the-price-of-one gladiators, so decrepit already that they'd have dropped if you blew at them. I've seen *bestiarii* give a better performance. As for the *equites* killed, he got them off a lamp – they ran round like cocks in a backyard. One was just a cart-horse, the other couldn't stand up, and the reserve was just one corpse instead of another – he was practically hamstrung. One boy did have a bit of spirit, a *Thraex*, and even he didn't show any initiative. In fact, they were all flogged afterwards, there were so many shouts of "Give it to them!" from the crowd. Pure cowards, that's all.

"Well, I've put on a show for you," he says. "And I'm clapping you," says I. "Reckon it up – I'm giving more than I got. So we're quits."

In Apuleius' novel, another set of games is anticipated very differently by part of the prospective audience, who reap unexpected dividends from the pre-production disaster that befell Demochares, the *editor*. As planned, the spectacle would have included gladiatorial combats and *venationes* with famous professionals as well as lavish preparations for executions of condemned criminals.

Source: Apuleius, *The Golden Ass* 4.13:[18] [in Plataea] we found everyone chattering about a certain Demochares who was sponsoring a gladiatorial show. For, being a man with the highest connections and celebrated for his wealth and generosity, he furnished amusements for the populace as splendidly as his position warranted . . . There were gladiators (the very best names), *venatores* well-known for their agility, and criminals who had forfeited all claim on society and who were being fattened to feast the wild beasts. There were stages built up with stakes, towers of joisted beams like movable houses frescoed richly on the outside, luxurious receptacles for the animals destined to be slain. And as for the animals, they were all kinds imaginable; for [Demochares] had taken no end of trouble in importing from abroad the noble creatures whose bellies were the tombs for the condemned men. But apart from all the other hugely costly items he had concentrated the resources of his estate on collecting a bevy of enormous bears. Besides those snared by his own huntsmen and those bought at heavy expense, others had been donated by his enthusiastic friends; and the whole set were being reared with unstinted care and cost . . . the bears, pining away in their protracted captivity, weakened by the broiling summer heat, and deteriorating in their narrowed quarters, were afflicted by a sudden plague; and their numbers dwindled considerably. Everywhere in the streets you could see the hulks of dying bears strewn about like wrecked ships; and as a result of this the dirty mob, forced by rude poverty and pinched bellies to gulp down any offal that came their way as long as it cost nothing, stole out and served themselves with fresh bear steaks.

The Other Show: Audiences at the Games

Romans enjoyed rooting for their favorites: it generated heightened emotions and the rush of adrenaline, it was not terribly complex or involved, and it engaged the individual, vicariously but powerfully, in the danger and glory of the competition. Gambling on the outcome of matches invested the spectators in the results, increasing one's personal interest in the matches. Gladiator enthusiasts followed specific fighters and often identified themselves by preference for armature categories: light-armed or heavy-armed. *Scutarii* favored the heavily armed gladiators, whose heavy, body-protecting large shields were called *scuta* as a group. *Parmularii* rooted for the light-armed fighter, carrying the smaller, more maneuverable *parma* or small shield.

Emperors were fans too, able to dispute knowledgeably about different kinds of armature for gladiators. Titus shows himself to be positively involved in the games, sharing the spectators' enthusiasms but moderating his behavior appropriately.

Source: Suetonius, *Titus* 8:[19] [Titus] openly acknowledged his partisanship of the Thracian-style gladiators and would gesture and argue vociferously with the crowd on this subject, though never losing either his dignity or his sense of justice.

The audience, of course, was not all-consumed by the spectacle in the arena. In the stands, spectators took the opportunity to interact with one another in interesting and inventive ways that registered greater or lesser engagement with the actual performance. The heightened emotions provided initiative for personal pursuits, be they romantic or intellectual.

Ovid provides a detailed (and tongue-in-cheek) manual on how to further a seduction as a spectator in the stands. Much attention is given to making use of the specifics of the venue for flirtation and "accidental" caresses: the crowding, the grime, the relative ease of contact in this mixed-sexes scenario. The emotional ambience is also an opportunity for Ovid's lothario: shared enthusiasms and cheering as much as moaning reactions to mortal wounds parallel the feelings of lovers' intimacies.

Source: Ovid, *The Art of Love* 1.135–170:[20] Furthermore, don't overlook the meetings when horses are running; in the crowds at the track opportunity waits. There is no need for a code of finger-signals or nodding. Sit as close as you like; no one will stop you at all. In fact, you will have to sit close – that's one of the rules, at a race track. Whether she likes it or not, contact is part of the game. Try to find something in common, to open the conversation; don't care too much what you say, just so that everyone hears. Ask her, "Whose colors are those?" – that's good for an opening gambit. Put your own bet down, fast, on whatever she plays. Then, when the gods come along in procession, ivory, golden, outcheer every young man, shouting for Venus, the queen. Often it happens that dust may fall on the blouse of the lady. If such dust should fall, carefully brush it away. Even if there's no dust, brush off whatever there isn't. Any excuse will do: why do you think you have hands? If her cloak hangs low, and the ground is getting it dirty, gather it up with care, lift it a little, so! Maybe, by the way of reward, and not without her indulgence, you'll be able to see ankle or possibly knee. Then look around and glare at the fellow who's sitting behind you, don't let him crowd his knees into her delicate spine. Girls, as everyone knows, adore these little attentions: getting the cushion just right, that's in itself quite an art; yes, and it takes a technique in making a fan of your program or in fixing a stool under the feet of a girl.

> Such is the chance of approach the race track can offer a lover.
> There is another good ground, the gladiatorial shows. On that sorrowful sand Cupid has often contested, and the watcher of wounds often has "had it" himself.[21] While he is talking, or touching a hand, or studying entries, asking which one is ahead after his bet has been laid, wounded himself, he groans to feel the shaft of the arrow; he is a victim himself, no more spectator, but show.

A real-life example of such flirtation is given by Plutarch in his biography of the dictator Sulla, who met his last wife at the games. Plutarch's description acknowledges that the venue enables this kind of interaction in the audience, combining proximity of the sexes with the possibility for social circulation and intersecting eye lines.

> Source: Plutarch, *Sulla* 35:[22] A few months later there was a show of gladiators and since at this time men and women used to sit all together in the theater, with no separate seating accommodation for the sexes, there happened to be sitting near Sulla a very beautiful woman of a most distinguished family. Her name was Valeria ... As she passed behind Sulla, she rested her hand on him, pulled off a little piece of wool from his toga and then went on to her seat. When Sulla looked round at her in surprise, she said: "There's no reason to be surprised, Dictator. I only want to have a little bit of your good luck for myself." Sulla was far from displeased ... After this they kept glancing at each other, constantly turning their heads to look, and exchanging smiles. And in the end negotiations began for marriage.

The air of seduction in the stands was considered one of its dangers by the early Christian author Tertullian, who noted that fans "on the prowl" paid much attention to clothing and at least pretended interest in what was happening in the arena, as an opening to banter and flirtation.

> Source: Tertullian, *On the Spectacles* 25.2:[23] No, indeed, in every kind of spectacle he will meet with no greater temptation than that over careful attire of women and men. That sharing of feelings and that agreement or disagreement over favorites fan the sparks of lust from their fellowship.

Clement, a second-century Christian author, went into minute detail on how best to lead a Christian life. His condemnation of the arena focuses on its sexualized ambience, concentrating on the audience's lack of control as the prime cause of the lascivious atmosphere.

Source: Clement of Alexandria, *The Instructor* 3.11.77:[24] These assemblies, indeed, are full of confusion and iniquity; and these pretexts for assembling are the cause of disorder – men and women assembling promiscuously in the sight of one another. In this respect the assembly has already shown itself bad: for when the eye is lascivious, the desires grow warm; and the eyes that are accustomed to look impudently at one's neighbors during the leisure granted to them, inflame the amatory desires. Let spectacles, therefore, and plays that are full of scurrility and of abundant gossip, be forbidden.

The passion stirred by such shows roused some to take extreme action; Petronius' novel attributes some of the frenzied female sexual excitement to the allure of the forbidden, the marginal status of the performers. Note the reference to seating by social status in the woman's avoidance of the elite section.

Source: Petronius, *Satyricon* 126:[25] Some women get heated up over the absolute dregs [of society] and can't feel any passion unless they see slaves or bare-legged messengers. The arena drives some of them into heat, or a mule-driver covered with dust, or actors displayed on the stage. My mistress is one of this type. She jumps across the first fourteen seats from the orchestra and looks for something to love among the lowest crowd.

Dangerous games

Dangers to spectators were typically minimized by the construction of the spectacle venues; efficient movement through entrances would cut back on crowding, nets and barriers protected them from wild animals, even the risk of sunburn was diminished by the awnings. Rowdiness in the stands was, however, a recurrent problem, perhaps the ancient equivalent of modern soccer hooliganism. In the early empire, soldiers were regularly stationed at the spectacles to keep competitive passions from turning to blows. Nero's adoption of a "popular" stance in his early years led him to ease up on this control; in fact, the rowdy behavior of a portion of the spectators in the stands was not only tolerated but encouraged by the relaxed and approving attitude of the emperor.

Source: Tacitus, *Annals* 13.25:[26] In the theater, there were brawls between gangs favoring rival performers. Nero converted these disorders into serious warfare. For he waived penalties and offered prizes – watching in person, secretly and on many occasions even openly. Finally, however, public animosities and fears of worse disturbances left no alternative but . . . to station troops in the theater again.

A reference in the corpus of Roman law suggests that a particular demographic, the *iuvenes* or "young men," was seen as primarily responsible for creating a public nuisance at spectacles. The *iuvenes* was also the name for the young men's clubs that were in part sponsored by the authorities, as a means of developing the proper attitudes toward tradition and responsibility among a network of the younger generation of future leaders. Some have seen in this law a reference to the breakdown of social order in the late Empire, beginning with the restless youth in the clubs.

Source: *Digest* 48.19.28.3:[27] From Callistratus, *Judicial Examinations*, book 6 . . . Certain persons, who commonly call themselves "the young men," in certain towns where there is unrest play to the cheap seats for the applause of the mob. If they do no more than this and have not previously been admonished by the governor, they are beaten with rods and dismissed, or also forbidden to attend public spectacles. But if after such correction they are caught doing the same again, they should be punished with exile; or sometimes capital punishment may be imposed, for example, when they have too often been guilty of seditious and riotous behavior and after repeated arrests and too-lenient treatment persist in the same rash attitude.

Fights could break out in the stands at the spectacle, as happened in 59 CE in Pompeii's amphitheater, with serious consequences. Tacitus' description of the incident connects it to local partisanship, competition between boosters of Pompeii and the neighboring Nuceria, with a disenfranchised Roman senator possibly involved in the dispute. The Senate's punishment banned not only spectacles in Pompeii but also private *collegia* or associations, which may be a recognition of the risky behavior of fan clubs.

Source: Tacitus, *Annals* 14.17:[28] About the same time a trifling beginning led to frightful bloodshed between the inhabitants of Nuceria and Pompeii, at a gladiatorial show exhibited by Livineius Regulus, who had been, as I have related, expelled from the Senate. With the unruly spirit of townsfolk, they began with abusive language of each other; then they took up stones and at last weapons, the advantage resting with the populace of Pompeii, where the show was being exhibited. And so there were brought to Rome a number of the people of Nuceria, with their bodies mutilated by wounds, and many lamented the deaths of children or of parents. The emperor entrusted the trial of the case to the Senate, and the Senate to the consuls, and then again the matter being referred back to the Senators, the inhabitants of Pompeii were forbidden to have any such public gathering for ten years, and all associations they had formed in defiance of the laws were dissolved. Livineius and the others who had excited the disturbance were punished with exile.

Figure 3.10 Fresco of riot at Pompeii. Scala/Art Resource, NY

A fresco found at Pompeii (see figure 3.10) depicts the riot of 59 in progress, as figures *not* in gladiatorial gear beat each other in the arena, in the
stands and in the streets of the city near the amphitheater. The artist has
tried to render something of a bird's-eye view of the setting, with some
care given to the representation of the *vela* or awning in use as well as
the distinctive exterior staircase of this early venue. More striking, however, are the clusters of out-of-scale figures committing mayhem upon each
other.

The actual venue of the spectacle might not be safe. Tacitus spends some
time on the enormous human costs of the tragedy at Fidenae in 27 CE, when
a badly built temporary amphitheater collapsed (see chapter 2). Tacitus finds
a moral value in the Romans' generous response to disaster – not unlike
modern-day media coverage of tragedy.

Source: Tacitus, *Annals* 4.62–63:[29] Those who were crushed to death in the first moment of the accident had at least under such dreadful circumstances the advantage of escaping torture. More to be pitied were they who with limbs torn from them still retained life, while they recognised their wives and children by seeing them during the day and by hearing in the night their screams and groans. Soon all the neighbors in their excitement at the report were bewailing brothers, kinsmen or parents. Even those whose friends or relatives were away from home for quite a different reason, still trembled for them, and as it was not yet known who had been destroyed by the crash, suspense made the alarm more widespread.

As soon as they began to remove the debris, there was a rush to see the lifeless forms and much embracing and kissing. Often a dispute would arise, when some distorted face, bearing however a general resemblance of form and age, had baffled their efforts at recognition. Fifty thousand persons were maimed or destroyed in this disaster . . . At the moment of the calamity the nobles threw open their houses and supplied indiscriminately medicines and physicians, so that Rome then, notwithstanding her sorrowful aspect, wore a likeness to the manners of our forefathers who after a great battle always relieved the wounded with their bounty and attentions.

Special treats

Ancient authors and surviving announcements of games often herald the attention to detail demonstrated by the *editor* of the spectacle. A magnanimous sponsor not only provided exciting and colorful shows and fierce competition; he also took care of the human needs of his audience. This took the form of special comforts for the spectator: shade, snacks, sprinkles, and door prizes. A frequent source of pleasure for the Pompeiian audience was the provision of *vela* or awnings, to provide cooling shade; the phrase *"vela erunt"* ("there will be awnings") is nearly a standard feature in the announcements of games painted on the walls of that town. The audience in Rome was also familiar with the *vela*; development of the concept in the capital improved on the material and the expanse of such awnings for spectators, as Pliny the Elder documents.

Source: Pliny, *Natural History* 19.23–25:[30] Linen cloths were used in the theaters as awnings, a plan first invented by Quintus Catulus[31] when dedicating the Capitol. Next Lentulus Spinther is recorded to have been the first to stretch awnings of cambric in the theater, at the *Ludi Apollinares*.[32] Soon afterwards Caesar when dictator stretched awnings over the whole of the Roman Forum, as well as the Sacred Way from his mansion, and the slope right up to the Capitol, a display recorded to have been thought more wonderful even than the show of gladiators which he gave . . . recently awnings actually of sky blue and spangled with stars have been stretched with ropes even in the emperor Nero's amphitheaters.

Food, spectacular food

Distribution of food items as largesse had a long tradition in Roman politics; patrons in the early Republic, for example, fed their clients who came to wish them a good morning at the *salutatio*. Redistribution of wealth through public banquets was a regular feature of public religion as well as private events, such as funerals, and those that straddled the dividing line between public and private, including triumphs and *munera*. Grandiose handouts of food and beverages formed part of the spectacle during the great imperial games; at a set of games under Domitian, Statius was impressed by the lush and tasty treats falling from overhead.

Source: Statius, *Silvae* 1.6.9–50:[33] Scarce was the new dawn stirring, when already sweetmeats were raining from the line, such was the dew the rising East wind was scattering; the famous fruit of Pontic nut groves or of Idume's fertile slopes, all that devout Damascus grows upon its boughs or thirsty Caunus ripens falls in a generous profusion. Biscuits and melting pastries, Amerian fruit[34] not over-ripe, must-cakes, and bursting dates from invisible palms were showering down. Not with such torrents do stormy Hyades overwhelm the earth or Pleiades dissolved in rain, as the hail that from a sunny sky lashed the people in the Latin spectacle seats . . . Behold another multitude, handsome and well-dressed, makes its way along all the rows. Some carry baskets of bread and white napkins and more luxurious fare; others serve languorous wine in abundant measure . . . you nourish alike the circle of the noble and austere and the folk that wear the toga and since, O generous lord, you feed so many multitudes, haughty Annona[35] knows nothing of this festival . . . One table serves each class alike: children, women, people, equestrians, and senators; freedom has loosed the bonds of awe. And even you as well – what god could have such leisure or promise as much – you came and shared our banquet. And now everyone, be he rich or poor, boasts himself the Emperor's guest.

Sparsiones

The Latin for sprinkles and door prizes uses the same fundamental word: *sparsio*. Alone, the word refers to a light cascade of water, most refreshing to a sweaty audience on a warm Mediterranean day. Sometimes the water could be mixed with balsam or saffron, to provide a pleasant scent. Pompey introduced these sprinkles into Rome for use in his theater, built during the

50s BCE. Seneca mentions a spraying contraption as an example of misdirected intelligence, human ingenuity used for frivolous purpose. His reference might be recognizable to a modern audience as "misters": water under pressure was distributed from a perforated pipe and floated gently onto the heads of the audience.

Source: Seneca *Letters* 90.15:[36] And today just tell me which of the following you consider the wiser man: the one who discovers a means of spraying saffron perfumes to a tremendous height from hidden pipes, who fills or empties channels in one sudden rush of water, who constructs a set of interchangeable ceilings for a dining room in such a way as to produce a constant succession of different patterns.

Sparsio missilium, in contrast to *sparsiones*, refers to a light "rain" of small wooden balls, tossed at spectators. These balls acted as vouchers, inscribed with the prizes the holder could collect from the sponsor. These prizes ran the gamut from food items to cash to the title to an apartment; the voucher would become part of the holder's estate, to be passed on to his heirs, even if not yet redeemed at the time of the owner's death.

Source: Dio Cassius 66.25:[37] Titus also furnished some things that were of practical use to the people. He would throw down into the theatre from aloft little wooden balls variously inscribed, one designating some article of food, another clothing, another a silver vessel or perhaps a gold one, or again horses, pack-animals, cattle or slaves. Those who seized them were to carry them to the dispensers of the bounty, from whom they would receive the article named.

With such desirable items literally up for grabs, the scramble to catch these "missiles" could turn to frenzy. Seneca compares the door prizes at the games to advantages distributed by Fortune to human beings; these tangible assets of possessions and advancement are not unproblematic but carry unsuspected risks, as do the *sparsiones missilium*, bringing joy and danger to those who try to catch them.

Source: Seneca, *Letters* 74.7:[38] Imagine now to yourself that Fortuna is presenting games and is showering down honors, riches, and influence upon this crowd of mortals; some of these prizes have already been torn to pieces in the hands of those who try to snatch them, others have been divided among untrustworthy partnerships, and still others have been snatched to the great detriment of those into whose possession they have come . . . others have been lost to their seekers because they were snatching too eagerly for them and, just because they are greedily seized upon, have been knocked from their hands . . . The most sensible man, therefore, runs from the theater as soon as he sees the little gifts being brought in; for he knows that one pays a high price for small favors. No one will grapple with him on the way out, or strike him as he departs; the quarrelling takes place where the prizes are.

Inaugural Games at the Flavian Amphitheater

The construction of the Colosseum was a key feature of the Flavian dynasty's imperial image. The family were "upstarts," their bloodlines lacking the patrician prestige that the Julio-Claudians had enjoyed. The change in imperial leadership was something of a test for the office of emperor as well. Much of the authority enjoyed by the first dynasty had been built up by the personal efforts of Augustus himself, with the best of his familial successors following established precedent very much in the name of their honored ancestor. Ignoring such traditions imperiled the emperor, as Nero had discovered to his detriment. After a period of civil war, the Flavians had to establish their legitimacy as rulers in the civil sphere, beyond the martial victory they'd already achieved. An important means of persuasion used by the Flavians was spectacle, to be housed in the enormous and lavish venue provided by Flavian generosity. The hundred days of games held by Titus to celebrate the opening of the Colosseum was an impressive way to demonstrate Flavian worthiness to their political constituencies. Descriptions of the events document repeated references to the cosmic or mythic level of Flavian power, power that was channeled positively toward leniency, accommodation, beneficence, but was nevertheless awe-inspiring.

Source: Dio Cassius 66.25:[39] Most that [Titus] did was not characterized by anything noteworthy, but in dedicating the hunting-theatre [amphitheater] and the baths that bear his name he produced many remarkable spectacles. There was a battle between cranes and also between four elephants; animals both tame and wild were slain to the number of nine thousand; and women (not those of any prominence, however) took part in despatching them. As for the men, several fought in single combat and several groups contended together both in infantry and naval battles. For Titus suddenly filled this same theatre with water and brought in horses and bulls and some other domesticated animals that had been taught to behave in the liquid element just as on land. He also brought in people on ships, who engaged in a sea-fight there, impersonating the Corcyreans and Corinthians; and others gave a similar exhibition outside the city in the grove of Gaius and Lucius, a place which Augustus had once excavated for this very purpose. There, too, on the first day there was a gladiatorial exhibition and wild-beast hunt, the lake in front of the images having first been covered over with a platform of planks and wooden stands erected around it. On the second day there was a horse-race, and on the third day a naval battle between three thousand men, followed by an infantry battle. The "Athenians" conquered the "Syracusans" (these were the names the combatants used), made a landing on the islet and assaulted and captured a wall that had been constructed around the monument. These were the spectacles that were offered, and they continued for a hundred days.

Martial's contemporary *Book of Spectacles* is a poetic celebration of the wonders displayed at the inaugural games sponsored by Titus. His "spin" on the games gives us an eyewitness' interpretation of what they meant and what sort of message the emperor was trying to convey to the spectators, who were the beneficiaries of this lavish gift. Repeatedly, Martial celebrates the universal authority of the emperor Titus. The fawning pachyderm in the following selection, possibly trained to curtsey for the procession, in this vignette reflects the peculiar status of the elephant in the Roman world, as an affiliate of power that could spontaneously recognize and submit to "natural" authority.

Source: Martial, *Spectacles* 20:[40] Devoted and suppliant the elephant adores you, Caesar, he who but lately was so formidable to the bull. He does it unbidden, no master teaches him. Believe me, he too feels our god.

Martial presents a comparison between Titus and Jupiter, referencing here the tale of Jupiter/Jove in eagle form abducting his favorite Ganymede. Titus' power is further demonstrated in this variation of the "lion and lamb" metaphor for the overturning of "natural" laws.

Source: Martial, *Epigrams* 1.6:[41] As the eagle bore the boy through the airs of heaven, the timid talons did not harm their clinging freight. Now Caesar's lions are won over by their prey and the hare plays safely in the massive jaws. Which do you think the greater marvel? Behind both stands the Highest. The one is Caesar's, the other Jove's.

Here the poet documents the occasionally unavoidable difficulties in work-ing with animals, here meant to defend the emperor's spectacle by suggesting the wait was worthwhile. The reluctance of the rhinoceros at Titus' games offers a context for the "miraculous" avoidance by the animals meant to destroy the Christian martyrs (see chapter 5).

Source: Martial, *Spectacles* 26:[42] While the trembling trainers were goading the rhinoceros and the great beast's anger was long a-gathering, men were giving up hope of the combats of promised warfare; but at length the fury we earlier knew returned. For with his double horn he tossed a heavy bear as a bull tosses dummies from his head to the stars. [With how sure a stroke does the strong hand of Carpophorus, still a youth, aim Norcian spears!] He lifted two steers with his mobile neck, to him yielded the fierce buffalo and the bison. A lion fleeting before him ran headlong upon the spears. Go now, you crowd, complain of tedious delays!

This is an example of Titus' balanced stance toward gladiatorial enthusiasm, here connected to respect for traditional procedure and display of skill, followed by generosity without precedent.

Source: Martial, *Spectacles* 31:[43] As Priscus and Verus each drew out the contest and the struggle between the pair long stood equal, shouts loud and often sought discharge for the combatants. But Caesar obeyed his own law (the law was that the bout go on without shield until a finger be raised).[44] What he could do, he did, often giving dishes and presents. But an end to the even strife was found: equal they fought, equal they yielded. To both Caesar sent wooden swords and to both palms. Thus valor and skill had their reward. This has happened under no prince but you, Caesar: two fought and both won.

Commodus' Games

The emperor Commodus carried on in the tradition of extraordinary imperial games by sponsoring a lavish spectacle for 14 days in 192 CE. Commodus was the first emperor born to a reigning emperor; all his life he had known the license of unbridled power, with little experience of discipline beyond, apparently, that of the *ludus* and the circus. Like other emperors, he tried to create an image of authority through the use of spectacle. He is not unlike Titus in his repeated references to mythology, a means of inserting the emperor into the superhuman narratives of power. The way in which this emperor interacts with the symbolic repertory is different; the emperor himself becomes a *venator* and a gladiator, taking upon himself the taint of such *infames*. He does not, however, please the crowd like a real performer; many of his actions in the arena are read by Dio Cassius, an eye-witness to these events, as a deliberate threat to the audience. The appropriate relationship of power is grotesquely twisted; the bears and ostriches are stand-ins for the victimized Roman people as the boundaries between the protected and the condemned are repeatedly violated.

Source: Dio Cassius 73.18–21:[45] On the first day [Commodus] killed a hundred bears all by himself, shooting down at them from the railing of the balustrade; for the whole amphitheater had been divided up by means of two intersecting cross-walls which supported the gallery that ran its entire length, the purpose being that the beasts, divided into four herds, might more easily be speared at short range from any point. In the midst of the struggle he became weary, and taking from a woman some chilled sweet wine in a cup shaped like a club,[46] he drank it at one gulp. At this both the populace and we [senators] all immediately shouted out the words so familiar at drinking-bouts, "Long life to you!" And let no one feel that I am sullying the dignity of history by recording such occurrences. On most accounts, to be sure, I should not have mentioned this exhibition; but since it was given by the emperor himself, and since I was present myself and took part in everything seen, heard and spoken, I have thought proper to suppress none of the details, but to hand them down, trivial as they are, to the memory of those who shall live hereafter, just like any events of the greatest weight and importance . . . On the first day, then, the events that I have described took place. On the other days he descended to the arena from his place above and cut down all the domestic animals that approached him and some also that were led up to him or were brought before him in nets. He also killed a tiger, a hippopotamus, and an elephant. Having performed these exploits, he would retire, but later, after luncheon, would fight as a gladiator. The form of contest that he practiced and the armor that he used were those of the *secutores* as they were called: he held the shield in his right hand and the wooden sword[47] in his left, and indeed took great pride in the fact that he was left-handed. His antagonist would be some athlete or perchance a gladiator armed with a wand; sometimes it was a man that he himself had challenged, sometimes one chosen by the people; for in this as well as other matters he put himself on equal footing with the other gladiators, except for the fact that they enter the lists for a very small sum, whereas Commodus received a million sesterces from the gladiatorial fund each day. Standing beside him as he fought were Aemilius Laetus, the prefect, and Eclectus, his *cubicularius*;[48] and when he had finished his sparring match, and of course won it, he would then, just as he was, kiss these companions through his helmet.[49] After this the regular contestants would fight. The first day he personally paired off all the combatants down in the arena, where he appeared with all the trappings of Mercury, including a gilded wand, and took his place on a gilded platform; and we regarded his doing this as an omen. Later he would ascend to his customary place and from there view the remainder of the spectacle with us. After that the contests no longer resembled child's play, but were so serious that great numbers of men were killed. Indeed, on one occasion, when some of the victors hesitated to slay the vanquished, he fastened the various contestants together and ordered them all to fight at once. Thereupon the men so bound fought man against man, and some killed even those who did not belong to their group at all, since the numbers and the limited space had brought them together.

That spectacle, of the general character I have described, lasted fourteen days. When the emperor was fighting, we senators together with the equestrians always attended. Only Claudius Pompeianus the elder never appeared, but sent his sons, while remaining away himself; for he preferred even to be killed for this rather than to behold the emperor, the son of Marcus, conducting himself in such a fashion. . . . of the populace in general, many did not enter the amphitheatre at all, and others departed after merely glancing inside, partly from shame at what was going on, partly also from fear, inasmuch as a report spread abroad that he would want to shoot a few of the spectators in imitation of Hercules and the Stymphalian birds. And this story was believed, too, because he had once got together all the men in the city who had lost their feet as the result of disease or some accident, and then, after fastening about their knees some likeness of serpents' bodies, and giving them sponges to throw instead of stones, had killed them with blows of a club, pretending that they were giants.[50]

This fear was shared by all, by us [senators] as well as by the rest. And here is another thing that he did to us senators which gave us every reason to look for our death. Having killed an ostrich and cut off its head, he came up to where we were sitting, holding the head in his left hand and in his right hand raising aloft his bloody sword; and though he spoke not a word, yet he wagged his head with a grin, indicating that he would treat us in the same way. And many would indeed have perished by the sword on the spot, for laughing at him (for it was laughter rather than indignation that overcame us), if I had not chewed some laurel leaves, which I got from my garland, myself, and persuaded the others who were sitting near me to do the same, so that in the steady movement of our jaws we might conceal the fact that we were laughing.

Tainted by the Crowd

Criticism of spectacle was relatively rare among the Romans, either the populace or the intelligentsia. Those who did perceive a negative effect of the games tended to focus on issues that may seem strange to a modern reader. Perhaps the most prominent of these is the perception that spending time in a crowd had a damaging impact. This is the main focus of a famous letter of Seneca that discusses the spectacles at some length with the argument that the intensity of the emotions at the *munera* make one particularly susceptible to ethical degradation; indeed, Seneca suggests that one is more likely to learn selfishness there than the selflessness celebrated as a major benefit of watching blood games.

Source: Seneca *Letters from a Stoic*, 7:[51] You ask me to say what you should consider it particularly important to avoid. My answer is this: a mass crowd. Associating with people in large numbers is actually harmful: there is not one of them that will not make some vice or other attractive to us, or leave us carrying the imprint of it or bedaubed all unawares with it. And inevitably enough, the larger the size of the crowd we mingle with, the greater the danger. But nothing is as ruinous to the character as sitting away one's time at a show – for it is then, through the medium of entertainment, that vices creep into one with more than usual ease. What do you take me to mean? That I go home more selfish, more self-seeking and more self-indulgent? Yes, and what is more, a person crueller and less humane through having been in contact with human beings . . . "But he was a highway robber, he killed a man." And what of it? Granted that as a murderer he deserved this punishment, what have you done, you wretched fellow, to deserve to watch it? "Kill him! Flog him! Burn him! Why does he run at the other man's weapon in such a cowardly way? Why isn't the other one less half-hearted about killing? Why isn't this one a bit more enthusiastic about dying? Whip him forward to get his wounds! Make them each offer the other a bare breast and trade blow for blow on them." And when there is an interval in the show: "Let's have some throats cut in the meantime, so that there's something happening!" Come now, I say, surely you people realize – if you realize nothing else – that bad examples have a way of recoiling on those who set them? Give thanks to the immortal gods that the men to whom you are giving a lesson in cruelty are not in a position to profit from it.

The relative rarity of amphitheaters in the Greek east long led scholars to assume that the cultured Hellenes scorned the crude spectacles of the Romans, that the horror provoked in the audience of Antiochus IV's *munera* reflected a general and lingering disgust at Roman-style blood events among the refined Greeks. Closer study of the evidence, especially material remains, offers a correction: Greek cities, like cities in the west, had an appetite for the Roman games and accommodated these spectacles within modified existing structures. Indeed, the criticism of the games offered by some Greek intellectuals points up their popularity among the general population of the eastern Mediterranean. Apollonius, a philosopher of the first century CE, condemns the contemporary use of Athens' Theater of Dionysus for gladiatorial events, noting with disapproval the enthusiasm of the crowd and the manipulation of the judicial system to acquire performers. The main thrust of his criticism seems to be the location itself: the theater, as a sacred space, was particularly vulnerable to the pollution of bloodshed, specifically, the ritual miasma created by the killing of human beings.

Source: Philostratus, *Life of Apollonius* 4.22:[52] The Athenians ran in crowds to the theater beneath the Acropolis to witness human slaughter, and the passion for such sports was stronger there than it is in Corinth today; for they would buy for large sums adulterers and fornicators and burglars and cut-purses and kidnappers and suchlike rabble, and then they took them and armed them and set them to fight with one another. Apollonius then attacked these practices, and when the Athenians invited him to attend their assembly, he refused to enter a place so impure and reeking with gore. And this he said in an epistle to them, that he was surprised "that the goddess had not already fled the Acropolis when you shed such blood under her eyes."

4

The Life of the Gladiator

The first *munera* were probably fairly simple and straightforward. With the growth of the combats in size, frequency and complexity, institutional support was needed to provide for such development, to locate, house and train likely gladiators and to arrange the facilities required for the show. Gladiatorial schools, or *ludi*, were established, run by a *lanista*, who was responsible for the acquisition and training of new gladiators. The importance of spectacle for Roman politics created new questions about what sort of relationship the spectacle professionals would have with the sources and agents of power. Would gladiators themselves eventually control the show? What kinds of life expectations did the arena performers have?

Where Did Gladiators Come From?

There were three main sources for the performers in the arena: slaves, criminals, and free volunteers. The chief supply of Roman slaves during the Republic and early empire was Roman warfare: enemies of Rome captured on the field of battle were typically sold as slaves. The skills gained as former soldiers could be adapted for performance in gladiatorial matches. As the population of slaves grew, the number of *vernae* or people born in slavery also increased, creating a local source of unfree labor that could, potentially, be channeled into the arena as into other occupations. Criminals also appeared on the sands, both those who had been condemned to death in the arena as well as those who had been condemned to the gladiatorial school, a lesser penalty. Some performers were neither slaves nor criminals, but chose freely to become gladiators; the legal liabilities this entailed may, for some, have been balanced by the positive benefits that came to some gladiators. Shockingly, some elites chose to enter the arena, including some emperors; the scandal generated by this reversal of social standing led to legislation against the occurrence.

Prisoners of war

Gladiators were created by the enactment of Roman justice and Roman authority: the first gladiators were probably prisoners of war, and war would prove to be an ongoing major source for combatants in the arena. The Junii and the Aemilii Lepidi, sponsors of the first recorded *munera* in Rome, had family members renowned among Roman generals and thus probably had access to such prisoners. Use of prisoners of war also seems to have been the custom at the early Campanian banquet combats. The armature of some gladiators may be connected to the specialized weaponry of enemy combatants, such as the Samnite, the *Gallus* and the *Thraex* as well as the *essedarius* introduced by Caesar, who had personal battlefield experience of this British style of fighting from chariots. Resistance to Rome in war had put these people beyond the circle of Roman obligation. They deserved nothing from Rome; granting them slavery instead of death was considered a gift by the Roman victors. For many of these prisoners, however, death was simply deferred until the spectacle was prepared. Death in such a setting could thus serve as an object lesson about those who opposed Rome's empire. In some instances, however, the use of prisoners of war in the arena was complicated, even for the Romans.

When the last survivors of the second Sicilian slave war surrendered to proconsul Manius Aquilius in 100 BCE, they were taken to Rome and made to fight animals; here the intent was to execute the captives, as punishment for their rebellion against Roman authority. Their resistance continued in the arena as they asserted the right to choose their own method of death and to deny Rome the power to kill them. The choice made by the defiant prisoners was recognized as an honorable one by some of the Roman witnesses; this notion of the "heroic" gladiatorial suicide is also found in other contexts (see below).

Source: Diodorus Siculus 36.10:[1] Aquillius was sent against the rebels, and by his personal valor won a resounding victory over them . . . a thousand were still left . . . Aquillius at first intended to subdue them by force of arms, but when later, after an exchange of envoys, they surrendered, he released them from immediate punishment and took them to Rome to do combat with wild beasts. There, as some report, they brought their lives to a most glorious end; for they avoided combat with the beasts and cut one another down at the public altars . . . the final survivor died heroically by his own hand.

The emperor Claudius celebrated his conquest of Britannia in 43 CE with a triumph, lavish spectacles, and annual commemorations of the achievement. He extended these honors to include Aulus Plautius, the field general who oversaw the invasion. Here, the prisoners channeled for this purpose seem to become a resource available for state "use."

Source: Dio Cassius 60.30:[2] Plautius for his skilful and successful conduct of the war in Britain not only was praised by Claudius but also obtained an ovation.[3] In the gladiatorial combats many persons took part, not only of the foreign freedmen but also the British captives. He used up many men in this part of the spectacle and took pride in the fact.

After the capture of Jerusalem in 70 CE, Titus delegated the duty of deciding what to do with all the survivors of the siege (those who hadn't been killed by Roman troops as they pillaged the city) to his friend Fronto Haterius. The children were sold as slaves, while the adults met various fates, thousands of them providing an object lesson on the danger of rebellion in the spectacles presented at town after town as the victorious general reasserted Roman control over Judaea. By combining these demonstrative shows with celebrations of the new imperial family, multiple purposes are served.

Source: Josephus, *The Jewish War*, 6. 418:[4] Fronto put to death all the seditious ones and the brigands, information being given by them against each other; he selected the tallest and most handsome of the youth and reserved them for the triumph; of the rest, those over seventeen years of age he sent in chains to the works in Egypt, while multitudes were presented by Titus to the various provinces, to be destroyed in the [arena], by sword [as gladiators] or by wild beasts.

Source: Josephus, *The Jewish War* 7.37–40, 96:[5] During his stay at Caesarea Maritima [in the fall of 70], Titus celebrated his brother's birthday[6] with great splendor, reserving for his honor much of the punishment of his Jewish captives. For the number of those destroyed in contests with wild beasts or with one another or in the flames was more than two thousand five hundred. Yet to the Romans, notwithstanding the myriad forms in which their victims perished, all this seemed too light a penalty. After this, [Titus] Caesar passed to Beirut, a city of Phoenicia and a Roman colony. Here he made a longer stay, displaying still greater magnificence on the occasion of his father's birthday, both in the costliness of the spectacles and in the ingenuity of the various other items of expenditure. Multitudes of captives perished in the same manner as before ... Leaving from Beirut, Titus exhibited costly spectacles in all the cities of Syria he passed through, making his Jewish captives serve to display their own destruction.

Condemned criminals

Executing, in a spectacular fashion, people who had proven to be dangers to the safety of the state was meant to demonstrate the power of the emperor and to restore the order that had been challenged by the criminal behavior. More and more elaborate contrivances for killing the condemned were developed under the emperors, culminating in the mythicized narratives seen in chapter 3. Criminals became a resource for spectacle, with more emphasis placed on the potential showmanship of the individual miscreant. The "best" criminals, those whose physical stamina or familiarity with combat promised a "good" show, were reserved for the games in the capital, with imperial administrators mandated to assess the spectacle value of those in custody. Legal evidence suggests that some unauthorized exchange of performance-worthy convicts may have been going on in the provinces; this was to be discouraged, as the emperor should determine the distribution of such resources.

Source: *Digest* 48.19.31:[7] Modestinus, *Punishments*, book 3 . . . The governor should not, at the whim of the people, release persons who have been condemned to the beasts; but if they are of such strength or skill that they can fittingly be displayed to the people of Rome, [the governor] should consult with the emperor [about transferring custody]. The deified Severus and Antoninus wrote in a rescript that condemned persons should not be transferred from one province to another without the emperor's permission.

Different crimes directed the condemned toward spectacle in different ways. Capital offenses entailed the exposure to lethal danger, as convicts were sentenced to the arena or the sword or to the beasts. Being sentenced to the *ludus* or gladiatorial school was a lesser penalty, one involving high-risk servitude but "only" for a limited time period, as spelled out in legislation by the emperor Hadrian.

Source: *Collatio Mosaicarum et Romanarum legum* 11.7:[8] Ulpian, in the eighth book of *The Proconsular Functions*. The late Emperor Hadrian, in a rescript to the Council of Baetica concerning the punishment of cattle-raiders, wrote as follows . . . The terms of the Emperor Hadrian's rescript would imply that labor in the mines is the severer punishment [in comparison to being sentenced to the sword]. Unless, possibly, the Emperor Hadrian meant by the phrase "punishment of the sword" the gladiatorial games. There is, however, a distinction between those sentenced to the sword and those sentenced to the *ludus*; the former are dispatched without delay, or at any rate ought to be dispatched within a year, and this instruction is contained in the Orders. But those condemned to the *ludus* are not necessarily dispatched; they may even, after a time, be restored to freedom, or be discharged from the obligation of being a gladiator; since, after five years, they may be restored to freedom, while, on the expiration of three years, they are permitted to receive their discharge (*rudis*) from the gladiatorial games.

"Bad" emperors were suspected of abusing the judicial supplies for the shows. Gaius Caligula is a particular target of such accusations, in which the excessive emperor reacts inappropriately to resulting shortages. The following two selections may refer to the same event, although different kinds of despotism are in play: in the first, Caligula dehumanizes the prisoners by making them into "food" for animals, even those whose lesser crimes may not have warranted death; in the second, Caligula reaches beyond the criminal supply to draw upon audience members as fodder for the shows.

Source: Suetonius, *Caligula* 27:[9] Having collected wild animals for one of his shows, [Caligula] found butcher's meat too expensive and decided to feed them with criminals instead. He paid no attention to the charge-sheets, but simply stood in the middle of a colonnade, glanced at the prisoners lined up before him, and gave the order; "Kill every man between that bald head and the other one over there!"

Source: Dio Cassius 59.10:[10] The same trait of cruelty led [Caligula] once, when there was a shortage of condemned criminals to be given to the wild beasts, to order that some of the mob standing near the benches should be seized and thrown to them; and to prevent the possibility of their making an outcry or uttering any reproaches, he first caused their tongues to be cut out.

Claudius also was blamed for his seemingly excessive presentation of *munera*, excessive in the high level of mortality exacted on the sands. Claudius tapped a new source of potential victims among the ranks of the low-status informers utilized by his predecessors. These people served in the prosecutions of those charged with *maiestas*, offenses against the "majesty" of Rome, a category of criminal behavior that could be expanded to include snide comments about the emperor or insufficient reverence shown to images of the current or former *princeps*. In exchange for their testimony, informers were eligible to receive a sizeable portion of the estate of those convicted. While slaves and freedmen may indeed have had access to secretive behavior of their owners, they may also have carried resentment because of harsh treatment received over the years and elected to serve as informers for personal motives beyond mere greed. Elite authors did not approve of the practice or the practitioners, but neither did they approve of excessive punishment like that attributed to Claudius.

Source: Dio Cassius:[11] [Claudius] was constantly giving gladiatorial contests; for he took great pleasure in them, so that he even aroused criticism on this score ... a great many human beings [perished], some of them fighting with one another and others being devoured by the animals. For the emperor detested the slaves and freedmen who in the reigns of Tiberius and Gaius had conspired against their masters, as well as those who had laid information against others without cause or had borne false witness against them, and he therefore got rid of most of them in the manner related ... Indeed, the number of those who were publicly executed was becoming so large, that the statue of Augustus which stood on the spot was taken elsewhere, so that it should not either seem to be witnessing the bloodshed or else always be covered up.

Slave gladiators and the Spartacan war

There is a good deal of overlap between this category of gladiator and the others; in part because prisoners of war were often sold as slaves to a gladiatorial school, just as those condemned to the *ludus* by criminal conviction were considered slaves legally. More importantly, the taint of becoming a gladiator essentially took away one's free status, even from those who entered the profession voluntarily. One could say that all gladiators were slaves.

Perhaps the most famous slave gladiator is Spartacus, leader of a notoriously dangerous rebellion against Rome from 73–71 BCE. The Spartacan war was the last and perhaps most memorable of a series of major slave wars in the later Roman Republic; this one took place in Italy and was a direct threat to the heartland of the Roman hegemony. Rome's military resources were being stretched thin by civil war and rebellion: Spartacus' efforts followed soon after the war between Rome and her Italian allies in 91–89 BCE and the military coup led by Sulla 83–82 BCE. Pompey was in Spain suppressing the rebellion of Sertorius from 77 and Lucullus was fighting Mithridates, king of Pontus and thorn in the side of Rome's eastern interests. M. Licinius Crassus would use the uprising to establish his military reputation: he and Pompey would jointly force the Senate to grant them the consulship in the wake of their success over the rebels. The prominence of gladiators in the Spartacan war fired the Roman imagination, because of the popularity of gladiatorial combat and its increasing identification with the machinery and imagery of Roman politics. It is after the Spartacan war that we see the first efforts to control gladiators in the capital city, as a recognized danger. And within a generation of Spartacus' death, Roman politicians would marshal gladiators to intimidate their rivals on the streets of Rome.

So what happened? Who was Spartacus and how did he manage to put together such a successful revolt? How and why did he eventually fail? The stories the Romans told themselves about Spartacus are shaped by what they needed to know about this blot on their impressive record of victory and control. None of the ancient authors are sympathetic to the rebellion, but they do find different nuances in their analyses of motivation and achievement and how they measured up against Roman expectations for authority and military success.

To a certain extent, Rome was culpable for Spartacus and the revolt. Appian claims he started as an auxiliary in the Roman army, while Plutarch suggests that mistreatment by the *lanista* was the catalyst for what was initially an unarmed outbreak.

Source: Appian, *Civil Wars* 1.116:[12] Spartacus, a Thracian by birth, who had once served as a soldier with the Romans, but had since been a prisoner and sold for a gladiator, and was in the gladiatorial training school at Capua, persuaded about seventy of his comrades to strike for their own freedom rather than for the amusement of spectators.

Source: Plutarch, *Crassus* 8:[13] A man called Lentulus Batiatus had an establishment for gladiators at Capua. Most of them were Gauls and Thracians. They had done nothing wrong, but, simply because of the cruelty of their owner, were kept in close confinement until the time came for them to engage in combat. Two hundred of them planned to escape, but their plan was betrayed and only seventy-eight, who realized this, managed to act in time and get away, armed with choppers and spits which they seized from some cookhouse.

Spartacus himself is singled out among the leaders of the revolt for praise: he is not bestial, not uneducated, not slave-like at all, but a civilized man, whom the gods have selected for an extraordinary event.

Source: Plutarch, *Crassus* 8:[14] He was a Thracian from the nomadic tribes and not only had a great spirit and great physical strength, but was, much more than one would expect from his condition, most intelligent and cultured, being more like a Greek than a Thracian. They say that when he was first taken to Rome to be sold, a snake was seen coiled around his head while he was asleep and his wife, who came from the same tribe and was a prophetess subject to possession by the frenzy of Dionysus, declared that this sign meant that he would have a great and terrible power which would end in misfortune.

The goals of the gladiators are initially to escape the bad treatment of confinement and to find a better life than one servicing, as Appian claims, the amusement of spectators. Soon they are joined by thousands of supporters, who do not come from gladiatorial schools nor entirely, it seems, from the slave class, but rather from those agricultural laborers and small farmers who had been displaced by changes in Rome's economy and land use that favored the growth of large plantations owned by the wealthy few.

Source: Appian, *Civil Wars* 1.116:[15] There many fugitive slaves and even some free-men from the fields joined Spartacus, and he plundered the neighboring country-side, having for subordinate officers two gladiators named Oenomaus and Crixus. Because he divided up the plunder impartially, he soon had plenty of men.

How many this "plenty of men" included varies in the ancient accounts, from 60,000 in Eutropius to 120,000 in Appian. The economic interest of these men is often noted; whether this reflects the hardship of the dis-enfranchised or the greed of the selfish thug depends on the author. Florus' analysis is fairly hostile toward the rebels, emphasizing not only their sinister and shameful origins but also their literally ludicrous pretensions.

Source: Florus *Abridgement* 2.8: [Spartacus] also celebrated the funerals of his officers who had died in battle with the rituals reserved to top generals and made prisoners of war fight to the death around the funeral pyre, as if he wanted in this way to wipe out all the previous shame of having been a gladiator by becoming the presenter of gladiatorial games.

Appian likewise notes the presentation of gladiatorial games, as well as sacrifice of prisoners, at the funeral of Crixus, one of Spartacus' fellow leaders. Absent the class-based condemnation in Florus, Appian's account allows for the calculated use of these shaming and terrifying procedures by Spartacus, meant specifically to have an emotional impact on his enemy's morale. The long-term goals of Spartacus and his army are only discussed in general terms, often addressing what must have been a powerful question at the time: why did they not march on Rome?

Source: Appian, *Civil Wars* 1.117:[16] Spartacus tried to make his way through the Apennines to the Alps and the Gallic country, but one of the consuls anticipated him and hindered his flight while the other hung upon his rear. He turned upon them one after the other and beat them in detail. They retreated in confusion in different directions. Spartacus sacrificed 300 Roman prisoners to the spirit of Crixus and marched toward Rome with 120,000 infantry, having burned all his useless material, killed all his prisoners, and butchered his pack animals in order to expedite his movement. Many deserters offered themselves to him, but he would not accept them. The consuls again met him in the country of Picenum. Here there was fought another great battle and there was, too, another great defeat for the Romans. Spartacus changed his intention of marching on Rome. He did not consider himself ready as yet for that kind of a fight, as his whole force was not suitably armed, for no city had joined him, but only slaves, deserters, and riff-raff. However, he occupied the mountains around Thurii and took the city itself.

Source: Plutarch, *Crassus* 9:[17] Spartacus had grown to be a great and formidable power, but he showed no signs of losing his head. He could not expect to prove superior to the whole power of Rome, and so he began to lead his army towards the Alps. His view was that they should cross the mountains and then disperse to their own homes, some to Thrace and some to Gaul. His men, however, would not listen to him. They were strong in numbers and full of confidence, and they went about Italy ravaging everything in their way.

The lack of discipline in the Spartacan army sounds an ominous tone, but would have been expected of such "riff-raff" by a Roman audience. The presence of deserters[18] suggests that Rome cannot retain the loyalty of its troops; given the recent repeated experiences of civil war, the problem may be systemic at this time. Yet, the deserters may be opportunistic support at best for Spartacus. The Roman leadership in the Spartacan war was apparently cursed by bad luck; certainly it was failing, until M. Licinius Crassus was granted the command.

Source: Appian, *Civil Wars* 1.118:[19] This war, so formidable to the Romans (although ridiculed and despised in the beginning, as being merely the work of gladiators), had now lasted three years. When the election of new praetors approached, fear fell upon everyone, and nobody offered himself as a candidate until Licinius Crassus, a man distinguished among the Romans for birth and wealth, assumed the praetorship and marched against Spartacus with six new legions.

A brief reference in Plutarch to a failed escape attempt by Spartacus is a rare link to some sort of anti-slavery ideology among the rebels, some universal fight for freedom for all slaves. Even this pushes the available evidence pretty far in terms of his motivation; long-term social change does not seem foremost on his mind.

Source: Plutarch *Crassus* 10:[20] Spartacus . . . marched through Lucania to the sea. At the Straits he fell in with some pirate ships from Cilicia and formed the plan of landing 2,000 men in Sicily and seizing the island; he would be able, he thought, to start another revolt of the slaves there, since the previous slave war had recently died down and only needed a little fuel to make it blaze out again. However, the Cilicians, after agreeing to his proposals and receiving gifts from him, failed to keep their promises and sailed off. So Spartacus marched back again from the sea.

Meanwhile, successful campaigns both east and west had made veteran Roman troops now available for the effort against Spartacus, and Lucullus and Pompey were recalled to Italy. Appian's Spartacus senses the reduction of options, but in Plutarch's account, Spartacus is forced to abandon a sustainable strategy by dissension among his followers, a motif that recurs throughout the ancient narrative.

> Source: Plutarch, *Crassus* 11:[21] Spartacus turned on his pursuers [and] the Romans were entirely routed ... this success turned out to be the undoing of Spartacus, since it filled his slaves with over-confidence. They refused any longer to avoid battle and would not even obey their officers. Instead they surrounded them with arms in their hands as soon as they began to march and forced them to lead them back through Lucania against the Romans. This was precisely what Crassus most wanted them to do ... Spartacus, realizing that he had no alternative, drew up his whole army in order of battle.

For the Romans, it was useful to blame Spartacus' failure on his army's inherent willfulness, short-sightedness and inability to recognize appropriate hierarchy. Spartacus' success then becomes more of a fluke, a result of the extraordinary capacity of one man, rather than a dangerous flaw in the Roman institution of slavery or the weakness in Roman leadership. The punishment for the survivors of the rebellion was typical for those who revolted against Roman rule; the choice of location would remind every gladiator moving between the training schools in Capua and the spectacular *munera* in Rome of the consequences of resisting the system.

> Source: Appian, *Civil Wars* 1.120:[22] The body of Spartacus was not found. A large number of his men fled from the battle-field to the mountains ... they continued to fight until they all perished except 6,000, who were captured and crucified along the whole road from Capua to Rome.

There were immediate political benefits for Crassus and for Pompey. The Spartacan war boosted them into the consulship for 70 BCE with coercion playing a role in the appointment. Gladiators were perceived as more of a security risk in the last years of the Republic, allegedly recruited to fight for a number of ambitious and radical politicians. "Escaped" gladiators had a very different experience in 31–30 CE, when a troupe of gladiators drafted to the cause of Antony were cut adrift in the days following Antony's catastrophic loss at the Battle of Actium. The presence of gladiators enrolled in the Roman legions was a sign of confused and desperate times; normally, Rome's generals scorned such *infames* people as unworthy of the honor of fighting for Rome. In Dio's account of this particular *familia*, however, the gladiators become models of loyalty, a commodity in short supply for Marcus Antonius.

Source: Dio Cassius 51.7:[23] Peoples and princes without exception refused their assistance to Antony ... yet the men who were being kept for gladiatorial combats, who were among the most despised, showed the utmost zeal in [Antony and Cleopatra's] behalf and fought most bravely. These men, I should explain, were training in Cyzicus for the triumphal games which they were expecting to hold in celebration of [Octavian's] overthrow, and as soon as they became aware of what had taken place, they set out for Egypt to bear aid to their rulers. Many were their exploits against Amyntas in Galatia and many against the sons of Tarcondimotus in Cilicia, who had been their strongest friends but now in view of the changes in circumstances had gone over to the other side; many also were their exploits against Didius, who undertook to prevent their passing through Syria; nevertheless they were unable to force their way through to Egypt. Yet, even when they were surrounded on all sides, not even then would they accept any terms of surrender, though Didius made them many promises. Instead, they sent for Antony, feeling that they would fight better even in Syria if he were with them; and then, when he neither came himself nor sent them any message, they at last decided that he had perished and reluctantly made terms, on condition that they were never again to fight as gladiators. And they received Daphne, the suburb of Antioch, from Didius, to live in until the matter should be brought to [Octavian's] attention. These men were later deceived by Messalla and sent to various places under the pretext that they were to be enlisted in the legions, and were then put out of the way in some convenient manner.

Gladiators and status

By law, gladiators were not entitled to the full range of rights guaranteed to other Romans. They were considered *infames*, a category of shame that also included actors, prostitutes, pimps, and *lanistae*, all occupations that involved the submission of the body to the pleasure of others. These others, be they the audience, the *lanista*, the pimp, or the sexual client, controlled the body of the *infamis*; the absence of basic authority this entailed indicated to Romans that the *infames* were incapable of control, of the proper use of authority. Thus they were legally prohibited from a range of privileges that involved power. *Infames* were barred from running for office and from voting. The testimony of *infames* was not allowed in court. Those condemned to the arena lost control over dispensation of their property; they could not make wills before their execution.

Source: *Digest* 28.3.6.5–6:[24] [from Ulpian] A will is rendered ineffectual whenever something has happened to the testator himself ... even if someone has been condemned to capital punishment, to fight with beasts or to be beheaded, or condemned to another punishment which deprives him of life, his testament will become ineffectual and that not as at the time when he is killed, but when he comes under sentence; for he is made a *servus poenae* [slave due to his punishment].

Condemnation to the *ludi* carried, in the eyes of Roman jurists, a double penalty: not only was the criminal bound to risk mutilation and possibly death, but the condemned also suffered a loss of status. Condemnation to the gladiatorial school was among those punishments that made one a slave, whatever one's status had been prior to sentencing. Slaves who received this sentence ceased, however, to be property of their former owners and became instead "slaves of the penalty."

Source: *Digest* 48.19.8.11–12[25]: [Ulpian, *Duties of Proconsul*, book 9] We must see whether all those who have been condemned to the wild beast hunts are made slaves of the penalty; of course, it is customary for the younger men to suffer this punishment. Therefore, we must see whether these are made slaves of the penalty or whether they retain their freedom. The prevailing view is that they too are made slaves; for they only differ from the others [condemned to life sentences] in this, that they are set to be *venatores* or Pyrrhic dancers or to provide some other kind of pleasure by pantomime or other movements of their bodies. There is no doubting that slaves are customarily condemned to the mines or to the mine-works[26], or again to the wild beast hunts; and if they are handed over for these they are made slaves of the penalty and will no longer belong to him whose property they were before their condemnation.

The legal status of all gladiators, whether condemned, purchased, or volunteer, is essentially that of slaves; their bodies were not theirs to control, due to the fact that they could be beaten, wounded, and subjected to the threat of death, all at the decision of the *lanista* with no institutional protection. Such *infames* were susceptible to public demonstrations of this vulnerability. Magistrates, for example, could arbitrarily abuse the bodies of *infames*, such as actors, who had no real recourse from such actions. Slave gladiators also were deprived of the right to make decisions about their own lives; this is illustrated by the example of Asiaticus, who, as slave of the future emperor Vitellius, had access to all sorts of physical comforts but, because he was a slave, he could lose them all on the whim of the emperor. Asiaticus' oscillation between privilege and degradation demonstrates the vulnerability of the slave, with, however, a "happy ending" in his elevation to equestrian status.

Source: Suetonius, *Vitellius* 12:[27] [Vitellius] based many important political decisions on what the lowest performers in the theater or arena told him, and relied particularly on the advice of his freedman Asiaticus. Asiaticus had been Vitellius' slave and boy lover, but soon grew tired of this role and ran away. After a while he was discovered selling cheap drinks at Puteoli, and put in chains until Vitellius ordered his release and made him his favorite again, However, Asiaticus behaved so insolently, and so thievishly as well, that Vitellius became irritated and sold him to an itinerant trainer of gladiators; but impulsively bought him back when he was just about to take part in the final match of a gladiatorial contest. When sent to govern Lower Germany, Vitellius freed Asiaticus, and on his first day as emperor presented him with the gold ring of the equestrian order; although that very morning he had rejected a popular demand for this award, with the emphatic statement that Asiaticus' appointment would disgrace the order.

Over time, some protections were built into the system. Hadrian was an important innovator in this regard, with measures introduced specifically to limit the practice of punishing slaves by sending them to the *ludus* without due process, strictly on the order of the owner. This was expanded under Antoninus Pius to include further limitations on the capacity of owners to punish disobedient slaves with condemnation *ad bestias*; in this case, specific penalties for the former owner and *lanista* would be imposed, for which the jurist Modestinus claimed the precedent of legislation from the reign of Tiberius. The development gradually would incorporate those of slave status into the Roman judicial system and remove them from utter dependence on the goodwill of their owners.

Source: Historia Augusta, *Hadrian* 18:[28] [Hadrian] prohibited the killing of slaves by their masters, and he ordered that they should be sentenced by judges if they deserved it. He prohibited the sale of a male or female slave to a pimp or a *lanista*, without the case being presented.

Source: *Digest* 48.8.11.1–2:[29] Modestinus, *Rules* book 6. If a slave be thrown to the beasts without having been before a judge, not only he who sold him but also he who bought him shall be liable to punishment. Following the *lex Petronia* [of 19 CE] and the senatorial decrees relating to it, masters have lost the power of handing over at their own discretion their slaves to fight with the beasts; but after the slave has been produced before a judge, if his master's complaint is just, he shall in this case be handed over to punishment.

Free gladiators

Some Romans of free status voluntarily became gladiators; in doing so, they bound themselves to the status of slaves, surrendering authority over their own bodies to the *lanista*. They were required to take a formal oath to allow themselves to be disciplined and subjected to physical abuse of the kind associated with training in the *ludus*. Seneca finds the selfless dedication implied by the gladiators' oath admirable, even if the gladiators themselves are socially repugnant.

Source: Seneca, *Letters* 37:[30] The words of this most honorable compact are the same as the words of that most disgraceful one, i.e. "Through burning, imprisonment, or death by the sword." From the men who hire out their strength for the arena, who must pay for what they eat and drink with their blood, security is demanded that they will endure such things even if unwilling . . . The gladiator may lower his weapon and try the pity of the people; but you will neither lower your weapon nor beg for life.

The fact that legal penalties were involved meant that free volunteers had to formally register with the Roman government to become gladiators. The *senatus consultum* on limiting prices of gladiators, promoted by Marcus Aurelius in 177 CE, suggests that this registration was typically for a limited period of time, after which the individual could re-enlist with his pay scale increased in recognition of his experience. This portion of the law is concerned about setting some limit on payments demanded for veteran gladiators with established reputations.

Source: *CIL* 2.6278, lines 62–63:[31] In the case of him, however, who voluntarily, in the presence of His Excellency the tribune of the plebs, may announce his intention to fight at the legal price of 2,000 sesterces, if this man, when he has obtained his release, reenters his dangerous occupation, his valuation thereafter shall not exceed 12,000 sesterces.

The presence of free men in the *ludus* is also documented by epitaphs and other monuments. Free status is indicated sometimes by an explicit reference to status, sometimes by the use of the *tria nomina*, the three names that marked the possession of Roman citizenship. On this tombstone from Rome, the career high points of the free Exochus (who bears the *tria nomina*) against an imperial slave, Araxes ("slave of Caesar" being a translation of "Caesaris"), and against a free competitor are detailed. Note that the games referred to here are the famously lavish ones of Trajan to commemorate success over the Dacians; 10,000 gladiators fought, including these three.

Source: *CIL* 6.10194: The Thraex Marcus Antonius Exochus, a native of Alexandria, fought as a *tiro* against Araxes Caesaris on the second day of the games for the triumph of the deified Trajan in Rome. He was dismissed while still standing. In Rome, on the ninth day of the same *munus*, he fought Fimbria, a free man who had fought in nine gladiatorial contests; Fimbria was dismissed while still standing. In Rome, at the same *munus*.

Choosing gladiatorial status

Why would anyone want to become a gladiator? What positive reasons were there for free people, even those of high status, to voluntarily choose this occupation? Strong motivations, surely, would be needed to outweigh the loss of honor, the risk of death, the regular infliction of corporal punishment, and the day-to-day inability to make decisions about one's own body, what to eat, where to go.

Money was an issue for some of these, according to the literary evidence. Sometimes the financial motivation is framed negatively, suggesting that people are forced by dire circumstances to enter the arena. When death by starvation threatened, perhaps the high costs of the gladiators' life were worth paying.

> Source: Tatian, *To the Greeks* 23:[32] Some, giving themselves up to idleness for the sake of profligacy, sell themselves to be killed; and the indigent barters himself away, while the rich man buys others to kill him.

The rhetorical schools, which debated this question as part of the education of young Romans, suggest that mere poverty is insufficient reason to become a gladiator, that this would just be the lowest point on a downward spiral of degradation. They emphasize exceptional circumstances that would mitigate the shame and give the choice moral weight. If the individual were not motivated solely by his own survival, but entered the arena in order to perform a filial duty, such as the proper burial of a parent, or a social duty, of rescuing a friend from poverty and death, then the choice would be a proper one.

> Source: Lucian, *Toxaris* 58–59:[33] We discussed the situation to see what we should do, now that we had become absolutely penniless in a strange country ... [my friend] begged me not to [commit suicide], for he himself would discover a means of our having enough to live on. ... we took our seats and first we saw wild beasts brought down by javelins, hunted with dogs, and loosed upon men in chains – criminals, we conjectured. Then the gladiators entered, and the herald, bringing in a tall youth, said that whoever wanted to fight with that man should come forward, and would receive ten thousand drachmas in payment for the fight. Thereupon [my friend] Sisinnes arose, and, leaping down, undertook to fight and asked for weapons. On receiving his pay, the ten thousand drachmas, he promptly put it in my hands, saying: "If I win, Toxaris, we shall go away together, with all that we need; but if I die, bury me and go back to Scythia."

The following passage, from a rhetorical exercise used to train young men in argumentation and persuasion, presents the pathetic story of two youthful friends, one wealthy, one poor, and the moral value of sacrifice. The wealthy young man is kidnapped and sold to a *ludus*. His friend comes to save him and enters the arena in his place, only to die on the sand. The surviving young man fulfills his promise to help the grieving father but, in so doing, provokes the anger of his own father, who despises the poorer family. The surviving young man argues in defense of his dead friend, asserting that there are good reasons to become a gladiator and that his friend had demonstrated them.

Source: Ps-Quintilian, *Declamations* 9:[34] It is a terrible shame that his courage and fervor were not employed in the army, in military combat . . . with what vigor did he rush out into the fray, enraged against his opponent as though he were still mine! . . . offering his bared body to his opponent's blows . . . he died standing up . . . he received the sword blow facing straight ahead . . . Neither a criminal nor down on his luck, he entered the arena. Gentlemen, when did you ever hear of such a thing? He became a gladiator because of his virtue!

Glory

Some authors suggest volunteer gladiators, especially those from the wealthier classes, went into the arena in the pursuit of "glory," weighting the acclaim of the crowds higher than the shame brought by the violation of traditional ways of measuring status, or the danger of wounds and death. Tertullian contrasts this kind of fleeting earthly fame to an eternal glory to be found in martyrs' piety (see chapter 5).

Source: Tertullian, *To the Martyrs* 4–5:[35] Earthly glory has so great power over the strength of body and mind, that men despise the sword, the fire, the cross, the beasts, the tortures, for the reward of the praise of men . . . How many men of leisure does a display of weapons hire to the sword! Truly they go down to the very beasts for the motive of display, and see themselves as more beautiful from their bites and their scars.

Some gladiators were real celebrities, immortalized in inscriptions, art, and in song. Pliny describes how this fame might be captured for permanent commemoration; gladiator art was very popular, both portraits of individual gladiators and representations of specific events. The mosaic portraits of performers at the Baths of Caracalla are surviving testimony to this kind of fame, however fleeting it might ultimately be (see figure 4.1).

Figure 4.1 Baths of Caracalla, portraits of spectacle stars. Scala/Art Resource, NY

Source: Pliny, *Natural History* 35.52:[36] When a freedman of Nero was putting on a gladiatorial show at Antium, paintings containing life-like portraits of all the gladiators and their assistants decorated the public porticoes. Portraits of gladiators have commanded the greatest interest in art for many generations. It was, however, Gaius Terentius Lucanus who began commissioning pictures of gladiatorial shows and having them publicly exhibited.

Martial's poem about the fighter Hermes may encapsulate some of the enthusiastic chants that rose on game day from stands stuffed with his fans. It also suggests some of the reasons for Hermes' fame, such as wins over rivals like Helius and Advolans, technical ability reaching beyond a single armature, sex appeal, and economic value.

Source: Martial 5.24:[37] Hermes, favorite fighter of the age; Hermes, skilled in all weaponry; Hermes, gladiator and trainer both; Hermes, tempest and tremor of his school; Hermes, who (but none other) makes Helius afraid; Hermes, before whom (but none other) Advolans falls; Hermes, taught to win without wounding; Hermes, himself his own substitute; Hermes, gold mine of seat-mongers; Hermes, darling and distress of gladiators' women; Hermes, proud with battling spear; Hermes, menacing with marine trident; Hermes, formidable in drooping helmet; Hermes, glory of Mars universal; Hermes, all things in one and thrice unique.

Tertullian acknowledges the fame and adoration given to the performers in the arena; he also finds it a target for his criticism, because of the ambiguity of the gladiator's position. The Christian author juxtaposes the admiration and desire directed toward gladiators with their degraded status to point up the hypocrisy of the situation, that someone can be both revered and reviled for the same action.

Source: Tertullian, *On the Spectacles* 22.3–4:[38] Take the treatment the very providers and managers of the spectacles accord to those idolized charioteers, actors, athletes, and gladiators, to whom men surrender their souls and women even their bodies, on whose account they commit the sins they censure: for the very same skill for which they glorify them, they debase and degrade them; worse, they publicly condemn them to dishonor and deprivation of civil rights, excluding them from the council chamber, the orator's platform, the senatorial and equestrian orders, from all other offices and certain distinctions. What perversity! They love whom they penalize; they bring into disrepute whom they applaud; they extol the art and brand the artist with disgrace. What sort of judgment is this – that a man should be vilified for the things that win him a reputation?

Strange though it may seem to a modern reader, some volunteer gladiators committed themselves to this risk without asking payment for their efforts. The presence of this group of "amateur" fighters is acknowledged in the corpus of Roman law, as decisions had to be made about their status. The absence of payment apparently removed some portion of the legal and social taint that was transmitted by performance in the arena. The jurist Ulpian discusses who is allowed to make claims before the magistrate, or rather, those who are limited in the demands they can make on the praetor's time. Some cannot make claims at all, some can make claims only for themselves, some can make claims for themselves and for a select number of others. The types of people being excluded here are those considered "disabled" by reason of age, sex, or incapacity and those considered "exceptionally disreputable" or *infamis*, into which falls the professional *venator*, but not the amateur.

Source: *Digest* 3.1.1.6:[39] [Ulpian, *Edict* book 6] . . . [the man] who has been condemned on a capital charge does not have the right to make legal claims on behalf of another . . . so too with the man who has hired out his services to fight against beasts. But we ought to interpret the term beasts by reference to the animal's ferocity rather than to its species. For what if it should be a lion, but a tame one, or some other tame carnivore? It is, then, only the man who has hired out his services who is blacklisted, whether he ends up by fighting or not. For if he fights when he had not hired out his services, he will not be liable. For it is not the man who has fought against beasts who will be liable, but only the man who has hired out his services for this purpose. Accordingly, the old authorities say that those who do this without pay to demonstrate their manliness are not liable, unless they have accepted [cash] prizes in the arena.

An epitaph of a retired gladiator from Ankara lists a number of achievements, including, interestingly, a list of cities that granted him honorary citizenship in recognition of his success as a combatant; the public awards here fall much more into the Greek tradition of esteem for successful athletes, in which the grant of civic honors was not uncommon. In the eastern Mediterranean, then, a competing tradition offered local rehabilitation from the legal limitations of the *infamis* status.

Source: Robert #90: To the gods below. Aelia to Publius Aelius, the illustrious Pergamene *summa rudis*, a member of the *collegium* of the *summae rudes* in Rome, to my own husband, happily joined to me in life, having lived 37 years, Aelia set this up in memory. And he was a citizen of these cities in order: Thessalonica, Nikomedia, Larissa, Philippopolis, Apros, Berga, Thasos.

Life in the *Ludi*

Soon after entering the *ludus*, the *tiro* or beginning gladiator was placed in an armature and assigned to a *doctor* for that particular specialization. The *lanista* oversaw the training process, hiring *doctores* (specialists in the various styles of combat) and *magistri* (former gladiators with experience in the arena). He then negotiated the performance contract with the *editor* of a given set of games, balancing skill level and showmanship of the fighters against risk of loss. Importantly for the gladiators, the *lanista*, in a real sense, owned them.

Training for gladiatorial combat was done using a wooden sword or *rudis*, to limit damage in practice. In addition to sparring with each other, the *tiros* used a wooden stake driven into the ground, with the remaining aboveground portion standing about man height. On this they could practice full-strength blows with the *rudis* as well as body slams with the shield. The rhetorician Quintilian compares the process of formal argumentation to the exchange of blows by gladiators; scholars have interpreted this passage to indicate that different kinds of strokes were numbered and that gladiators were trained to parry specific attacks with specific counter-attacks, much as is done in more recent fencing.

Source: Quintilian, *Oratorical Institute* 5.13.54:[40] But from our answers to objections fresh objections will arise, a process which may be carried to some length. The strokes of gladiators provide a parallel. If the first stroke was intended to provoke the adversary to strike, the second will lead to the third, while if the challenge be repeated it will lead to the fourth stroke, so that there will be two parries and two attacks. And the process may be prolonged still further.

Gladiatorial training involved a number of regimens, from the learning of specific weapons techniques to specific kinds of physical discipline, meant to develop strength and endurance. Epictetus compares the conditions of the *ludus* to the training of the rhetorician, in terms of commitment to a set of rules for success.

Source: Epictetus, *Discourse* 3.15:[41] In every affair consider what precedes and follows, and then undertake it . . . consider what precedes and follows, and then, if it be for your advantage, engage in the affair. You must conform to rules, submit to a diet, refrain from dainties; exercise your body, whether you choose it or not, at a stated hour, in heat and cold; you must drink no cold water, and sometimes no wine, – in a word, you must give yourself up to your trainer as to a physician. Then, in the combat, you may be thrown into a ditch, dislocate your arm, turn your ankle, swallow abundance of dust, receive stripes [for negligence], and, after all, lose the victory. When you have reckoned up all this, if your inclination still holds, set about the combat. Otherwise, take notice, you will behave like children who sometimes play wrestlers, sometimes gladiators; sometimes blow a trumpet, and sometimes act a tragedy, when they happen to have seen and admired these shows . . . For you have never entered upon anything considerately, nor after having surveyed and tested the whole matter; but carelessly, and with a half-way zeal.

The kind of blows wielded by gladiators were supposed to be controlled, even elegant, to maximize accuracy and to save their strength for an extended combat. This is acknowledged by Cicero, who also compares this economy of motion to training in rhetoric.

Source: Cicero, *Orator* 228:[42] For as we observe that boxers, and gladiators not much less, do not make any motion, either in cautious parrying or vigorous thrusting, which does not have a certain grace, so that whatever is useful for the combat is also attractive to look upon, so the orator does not strike a heavy blow unless the thrust has been properly directed.

In addition to training in wounding and in wielding death, gladiators were trained in how to die, i.e. how to properly submit to a death blow when the judgment of the *editor* and crowd has made that decision. Numerous pieces of visual art depict this crucial moment, just before the fatal strike, the moment engaging the peak of control for all concerned: the *editor*'s well-considered determination of death, the victor's clean kill and the loser's proper positioning, breast exposed, steeled not to flinch, face betraying no fear nor pain.

Source: Cicero, *Tusculan Disputations*, 2.17:[43] Look at gladiators, who are either ruined men or barbarians, what blows they endure! See, how men, who have been well trained, prefer to receive a blow rather than basely avoid it! How frequently it is made evident that there is nothing they put higher than giving satisfaction to their owner or to the people! Even when weakened with wounds they send word to their owners to ascertain their pleasure: if they have given satisfaction to them they are content to fall. What gladiator of ordinary merit has ever uttered a groan or changed countenance? Who of them has disgraced himself, I will not say upon his feet, but who has disgraced himself in his fall? Who after falling has drawn in his neck when ordered to suffer the fatal stroke? Such is the force of training, practice, and habit. Shall then the Samnite, filthy fellow, worthy of his life and place, be capable of this and shall a man born to fame have any portion of his soul so weak that he cannot strengthen it by systematic preparation?

Veteran gladiators became practiced at dealing with death, not just the careful infliction of it, but how to deal with the effects of potentially mortal combat. The danger lay not just in being wounded oneself, but in how the opponent's wounds shaped the fight.

Source: Seneca, *Controversies* 9.6: Among gladiators the worst position for a victor is to have to fight a dying opponent. You should fear no adversary more than one who cannot live, but can still kill . . . when his chance of *missio* is removed, a gladiator will pursue naked the opponent he had fled under arms.

Galen the physician, writing in the late second century CE, had more understanding than most of the costs of the gladiatorial lifestyle: he had received a good portion of his medical training in practice at a *ludus*, where he would have daily evidence of the long-term effect of the arena on the bodies of athletes. His discussion of the choice of profession argues against the life of the athlete and the fighter, not just because of the danger of trauma, but because of the unhealthy lack of balance he finds in their physical training and dietary regimen.

Source: Galen, *Exhortation to the Study of the Arts* 4:[44] In the amassing of [the athletes'] great quantity of flesh and blood their mind is lost in the vast mire. Receiving no stimulation to develop, it remains as stupid as that of brutes ... They fatigue themselves to the limit and then gourmandize to excess, prolonging their repast often into the middle of the night. Analogous rules to those guiding their exercise and eating regulate also their sleep. At the hour when people who live according to the laws of nature quit work to take their lunch, the athletes are rising ... While athletes pursue their profession their body remains in this dangerous state [of hyperdevelopment]. When they quit it, they fall into a state even more dangerous. Some die shortly after, others live a little longer, but never reach old age ... their bodies enfeebled by the jolts they have received, [they] are predisposed to become sick on the least provocation. Their eyes, ordinarily sunken, readily become the seat of fluxions; their teeth, so readily injured, fall out. With muscles and tendons frequently torn, their articulations become incapable of resisting strain and readily dislocate. From the standpoint of health no condition is more wretched ... many who have been perfectly proportioned fall into the hands of trainers who develop them beyond measure, overload them with flesh and blood, and make them just the opposite ... [fighters] develop a disfigured countenance hideous to look upon. Limbs broken or dislocated and eyes gouged out of sockets show the kind of beauty produced. These are the fruits they gather. When they no longer exercise their profession, they lose sensation, their limbs become dislocated, and, as I have said, they become completely deformed.

Against this pessimistic view of the gladiator's life experience, the personal suffering caused by the wounds and beatings in training and the risk of death in the arena, one must weigh the fact that the *lanista* had an economic interest in maximizing his investment. A well-fed, well-exercised, well-rested gladiator was more likely to fight well and thus return the costs expended. An appearance of health and strength also drew the favor of the crowd, which could bring in additional prize money and lead to repeat performances. Cyprian's Christian condemnation of the *munera* emphasizes the physical development of gladiators and the care taken to enhance their appearance.

Source: Cyprian, *Letter to Donatus* 7:[45] The gladiatorial games are prepared, that blood may gladden the lust of cruel eyes. The body is fed up with stronger food, and the vigorous mass of limbs is enriched with brawn and muscle, that the wretch fattened for punishment may die a harder death. Man is slaughtered that man may be gratified, and the skill that is best able to kill is an exercise and an art ... What state of things, I pray you, can that be, and what can it be like, in which men, whom none have condemned, offer themselves to the wild beasts – men of ripe age, of sufficiently beautiful person, clad in costly garments? Living men, they are adorned for a voluntary death.

Evidence points to some positive amenities to be found in the gladiatorial schools. *Ludi* employed *unctores*, who used oil to massage the gladiators after a workout. Buildings of the *ludus* were sited in healthful locations. Morsels of information about the gladiatorial diet lurk in the ancient texts. A number of references to the consumption of carbohydrates and fatty foods, such as the "stronger food" Cyprian mentions, suggest that trainers may have made some connection between food and endurance. Gladiators ate grains, as Pliny tells us.

Source: Pliny, *Natural History* 18.14:[46] Barley is the oldest among human foods, as is proved by the Athenian ceremony recorded by Menander [i.e. its use as a prize in the Eleusinian Games], and by the name given to gladiators, who used to be called "barley-men" (*hordearii*).

There were separate quarters for different armatures and for those who arrived in the *ludus* for different reasons. Still, the *ludus*, as the residence of *infames*, was understood by Roman norms to be a squalid place, whatever the physical amenities. This expectation is used by the satirist Juvenal for shock value, as he condemns the licentiousness of Roman women in their preference for lovers outside their class and culture.

Source: Juvenal, *Satire* 6. Oxford fragment 7–13:[47] The *lanista* runs a cleaner, more decent house than yours: he quarters the fag targeteers and the armored heavies well away from each other; *retiarii* aren't required to mess with convicted felons, nor in the same cell does he who strips off to fight discard his shoulder-guards and defensive trident. Even the lowest scum of the arena observe this rule; even in prison they're separate.

Two structures at Pompeii have been identified as gladiatorial barracks. The older of these is a private dwelling converted to this use, in which perhaps fifteen to twenty performers could be accommodated. The barracks were then moved to another, larger remodeled structure; previously a quad-roportico or colonnaded plaza in the theater district, this was converted after the earthquake of 62 CE to provide basic sleeping rooms and training areas for as many as 100 gladiators (see figure 4.2). Storage areas for weapons and armor were created, along with a kitchen and a new access way, after the passage into the theater was blocked up. There seems to be little structural effort to limit the mobility of the residents of the *ludus*; a possible guard post may have served to monitor movements of gladiators and visitors, rather than bar access in either direction. A small room found in the complex may have been used for disciplinary measures; built along the lines of the medieval

Figure 4.2 Pompeii, barracks of gladiators

"small ease" chambers, a person placed in this cell could neither stand nor stretch out fully inside. Graffiti recovered from the barracks were written by and about the gladiators, giving us glimpses into their lives.

Source: *CIL* 4.4304: Servilius is in love: may he have no success. Servilius the sucker.

Death or Survival

Calculating the individual mortality rates for gladiators is heavily dependent on the existing database, which is minimal at best. Information about surviving the arena comes mostly from epitaphs of gladiators, graffiti, and edicts from Pompeii, and occasional references in the literary sources. The inscriptions carry an important bias: money. Erecting any kind of tomb monument required a substantial financial investment. Those individual gladiators documented by such inscriptions are more likely to have been successful, to accumulate the needed resources. Georges Ville has done the most work on estimating the rates of survival, focusing in particular on the first century CE. One hundred bouts, by his calculations, would likely result in nineteen fatalities. Assuming that one hundred combatants lost their match, the death rate for losers would be about one in five, while the risk of death for all who entered the arena was about one in ten. Whether these nineteen were actually killed in the arena and not granted *missio* by the editor, or they died shortly after the match of blood loss, shock or infection is not known. Ville suggested that the odds of survival got worse in the second and third centuries. This later evidence indicates that half of all matches ended in the death of one of the gladiators. Those entering the arena in this later period had a one in four likelihood of death. This may suggest that the audiences of the later empire were more sophisticated, perhaps, with very demanding standards for gladiatorial performance. *Missio* was thus more difficult to achieve, more rarely given.[48]

Paradoxically, the longer one was a gladiator, the less likely was death in the arena. Experience of combat and years of training paid off in honed fighting skills, of course. Because of the audience's preference for equal matches, a veteran of twenty or thirty bouts had fewer opponents at his level; he also was more costly for an *editor* to acquire. The frequency of matches for him was thus lower. His success over time had also built a reputation among the fans, who were thus more likely to call for *missio*, should he be defeated. Inscriptions and graffiti referring to such veterans have been found in various parts of the empire. This pattern is supported as well by the career records of gladiators from Pompeii that document the ongoing careers of combatants with dozens of matches they'd survived, not always by winning. These were fighters whose skill or showmanship had won them reprieve or *missio*, even though they'd been disarmed or downed by their opponents.

Source: *CIL* 12.5837: To the ... spirits. Asiaticus, first fighter, released after 53 combats. His wife had this made.

Source: *CIL* 6.33952: Maximus, *essedarius* from the Julian *ludus*, 40 combats, 36 victories.

Source: *CIL* 4.2387: Pinna of the Neronian *ludus*, 16 combats, winner. Columbus, released, 88 combats, died.

Source: *CIL* 4.5306: Auctus of the Julian *ludus*, 50 combats.

Source: *CIL* 4.2451: Viriotas, 150 combats, against Sextius, 100 combats. Valerius, 25 combats, against Viriotas, 150 combats. Amon . . . 75 combats, against Valerius, 75 combats. Servilius, 100 combats, against Valerius, 75 combats. Marcus, 50 combats. Sequanus, 75 combats. Sedulatus, 25 combats.

The fact that *editores* had to make the effort to specify that some games were *sine missione* likewise argues that mandatory death was not typical of matches in the arena. The pattern of praise and blame for emperors' stances on the issue of *missio* suggest that the possibility of release was regarded as a positive element.

Source: Suetonius, *Augustus* 45:[49] [Augustus] banned gladiatorial contests if the defeated fighter were forbidden to plead for mercy.

Forcing death in the arena was interpreted as the action of a cruel emperor; to some extent, this diminished the importance of skill and the role of fortune in combats. The risks of combat could be prepared for; death that resulted from the whimsy of the emperor could not and presented a real danger for performers in the arena.

Source: Suetonius, *Caligula* 30:[50] A group of *retiarii*, dressed in tunics, put up a very poor fight against the five *secutores* with whom they were matched; but when [Caligula] sentenced them to death, one of them seized a trident and killed each of the victorious team in turn. Gaius then publicly expressed his horror at what he called "this most bloody murder" and his disgust with those who had been able to stomach the sight.

Claudius' *sine missione* games emphasized the punishment of error, not only on the part of combatants but also for the support personnel.

Source: Suetonius, *Claudius* 34:[51] His cruelty and bloodthirstiness appeared equally in great and small matters . . . At gladiatorial shows, whether or not they were staged by himself, he ruled that all combatants who fell accidentally should have their throats cut – above all *retiarii* so that he could gaze on their death agony . . . after he had spent the whole morning in the amphitheater from daybreak until noon, he would dismiss the audience, keep his seat, and not only watch the regular combats but extemporize others between the stage carpenters and similar members of the theater staff, as a punishment for the failure of any mechanical device to work as it should.

Sexy Gladiators

A fringe benefit for surviving combatants was the sexual glamour that surrounded winning performers. The graffiti of Pompeii document the sexual allure of the gladiators, with repeated connections between specific combatants and "the girls" or "the dollies." Without knowing the writers of these comments, it's hard to say whether these are boasts by the gladiators or appreciative accolades by fans, male or female.

> Source: *CIL* 4.4342: Celadus the *Thraex*, the sigh of the girls, three combats, three victories.

> Source: *CIL* 4.4345: Celadus the *Thraex*, the glory of the girls.

> Source: *CIL* 4.4353: Crescens the *retiarius, doctor* . . . of nighttime dollies.

A notorious scandal is recounted by Juvenal in his detailed critique of Rome's immoral women. The appeal of the arena performer for an elite woman was probably intensified by his degraded status, his difference; the risk of his profession also probably added savor to the relationship.

> Source: Juvenal, *Satire* 6.102–112:[52] What beauty set Eppia [a senator's wife] on fire? What youth captured her? What did she see that made her endured being called a *ludia* [gladiator's woman]? For her darling Sergius had already begun to shave [i.e., he was middle-aged], and to hope for retirement due to a wounded arm. Moreover, there were many deformities on his face; for instance, there was a huge wart on the middle of his nose which was rubbed by his helmet, and a bitter matter dripped continually from one eye. But he was a gladiator: this makes them Hyacinthuses. She preferred this to her children and her country, that woman preferred this to her sister and her husband. The sword is what they love.

These beloved "swords" gained symbolic power; the actions of the arena became metaphors for sex and conjugal interaction, a linkage firmly embedded in the Roman worldview. In Artemidorus' book of dream interpretation, a man dreaming of being a gladiator could anticipate a marriage in the near future. More than that, the specifics of his dream combat had significance for the upcoming marital pairing.

Source: Artemidorus 2.32:[53] I have often observed that this dream indicates that a man will marry a woman whose character corresponds to the armature that he dreams he is using or to the type of opponent against whom he is fighting ... For example, if a man fights a *Thraex*, he will marry a wife who is rich, crafty and fond of being first. She will be rich because the *Thraex's* body is entirely covered by his armor; crafty, because his sword is not straight; and fond of being first, because this fighter employs the advancing technique.

Rumors abounded about high-born ladies and the low-born objects of their desires, rendered even more desirable because of the thrill of violating status expectations by associating with one so vile. Even the empress could be suspected of harboring such desires, especially the mother of Commodus, the notorious gladiator emperor (see below). Faustina's lusts, in one of the numerous rumors in circulation, proved a danger to one particular gladiator, demonstrating the tremendous vulnerability of his status, alongside the potential benefit of being "noticed" by the powerful.

Source; Historia Augusta, *Marcus Antoninus* 19:[54] Some say, and this seems plausible, that Commodus Antoninus, [Marcus Aurelius'] son and successor, was not begotten by him but from an adulterous union, and they embroider such a tale with a story current among the common people. Allegedly Faustina, Pius' daughter and Marcus' wife, had once seen gladiators pass by and was inflamed with passion for one of them. While troubled by a long illness she confessed to her husband about her passion. When Marcus had related this to the Chaldaean [soothsayers], it was their advice that the gladiator be killed and that Faustina should wash herself from beneath in his blood and in this state lie with her husband. When this had been done the passion was indeed abated, but Commodus was born a gladiator not a *princeps*; for as emperor he put on nearly a thousand gladiatorial fights, with the people looking on ... Many relate, however, that Commodus was actually begotten in adultery, since it is reasonably well known that Faustina chose both sailors and gladiators as paramours for herself at Caieta.

Death and Choice

The suicide of a gladiator became a philosophical trope, particularly powerful because of the legal and social powerlessness of the gladiator. One of Seneca's moralizing letters to his friend Lucilius cites a number of examples of suicides at the *ludi*, which can be interpreted a number of ways. Some have suggested that these document the abject misery of these performers' lives, including the constant scrutiny that deprived them of privacy. Seneca does not, however, focus on the poor quality of life available in the *ludus*. His point is that value of life comes with self-determination, with choosing the proper moment for death and acting upon that decision. Seneca does, however, imply that there are minimal standards to be met for life to be worth living. General circumstances of the gladiator's life, such as the forced daily submission as well as the shame of display, would be part of the calculation.[55]

> Source: Seneca, *Letters* 70.20–27:[56] You need not think that none but great men have had the strength to break the bonds of human servitude . . . For example, there was lately in a *ludus* for *bestiarii* a German, who was preparing for the morning exhibition; he withdrew in order to relieve himself – the only thing he was allowed to do in secret and without the presence of a guard. While so engaged, he seized the stick of wood, tipped with a sponge, which was used for the vilest purposes[57], and stuffed it, just as it was, down his throat; thus he blocked up his windpipe and choked the breath from his body . . . what a brave fellow! He surely deserved to be allowed to choose his fate! How bravely he would have wielded a sword . . . cut off from resources on every hand, he yet found a way to furnish himself with death, and with a weapon for death . . . the virtue of which I speak is found as frequently in the *ludus* for the *bestiarii* as among the leaders in a civil war. Recently a certain fighter, who had been sent for the morning spectacle, was being transported in a cart along with the other prisoners; nodding as if he were heavy with sleep, he let his head fall over so far that it was caught in the spokes, then he kept his body in position long enough to break his neck by the rotation of the wheel. So he made his escape by means of the very wagon which was carrying him to his punishment . . . more illustrations drawn from the same games. During the second event in a mock sea battle one of the barbarians sank deep into his own throat a spear which had been given him for use against his foe. "Why oh why," he said, "have I not long ago escaped from all this torture, all this humiliation? Why should I be armed and yet wait for death to come?" This exhibition was all the more striking because of the lesson men learn from it that dying is more honorable than killing.

Gladiator *Familiae*

The gladiatorial *familia*, the group of fighters who all belonged to the same *ludus*, formed a communal bond of some complexity. Typically, only one *ludus* supplied performers for a given set of games, so members of the same *familia* fought against each other in the arena, wounding and even killing the people they lived and worked with. At the same time, the gladiatorial *familia* was the social support network for its members; the familial relationship formed here was on display in the final meal before the *munera* and is evidenced in the monuments set up to honor *familia* members. The following inscriptions are epitaphs from the eastern part of the empire, from such towns as Smyrna and Thessalonika, set up by *familiae* as a whole or by fellow-gladiators for their fallen friends. Victor's monument indicates the emotional investment of the *familia* in defending the reputation of its members.

Source: Robert #241: The *familia* set this up in memory of Saturnilos.

Source: Robert #12:[58] For Nikephoros, son of Synetos, Lakedaimonian, and for Narcissus the *secutor*. Titus Flavius Satyrus set up this monument in his memory from his own money.

Source: Robert #109: For Hermes. Paitraeites with his cell-mates set this up in memory.

Source: Robert #34: I, Victor, left-handed, lie here, but my homeland was Thessalonica. Doom killed me, not the liar Pinnas. No longer let him boast. I had a fellow gladiator, Polyneikes, who killed Pinnas and avenged me. Claudius Thallus set up this memorial from what I left behind as a legacy.

Outside Italy, a connection between the priests of the Imperial Cult and support of gladiatorial troupes can be traced. *Munera* were regularly included in the festivals celebrating the deified emperor, so maintaining the necessary personnel and expertise may have made economic sense for the long run. Inscriptions erected by these *familiae* at Aphrodisias celebrate the range of expertise assembled by the troupe owner as well as his efforts on behalf of the city. The series of monuments commemorating such *familiae* suggests that this responsibility was passed down through multiple successions of priesthoods. The inscription set up by the *familia* of Zeno Hypsicles is dated to the late first or early second century. Interesting to note is the explicit reference to *katadikoi* or convicts.

Source: Roueche #14 = Robert #157:[59] The *familia* of Zeno Hypsicles, son of Hypsicles, son of Hypsicles the natural son of Zeno, high-priest, [the *familia*] of gladiators and convicts and bull-catchers.

The monument set up for M. Antonius Apellas Severinus incorporates some of the symbology common to the arena. The panel on which the inscription is carved is held up by a pair of winged Nikes, sculpted in relief, who flank a female figure holding a wheel, identified as Nemesis with her wheel of fortune, one of the primary deities of the amphitheater.

Source: Roueche #15 = Robert #156:[60] To Good Fortune. Memorial of the *familia* and of the *venatores* of Marcus Antonius Apellas Severinus, son of Marcus Antonius Hypsicles, high priest.

The ties between gladiators and their blood relatives are likewise assessed by the ancient evidence. An incident from the reign of Claudius suggests the strength of these bonds endured despite the degradation of status, a valuable asset indeed.

Source: Suetonius, *Claudius* 21:[61] When four brothers pleaded for the discharge of their father, an *essedarius*, Claudius presented him with the customary wooden sword amid resounding cheers, and then circulated a placard: "You now see the great advantage of having a large family; it can win favor and protection even for a gladiator."

The following epitaphs document these kinds of relationships, as well as the fact that gladiators had spouses and children who likewise registered their devotion with permanent monuments. Here, a gladiator honors his youthful dead wife.

Source: *CIL* 6.10167: To the departed spirits of Publicia Aromtis. Albanus, a veteran *eques* gladiator from the *Ludus Magnus* had this made for his dearest wife, who lived twenty-two years, five months and eight days. The tomb is allocated a space of three by eight feet.

A two-sided tombstone provides evidence of a family unit for one gladiator, who, with his wife, commemorated the passing of their toddler-age son, and then honored his deceased wife with an inscription on the other side.

Source: *CIL* 6.10176: Side 1: To the departed spirits of Alcibiades, dearest son, who lived two years, eleven months, seventeen days, eleven hours. His extremely devoted parents had this made.
    Side 2: To the departed spirits of Julia Procula. Gaesus, a veteran *murmillo* gladiator, put this up for his well-deserving spouse.

On another tombstone, a couple shares commemoration by their adult daughter; the veteran gladiator in this case was discharged from the arena with its highest honor, the *summa rudis*. The fact that this gladiator and his wife shared the same *nomen* suggests that they were former slaves.

> Source: *CIL* 6.10201: To the departed spirits of Cornelius Eugenianus, awarded the *summa rudis*, and of Cornelia Rufina. Their daughter had this made for her well-deserving and sweetest parents.

This tombstone, also from Rome, includes an unusually effusive tribute to the wife of a gladiator.

> Source: *CIL* 6.10193: To the departed spirits of Maria Thesidis. Publius Aelius, a veteran *Thraex* gladiator from the Troad, put this up for his most holy, most devoted, well-deserving wife.

This epitaph, from Rome, documents the long-term connection between an apparently freeborn gladiator and his wife; the son of this union joined his mother in this tribute to the dead *murmillo*.

> Source; *CIL* 6.10177: To the departed spirits of Marcus Ulpius Felix, veteran *murmillo* gladiator, who lived forty-five years. From the Tunger nation. Ulpia Syntyche, a freedwoman, along with Justus, his son, had this made for her sweetest and well-deserving spouse.

The family of Danaos, a gladiator from Cyzicus (figure 4.3) is represented visually on the tombstone, which depicts a family banquet, possibly meant to represent anticipated comforts of the afterlife. The father and his youthfully beardless son, Asklepiades, share a couch, while the matron, Eorta, sits on a chair, as respectable matrons did. A dog joins them near the table. The family scene is framed by nine crowns, representing the nine victories won by Danaos, along with some of his armature; the crowns and weapons are more crudely carved than the banquet and were probably done specifically for the customer, while the more generic funeral scene may have been ready-made.

> Source: Robert #293: Eorta his wife and Asklepiades his son set this up in memory of Danaos, second *palus*, *Thraex*. After nine combats he departed to Hades.

Figure 4.3 Tomb monument of Danaos. Erich Lessing/Art Resource, NY

Three tombstones from Gaul were built by the wives of the gladiatorial deceased. One notes that the money used was hers, which likely indicates she was a free woman of substance, even though her name does not survive.

Source: *CIL* 12.3323: [For] Beryllus, an *essedarius*, freed after the twentieth combat, a Greek, twenty-five years old. Nomas, his wife, set this up for her well-deserving husband.

Source: *CIL* 12.3327: [For] the *retiarius*, L. Pompeius, winner of nine crowns, born in Vienna, twenty-five years of age. His wife put this up with her own money for her wonderful spouse.

Source: *CIL* 12.5836: [For] M. Quintus Ducenius, best. Three combats, three victories. Hateria Potita, his wife, had this made.

The tombstone of Glauco fits into the "advice from the deceased" pattern of Roman commemoration; here, the dead person "recommends" caution in relying on Nemesis, one of the prominent deities of the amphitheater, who was supposed to see that events transpired as they should.

> Source: *CIL* 5.3466: To the revered spirits of the dead. Glauco, a native of Mutina, fought in seven fights and died in the eighth. He lived twenty-three years and five days. Aurelia and his friends [set up this epitaph] for her well-deserving husband. I [Glauco] advise you to find your own star: do not trust Nemesis: that's how I was deceived. Hail and farewell.

Female Performers: *Gladiatrices* and *Ludia*

Women did appear as combatants in the Roman games, fighting other women as well as animals with mixed reactions to their presence. How frequently this occurred and when this practice began is unclear. Likewise confusing is the use of the term *ludia* as well as *gladiatrix*: the latter seems to be a female gladiator, but is a *ludia*, literally a woman of the *ludus*, a performer or a woman who services the various needs of members of the *familia*?

Female performers often appear in the ancient texts as exotic markers of truly lavish spectacle. The following references in Martial seem to allude to vignettes at the spectacles of Titus in which women played the main role: in one instance, the performer was apparently clothed as the goddess of love, ancestress of the Roman people, and in another a female fighter overcame a lion.

> Source: Martial, *On the Spectacles* 7:[62] It is not enough that warrior Mars serves you in unconquered arms, Caesar. Venus herself serves you too.

> Source: Martial, *On the Spectacles* 8:[63] Illustrious Fame used to sing of the lion laid low in Nemea's spacious vale, Hercules' work. Let ancient testimony be silent, for after your shows, Caesar, we have now seen such things done by women's valor.

The dour emperor Domitian showed some innovative qualities in his arrangement of shows, as Suetonius notes, in which the combats of women were enhanced by special lighting.

Source: Suetonius, *Domitian* 4:[64] Domitian presented many extravagant entertainments in the Colosseum and the Circus...a sea-fight in the amphitheatre; wild-beast hunts; gladiatorial shows by torchlight in which women as well as men took part.

Statius may refer to the same set of games given by Domitian; the poet emphasizes the strangeness of the combats, soft women and tiny dwarves being inherently un-virile and thus un-warlike in Roman expectations.

Source: Statius, *Silvae* 1.6.53–64:[65] Women untrained to the *rudis* take their stand, daring, how recklessly, virile battles! You would think Thermodon's bands were furiously fighting by Tanais or barbarous Phasis. Then comes a bold array of dwarves, whose term of growth abruptly ended has bound them once and for all into a knotted lump. They give and suffer wounds and threaten death – with fists how tiny! Father Mars and Bloody Virtus laugh, and cranes, waiting to swoop on scattered booty, marvel at the fiercer pugilists.

Women from the elite class performed in *munera* during the reign of Nero; Tacitus acknowledges the lavishness of this display but also assigns a negative moral value to the spectacles. These are not the only crimes against class associated with Nero.

Source: Tacitus, *Annals* 15.32:[66] The same year [64 CE] witnessed shows of gladiators as magnificent as those of the past. Many ladies of distinction, however, and senators, disgraced themselves by appearing in the amphitheater.

Juvenal's tirade against depraved matrons notes with contempt the amateur *gladiatrix*. The problem here is not necessarily that these female combat enthusiasts will actually appear in public games, so much as the transgression of gender norms. These are, after all, married women, whose pursuit of "manly" skills unbalances the distribution of authority in the marital relationship. It also represents to Juvenal a betrayal of Roman tradition, an absence of matronly dignity inappropriate to the noble descendants of worthy ancestors.

Source: Juvenal, *Satire* 6.246–67:[67] Women in purple exercise clothes, women who wrestle – these are a common sight. So are our lady-fencers – we've all seen them, stabbing the practice stump with a *rudis*, shield well-advanced – just the right training needed to blow a matronly horn at the Floralia, unless their aim is higher, to make the real arena. But then, what modesty is there in some helmeted hoyden, a renegade from her sex, who adores male violence – yet wouldn't want to be a man, since the pleasure is so much less? What a sight, if one's wife's Samnite equipment were sold at auction, helmet crest, *balteus*, armlets, and one half of the left-leg shin-guard! Or if the other armature attracts her, how happy you'll be when the dear girl sells off her greaves! . . . Hark how she snorts at each practice thrust, bowed down by the weight of her helmet; see the big coarse *fascia* wrapped round her ample hams . . . Tell me, you noble ladies, descendants of Lepidus, blind Metellus, Fabius Gurges – what gladiator's woman ever dressed up like this, or gasped at the practice-stump?

Blame accrued to emperors that allowed inappropriate performers to debase themselves by appearing in the arena. In describing the inaugural games of Titus, Dio is careful to mention that the female *venatores*, the same noted by Martial in poetic form, are not from an elite background. Their presence in the shows is thus titillating but not necessarily shameful and Titus escapes moral culpability in his sponsorship of such fights.

Source: Dio Cassius 66.25:[68] In dedicating the amphitheater and the baths that bear his name [Titus] produced many remarkable spectacles . . . animals both tame and wild were slain to the number of nine thousand, and women (not those of any prominence, however) took part in dispatching them.

A ban on the appearance of women in the arena was mandated under Septimius Severus, provoked not so much by unusually high numbers of women in blood games, but rather because of disrespectful comments about high-born women that were made in conjunction with competitions.

Source: Dio Cassius 76.16:[69] There took place also during those days a gymnastic contest, at which so great a multitude of athletes assembled, under compulsion, that we wondered how the course could contain them all. And in this contest women took part, vying with one another most fiercely, with the result that jokes were made about other very distinguished women as well. Therefore it was henceforth forbidden for any woman, no matter what her origin, to fight in single combat.

Crimes of Status: Elites in the Arena

An individual's radical deterioration in status challenged the perceived stability of Roman order, as well as the reigning emperor's ability to preserve the status quo. If the empire were really stable, really ordered, such things could not happen at all. It also challenged the moral basis by which the Roman hierarchy was legitimized. Elites were supposed to control their social and political inferiors, not be controlled by the *lanista* and the shrieking crowd at the arena. To see senatorials and equestrians in the arena was bad enough; it was worse to see the emperor make himself into a performer. Nepos says this is the difference between Romans and others, that non-Romans can see elites on the stage with some equanimity, whereas for Romans this is a source of shame.

> Source: Cornelius Nepos, *Lives* pref 5: While all Greece honored an Olympic victor and to go onstage as a spectacle for the people was held in no way shameful to them, all these things are considered by us to be *infamia, humilia* and far from honorable.

The first known prohibition of Roman elites from appearing as performers in spectacle dates to 46 BCE and the triumphal games sponsored by Julius Caesar as dictator. It is unknown whether this was a formalization of earlier practice or if this was an innovation, perhaps prompted by the civil war context that made boundaries between different statuses in Roman society distressingly fluid. Roman populists, such as Caesar and the more radical Clodius, intensively wooed the lower classes as a useful political constituency, using measures that tended to act against traditional elite privilege. The power of mob politics degraded the cachet of Rome's elite, a slippage that many found troubling, including even those of lower status who might be considered to benefit from this leveling trend. Throughout the rest of the Republic period and the reign of Augustus, various efforts were made to spell out which elites, under which circumstances, could appear in the arena.

A bronze tablet found in Larinum gives the text of a law passed by the Senate under Tiberius that categorizes the performance of equestrians in theatrical presentations and in *munera* as violations of the status ideals established by Augustus in much of his social reform legislation. The prohibition here extends beyond the actual performance to include practice bouts, seemingly, and possibly non-lethal "demonstration" performances. The law also refers to fraud as a motivation for elites to engage in such shameful practices; some suggest that becoming an actor or gladiator may have been a means for some to evade the elite behavioral restrictions of the Augustan legislation on marriage, for example.

Source: Senatorial Decree of 19 CE:[70] Whereas M. Silanus and L. Norbanus Balbus the consuls declared that in accordance with the commission given them they had drawn up a memorandum on . . . those who, contrary to the dignity of the order to which they belonged, were appearing on the stage or at games or were pledging themselves to fight as gladiators, as forbidden by the senatorial decrees that had been passed on that subject in previous years, employing fraudulent evasion to the detriment of the majesty of the senate: on this matter, the senate's recommendation was as follows: no one should bring on to the stage a senator's son, daughter, grandson, granddaughter, great-grandson, great-granddaughter or any male whose father or grandfather (paternal or maternal) or brother or female whose husband or father or grandfather (paternal or maternal) or brother had ever possessed the right of sitting in the seats reserved for the equestrians; or induce them by means of a fee to fight to the death in the arena or to snatch the helmet-crests of gladiators or to take the practice-sword off anyone or to take part in any way in any similar subordinate capacity; nor, if anyone offered himself to do this, should he hire him; nor should any of these persons hire himself out; and that particular precautions were necessary because certain persons of equestrian standing had, for the sake of diminishing the authority of that order, seen to it that they either suffered public disgrace or were condemned in a case involving them in *infamia* and, after they had withdrawn of their own free will from the equestrian seats, had pledged themselves as gladiators or had appeared on the stage; nor should any of these persons, if they were taking that action in contravention of the dignity of their order, have due burial, unless they had already appeared on the stage or hired out their services for the arena or were the offspring male or female of an actor, gladiator, *lanista* or pimp. And with regard to the provisions of the senatorial decree passed by the consuls Manius Lepidus and Titus Statilius Taurus, namely that it should be permissible for no female of free birth of less than twenty years of age and for no male of free birth of less than twenty-five years of age to pledge himself as a gladiator or hire out his services for the arena or stage.

Later references to elites in the arena register shock, indicating their presence there was not typical, and identify this as a sign that behavioral standards have slipped, a failure usually attributed to poor leadership at the top. Juvenal recounts a series of scandals in which scions of noble families bring disgrace by venturing into the arena. In the case of Rutilus, at least, the reason stipulated for this shameful action is poverty following extravagance.

Source: Juvenal, *Satire* 11.3–8, 18–20:[71] Every dinner-party, all the baths and arcades and theater foyers are humming with the Rutilus scandal. He's young still, physically fit to bear arms, and hot-blooded. Gossip claims that with no official compulsion, but no ban either, he'll sign his freedom away to some tyrant of a *lanista*, take the gladiator's oath . . . they'll hock the family plate, or pledge poor Mummy's portrait, and spend their last fiver to add relish to their gourmet earthenware: thus they're reduced to the gladiators' mess-stew.

Imperial Gladiators

Some emperors became notorious not merely as fans of the arena, but as actual participants in spectacular events. This is strongly criticized in the ancient authors, as a horrific violation of the hierarchy of power and as evidence of moral failure. Nero and Commodus were the most reviled for their gladiatorial tendencies.

Nero's own need to perform (and to be acclaimed as a performer) finds satisfaction first indirectly, by staging elaborate yet technically "private" shows. He then creates "cover" for his own actions by exploiting the circumstances and fears of other elites, to make them perform.

> Source: Tacitus, *Annals* 14.14:[72] Imagining that he mitigated the scandal by disgracing many others, he brought on the stage descendants of noble families, who sold themselves because they were paupers. As they have ended their days, I think it due to their ancestors not to hand down their names. And indeed the infamy is his who gave them wealth to reward their degradation rather than to deter them from degrading themselves. He prevailed too on some well-known Roman equestrians, by immense presents, to offer their services in the amphitheater; only pay from one who is able to command, carries with it the force of compulsion.

Commodus was the first emperor born to the purple, i.e. born to a reigning emperor. His entire life was spent in privilege, a fact that probably affected his sense of entitlement and of license. Much of the ancient criticism levied against his rule focuses on what have, by the time of Commodus, become standard targets of imperial blame: excesses of self-indulgence, lack of discipline, and corresponding inattention to the tasks of government. Much of the description of Commodus' arena excess parallels similar activities attributed to Nero and to other "bad" emperors. Unlike Nero, however, Commodus seems to have performed in public *munera* himself, although some have questioned the extent of that performance. Dio Cassius was a senator in Rome under Commodus and thus an eye-witness to his rule. His description may suggest that Commodus' public performances were set apart from the regular shows as special "exhibitions" and consisted of stylized killing of select criminals and exotic animals, with the specific intent to compare the emperor's efforts to the labors of Hercules, Commodus' patron deity. The concentration on this kind of activity and the huge sums paid to support such grand gestures as spectacle and *sparsiones* (see chapter 3) eventually proved an intolerable strain on Commodus' rule.

Source: Dio Cassius 73.16–17:[73] Now this "Golden One," this "Hercules," this "god" (for he was even given this name, too)... was also fond, it is true, of bestowing gifts, and frequently gave largesses to the populace at the rate of one hundred and forty denarii per man; but most of his expenditures were for the objects I have mentioned... he saved nothing, but spent it all disgracefully on his wild beasts and his gladiators... As for wild beasts, however, he slew many both in private and in public. Moreover, he used to contend as a gladiator; in doing this at home he managed to kill a man now and then, and in making close passes with others, as if trying to clip off a bit of their hair, he sliced off the noses of some, the ears of others, and sundry features of still others; but in public he refrained from using steel and shedding human blood... As for the lion-skin and club, in the street they were carried before him, and in the amphitheatres they were placed on a gilded chair, whether he was present or not. He himself would enter the arena in the garb of Mercury, and casting aside all his other garments, would begin his exhibition wearing only a tunic and unshod.

Why did emperors do this? Individual reasons probably varied, from thrill-seeking in a fishbowl existence to the need for demonstrations of approval, of "love," to a display of power not just in the use of weapons but in the deliberate flouting of social norms. The emperor proved he was so powerful that rules no longer applied to him.

5

Christians and the Arena

This section begins with some basic establishing material about the interaction between the Roman state and early Christianity, starting with the targeting of Christians by Nero in the wake of the Great Fire of 64 CE. This would become a model for Roman initiative, which typically took action only in "crisis" situations, searching for a reason for the eruption of disorder and finding a solution in the disruption presented by the Christians. Pliny's exchange of letters with the emperor Trajan is vital to understanding the Roman perception of Christians and the official treatment of those accused of this offense; the formal procedure laid out by Trajan and Pliny is essential background to both the denunciation of the spectacles by early Christian authors and the Martyr Acts, which document Christian reactions to the persecution from a partisan perspective. The Martyr Acts offer a window into the ways in which the arena served as a venue for Christian construction of identity and faith. This process partly involved a reworking of the Roman values system embedded in the spectacle, redefining the terms of the performance so that the social stigma attached to those appearing in the arena was now to be understood as a sign of spiritual transcendence, a special elevation conferred by divine favor. Much of the "value" early Christians took from the arena did not, however, require this kind of inversion of Roman standards. Patterns of moral critique of gladiatorial behavior and of the degradation of the audience already existed that could be readily adapted to celebrate the martyrs' unearthly endurance and the evil of the pagan mob in attendance at the spectacles.

Rome and the Christians: The Official Relationship

During the years immediately after the crucifixion of Christ, the Roman government had no official opposition to Christianity; the legal troubles documented in *Acts of the Apostles* and alluded to in the letters of Paul seem to be local disputes mostly within Jewish communities of the Diaspora. The differences of practice and doctrine advocated by previously Jewish Christian proselytizers, like Paul, provoked more mainstream Jews to seek out official redress from Roman administrators, charging the proselytizers with "defying the edicts of Caesar" and worshipping in a way contrary to law. Even the deportation of Paul to Rome around 60 CE was the result of escalating tensions in Judaea that had resulted in charges of sedition being claimed against Paul; Paul made use of his right, as a Roman citizen, to appeal local judgment to the emperor.

Four years later, according to Christian tradition, Paul had successfully defended himself and resumed his missionary efforts, only to be caught up in Nero's persecution, the first officially sanctioned action against Christians.

The Neronian persecution

This represented a shift in Roman policy from the hands-off stance documented in Acts. What catalyzed the change? The most extensive account comes from Tacitus, who places the action in the aftermath of the Great Fire of 64. Tacitus' focus, however, is not on the Christians so much as the emperor; the Christian incident is added to a long list of Nero's abuses of power. In order to deflect hostile suspicion from himself, Nero targeted a group despised by the population to take the blame.

Source: Tacitus, *Annals* 15.44:[1] But all human efforts, all the lavish gifts of the emperor, and the propitiations of the gods, did not banish the sinister belief that the conflagration was the result of an order. Consequently, to get rid of the report, Nero fastened the guilt and inflicted the most exquisite tortures on a class hated for their abominations, called Christians by the populace. Christus, from whom the name had its origin, suffered the extreme penalty during the reign of Tiberius at the hands of one of our procurators, Pontius Pilatus, and a most mischievous superstition, thus checked for the moment, again broke out not only in Judaea, the first source of the evil, but even in Rome, where all things hideous and shameful from every part of the world find their center and become popular. Accordingly, an arrest was first made of all who pleaded guilty; then, upon their information, an immense multitude was convicted, not so much of the crime of firing the city, as of hatred against mankind. Mockery of every sort was added to their deaths. Covered with the skins of beasts, they were torn by dogs and perished, or were nailed to crosses, or were doomed to the flames and burnt, to serve as a nightly illumination, when daylight had expired. Nero offered his gardens for the spectacle, and was exhibiting a show in the circus, while he mingled with the people in the dress of a charioteer or stood aloft on a car. Hence, even for criminals who deserved extreme and exemplary punishment, there arose a feeling of compassion; for it was not, as it seemed, for the public good, but to glut one man's cruelty, that they were being destroyed.

Tacitus' version of events raises some questions: to what did the first people arrested confess? What were they guilty of? Tacitus is the only ancient author to connect the Christians to the fire at all and even he finds the arson connection unlikely. He does, however, believe they deserve execution, although not the spectacle to which they were subjected by Nero's "cruelty." Tacitus says they were condemned because of their known *odium humani generis*, hatred of the human race. His narrative of the Christian persecution follows his description of the traditional religious response to disaster, in which Nero, quite appropriately, tried to propitiate the gods who had punished the Romans with the Great Fire, tried to restore the positive relationship with deity by offering public prayers and ritual banquets to make up for some perceived neglect in pious duty. The real crime committed by the Christians is their sociopathic dereliction of their responsibilities toward the human community. By refusing to participate in public religion, Christians threatened everyone by provoking the rage of the gods. The Christians are guilty of organized misanthropy. Under Nero, Christianity became a crime against the Roman state, punishable, like sedition and treason, by death.

Christian sources interpreted the policy as the height of Nero's perversion, emphasizing the emperor's notoriety and lack of moral grounding as the "reason" behind his hostility toward Christians. Nero is evil, through and through, is their argument; he is engaged in a cosmic battle against all goodness. Opposition by such an emperor serves as proof, therefore, of Christian righteousness. Persecution of Christians becomes part of the pattern of praise and blame of Christian historians in their interpretation of the imperial past. Interesting as well is the frequency of a combat metaphor to describe this opposition, used here by Eusebius in the fourth century. Persecuting emperors become killer gladiators in a metaphysical arena.

Source: Eusebius, *Ecclesiastical History* 2.25:[2] When the rule of Nero was now gathering strength for unholy objects he began to take up arms against the worship of the God of the universe. It is not part of the present work to describe his depravity: many indeed have related his story in accurate narrative, and from them he who wishes can study the perversity of his degenerate madness, which made him compass the unreasonable destruction of so many thousands ... But with all this there was still lacking to him this – that it should be attributed to him that he was the first of the emperors to be pointed out as a foe of divine religion ... "We boast that such a man was the author of our chastisement; for he who knows him can understand that nothing would have been condemned by Nero had it not been great and good."[3] In this way then was he the first to be heralded as above all a fighter against God, and raised up to slaughter against the Apostles.

Trajan's policy

Roman criminal law was not very proactive. The absence of something approximating a public prosecutor meant that criminal procedures were usually initiated by individuals taking it upon themselves to press charges against the alleged malefactor. The criminalization of Christians did not mean, therefore, that the Roman state launched a house-to-house search to hunt down and destroy all believers. The pattern followed by most procedures against Christians, and the reasoning behind it, is laid out in correspondence between the emperor Trajan and Pliny the Younger. From about 109 CE, Pliny was acting as an imperial procurator in Bithynia, particularly charged with cleaning up financial corruption and administrative neglect. In this situation, Pliny serves as an agent of Roman law when a group of locals are accused of Christianity; the rarity of the action means that Pliny has no standard procedure to follow. The issue becomes more complicated, as Pliny wonders about the specific relationship these people have with Christianity, and whether this secret cult would involve them in other kinds of criminal activity, and how Roman justice should deal with what may constitute a number of different dangers to the state.

Source: Pliny *Letters* 10.96–7:[4] I have never been present at an examination of Christians. Consequently, I do not know the nature of the extent of the punishments usually meted out to them, nor the grounds for starting an investigation and how far it should be pressed. Nor am I at all sure whether any distinction should be made between them on the grounds of age, or if young people and adults should be treated alike; whether a pardon ought to be granted to anyone retracting his beliefs, or if he has once professed Christianity, he shall gain nothing by renouncing it; and whether it is the mere name of Christian which is punishable, even innocent of crime, or rather the crimes associated with the name. For the moment this is the line I have taken with all persons brought before me on the charge of being Christians. I have asked them in person if they are Christians, and if they admit it, I repeat the question a second and third time, with a warning of the punishment awaiting them. If they persist, I order them to be led away for execution; for, whatever the nature of their admission, I am convinced that their stubbornness and unshakeable obstinacy ought not to go unpunished. There have been others similarly fanatical who are Roman citizens. I have entered them on the list of persons to be sent to Rome for trial. Now that I have begun to deal with this problem, as so often happens, the charges are becoming more widespread and increasing in variety. An anonymous pamphlet has been circulated which contains the names of a number of accused persons. Amongst these I considered that I should dismiss any who denied that they were or ever had been Christians when they had repeated after me a formula of invocation to the gods and had made offerings of wine and incense to your statue (which I had ordered to be brought into court for this purpose along with the images of the gods), and furthermore had reviled the name of Christ: none of which things, I understand, any genuine Christian can be induced to do. Others, whose names were given to me by an informer, first admitted the charge and then denied it; they said that they had ceased to be Christians two or more years previously, and some of them even twenty years ago. They all did reverence to your statue and the images of the gods in the same way as the others, and reviled the name of Christ. They also declared that the sum total of their guilt or error amounted to no more than this: they had met regularly before dawn on a fixed day to chant verses alternately amongst themselves in honor of Christ as if to a god, and also to bind themselves by oath, not for any criminal purpose, but to abstain from theft, robbery, and adultery, to commit no breach of trust and not to deny a deposit when called upon to restore it. After this ceremony it had been their custom to disperse and reassemble later to take food of an ordinary, harmless kind; but they had in fact given up this practice since my edict, issued on your instructions, which banned all political societies. This made me decide it was all the more necessary to extract the truth by torture from two slave-women, whom they call deaconesses. I found nothing but a degenerate sort of cult carried to extravagant lengths. I have therefore postponed any further examination and hastened to consult you. The question seems to me to be worthy of your consideration, especially in view of the number of persons endangered; for a great many individuals of every age and class, both men and women, are being brought to trial, and this is likely to continue. It is not only the towns, but villages and rural districts too which are infected through contact with this wretched cult. I think though that it is still possible for it to be checked and directed to better ends, for there is no doubt that people have begun to throng the temples which had been almost entirely deserted for a long time; the sacred rites which had been allowed to lapse are being performed again, and flesh of sacrificial victims is on sale everywhere, though up till recently scarcely anyone could be found to buy it. It is easy to infer from this that a great many people could be reformed if they were given an opportunity to repent.

[Trajan to Pliny]: You have followed the right course of procedure, my dear Pliny, in your examination of the cases of persons charged with being Christians, for it is impossible to lay down a general rule to a fixed formula. These people must not be hunted out; if they are brought before you and the charge against them is proved, they must be punished, but in the case of anyone who denies that he is a Christian, and makes it clear that he is not by offering prayers to our gods, he is to be pardoned as a result of his repentance however suspect his past conduct may be. But pamphlets circulated anonymously must play no part in any accusation. They create the worst sort of precedent and are quite out of keeping with the spirit of our age.

Trajan's rescript becomes imperial policy, validating the actions of Pliny as standard procedure. The criminality of Christians is focused on the name itself, rather than any sinister behavior taking place at their meetings. Pliny's investigation of food and ritual points to the accusations of incest and cannibalism usually leveled against mystery cults like Christianity; it was feared that these cults of initiation kept their ritual acts private because they were shameful, disgusting and dangerous to the well-being of the community. Trajan's response means that Roman governors should focus on the sole charge of Christianity, rather than the additional alleged crimes.[5] They should also only condemn those who are presently and persistently Christian. Pliny had given the accused the opportunity to recant, requiring a small proof of their change in orientation, and then executed those who stubbornly clung to the cult, heedless of the threat of punishment.[6] Former Christians and those who denied the charge presented no danger to the state.

The correspondence between Pliny and Trajan points to what was dangerous about Christianity: atheism, here, the rejection of the Graeco-Roman gods. The belief in Christ as sole god defied the positive connection Rome maintained with the pantheon of divine powers and as such acted as a potential catalyst for divine retribution. This atheism had political overtones at a time when the head of the government was himself worshipped as a living god; denying his divinity was at the very least *lèse-majesté*.

During the second century, persecution of the Christians took place usually on a local level, usually as a result of popular agitation in the wake of some sort of crisis. Apparently arguing that the Christians were the source of this disruption, the crowd demanded that the officials take decisive action to resolve the situation.

Eusebius notes that basic premise of Trajan's rescript, i.e. that Christians were not to be sought out. He then discusses the overall effect of the policy to localize persecution of Christians.

Source: Eusebius *Ecclesiastical History* 3.33:[7] By this means the imminent threat of persecution was extinguished to some extent, but none the less opportunities remained to those who wished to harm us. Sometimes the populace, sometimes even the local authorities contrived plots against us, so that with no open persecution partial attacks broke out in various provinces and many of the faithful endured martyrdom in various ways.

Christian Denunciation of the Arena

Tertullian provides us with much of the specific reasoning for a Christian stance regarding the arena. In his defense of Christianity, Tertullian launches a counter-offensive against Roman polytheism, questioning the validity of the gods by noting the problematic uses and affiliations of religious symbols in Roman institutions. He frequently makes use of the arena to challenge paganism, referring, here, to the use of gods as characters in the fatal charades of the noon executions and to the arena personnel dressed as Mercury and

Pluto. His implication is that this constitutes disrespect, at the least, but who should respect such sordid characters as these?

> Source: Tertullian, *Apology* 15.4–5:[8] Of course, you are more devout in the seats of the amphitheater where, over human blood and the filth resulting from the tortures inflicted, your gods do their dancing and provide plots and stories for the guilty – except that the guilty, too, often assume the roles of your gods. We once saw Attis, that god from Pessinus, castrated, and a man who was being burned alive played the role of Hercules. Then, too, at the gladiators' midday performance, in the midst of the cruelties of the entertainment, we laughed at Mercury testing the dead with his red-hot iron. We watched Jupiter's brother, too, hammer in hand, dragging away the corpses of the gladiators.

The duty of a Christian is to avoid the taint of spectacle, primarily because of the polytheistic overtones of the shows, but also because the sensationalism of the presentation fosters inappropriate emotional responses, such as rage, desire, and bloodlust. Christians are to remain separate from those institutions of pagan Rome that clash with Christian norms.

> Source: Tertullian, *Apology*, 38.4–5:[9] Likewise, we renounce your public shows just as we do their origins which we know were begotten of superstition, while we are completely aloof from those matters with which they are concerned. Our tongues, our eyes, our ears have nothing to do with the madness of the circus, the shamelessness of the theater, the brutality of the arena, the vanity of the gymnasium. How, then, do we offend you? If we prefer different pleasures, if, in fine, we do not want to be amused, that is our loss – if loss there be – not yours.

Minucius Felix also rejects the polytheistic foundations of the spectacles as well as the emotional impact. Here, he emphasizes the seductive capacities of the shows, their capacity to engage the spectators' feelings with the artifice of performance. The spectator is thus intensely affected, even moved to action, by something that is not real, that is unworthy of such focus.

> Source: Minucius Felix, *Octavius* 37.11–12:[10] As a logical result, we, who judge ourselves by our conduct and purity of morals, keep aloof from your wicked amusements, processions, and public shows; we know that they have sprung from your sacred rites, and we condemn their obnoxious seduction. At the chariot races in the circus, who would not be horrified at the frenzy of the brawling populace, or at the fine art of manslaughter in the gladiatorial combats? Nor does raving madness subside in the stage plays, where indecencies are even more luxuriant: at one, a mimic player describes and exhibits ways of adultery;

at another, an effeminate actor arouses feelings of love while he is only playing a role: he vilifies your gods by mimicking their lewd love affairs, their sighs, their hates; feigning grief, he moves you to tears by senseless gestures and motions. Thus, you call for real murder and weep over fictitious ones on the stage.

Some of Tertullian's critique of the arena parallels that found in Seneca, where the passions of the mob act as a corruptive agent on the equanimity and virtue of the individual spectator. The pleasure of the visual stimulation awakens a host of overlapping emotions, such as yearning, aggression, frustration, casting the human spirit into wild turmoil. For Tertullian, such frenzy is the antipathy of the serenity offered by Christian conviction.

Source: Tertullian, *On the Spectacles* 15.2–6:[11] God has given us the command both to deal with the Holy Spirit in tranquillity, gentleness, quiet, and peace, inasmuch as, in accordance with the goodness of His nature, He is tender and sensitive, and also not to vex Him by frenzy, bitterness of feeling, anger, and grief. How, then, can the Holy Spirit have anything to do with spectacles? There is no spectacle without violent agitation of the soul. For, where you have pleasure, there also is desire which gives pleasure its savor; where you have desire, there is rivalry which gives desire its savor. And where, in turn, you have rivalry, there also are frenzy and bitterness of feeling and anger and grief and the other effects that spring from them, and, moreover, are incompatible with our moral discipline. For, even if a man enjoys spectacles modestly and soberly, as befits his rank, age, and natural disposition, he cannot go to them without his mind being roused and his soul being stirred by some unspoken agitation. No one ever approaches a pleasure such as this without passion; no one experiences this passion without its damaging effects. These very effects are incitements to passion. On the other hand, if the passion ceases, there is no pleasure, and he who goes where he gains nothing is convicted of foolishness.

Athenagoras, a second-century apologist for Christianity, wrote his *Embassy* as a letter to the emperor Marcus Aurelius around 176–177 CE. He expends some effort defending Christianity as an ethical system, arguing against the allegations of cannibalism and incest and claiming a higher moral ground. Rejection of the arena is part of this claim; he asserts that the audience at an execution is culpable for the death of the criminal.

Source: Athenagoras, *Embassy for the Christians* 35:[12] Who does not reckon among the things of greatest interest the contests of gladiators and wild beasts, especially those which are given by you? But we, deeming that to see a man put to death is much the same as killing him, have abjured such spectacles.

Tertullian also condemns the amphitheater as a noxious means of punishing wrong-doers, because it spreads criminality instead of limiting it. There is always the risk of inflicting fatal punishment upon the innocent, which makes the Roman spectator complicitous in murder. Even for those who are guilty, the actions forced upon them in the arena compound their guilt. The pleasure of the audience, whether it be awakened by a sense of righteous justice or simply arise from the excitement and horror, spreads the infection of crime among the spectators.

Source: Tertullian, *On the Spectacles* 19.1–4:[13] If we can claim that cruelty, impiety, and brutality are permitted us, let us by all means go to the amphitheater. If we are what people say we are, let us take delight in human blood. It is a good thing when the guilty are punished. Who will deny this but the guilty? Yet it is not becoming for the guiltless to take pleasure in the punishment of another; rather, it befits the guiltless to grieve that a man like himself, has become so guilty that he is treated with such cruelty. And who is my voucher that it is the guilty always who are condemned to the beasts, or whatever punishment, and that it is never inflicted on innocence, too, through the vindictiveness of the judge or the weakness of the defense or the intensity of the torture? How much better it is, then, not to know when the wicked are punished, lest I come to know also when the good are destroyed, provided, of course, that there is savor of good in them. Certain it is that innocent men are sold as gladiators to serve as victims of public pleasure. Even in the case of those who are condemned to the games, what a preposterous idea is it that, in atonement for a smaller offense, they should be driven to the extreme of murder!

Tertullian extends his argument on the audience's complicity in crime: a spectator who would not dream of engaging in mayhem outside the amphitheater is embedded in such activity because of his active participation in the spectacles. Here Tertullian indicts the law-abiding, peaceful citizen who applauds fights to the death; he has vicariously participated in homicide.

Source: Tertullian, *On the Spectacles* 21.3–4:[14] The same man who tries to break up or denounces a quarrel in the streets which has come to fisticuffs will in the stadium applaud fights far more dangerous; and the same man who shudders at the sight of the body of a man who died in accordance with nature's law common to all will in the amphitheater look down with tolerant eyes upon bodies mangled, rent asunder, and smeared with their own blood. What is more, the same man who allegedly comes to the spectacle to show his approval of the punishment for murder will have a reluctant gladiator driven on with lashes and with rods to commit murder; and the same man who wants every more notorious murderer to be cast before the lion will have the staff and cap of liberty granted as a reward to a savage gladiator, while he will demand that the other man who has been slain be dragged back to feast his eyes upon him, taking delight in scrutinizing close at hand the man he wished killed at a distance – and, if that was not his wish, so much more heartless he!

Tatian's denunciation of the games condemns the sociopolitical institution as a whole: *editor*, performers, spectators, all are murderers. Tatian became the founder of a sternly ascetic sect of Christianity in the last quarter of the second century; some of this asceticism appears in the connection he draws between the eating of meat and the spiritual cannibalism of the *munera*.

Source: Tatian, *To the Greeks* 23:[15] He who is chief among you collects a legion of blood-stained murderers, engaging to maintain them; and these ruffians are sent forth by him, and you assemble at the spectacle to be judges, partly of the wickedness of the adjudicator, and partly of that of the men who engage in the combat. And he who misses the murderous exhibition is grieved, because he was not doomed to be a spectator of wicked and impious and abominable deeds. You slaughter animals for the purpose of eating their flesh, and you purchase men to supply a cannibal banquet for the soul, nourishing it by the most impious bloodshedding. The robber commits murder for the sake of plunder, but the rich man purchases gladiators for the sake of their being killed.

The Arena and Christian Identity

Despite its problematic characteristics, the arena served as a venue for Christian construction of identity and faith. This is due primarily to the strong association between Roman spectacle and the highly visible, if relatively infrequent, executions of Christian martyrs. Claiming the arena as a crucial and positive element of Christian symbolism partly involved inverting Roman assumptions about hierarchy and honor, as demonstrated by spectacle, transforming the social stigma transmitted by the arena into marks of "glory." Much of the Christian "value" in the arena is, however, the reworking of patterns of praise and blame for individual achievement already established in Rome. The celebrated indifference to wounds of early martyrs, for example, finds a match with the behavior of "good" gladiators, as does the eager rushing to meet the beasts. The meaning attributed to these actions is what has been transformed.

For Justin, who would himself be martyred, the fearlessness of Christians in the arena was a demonstration that they were innocent of the "other crimes," e.g. incest and cannibalism, that outsiders associated with Christianity and other mystery religions.

Source: Justin *Apology* 2.12:[16] But I saw that [the Christians] were afraid neither of death, nor of anything usually thought fearful, and I considered it was impossible that they were living in wickedness and libertinism. For what libertine or incontinent person, or one who finds good in the eating of human flesh, could greet death, that it might take away all his lusts, and would not try to prolong by all means his present life and to avoid the notice of the rulers, and not give himself up to be murdered?

Minucius Felix compared the heroism of martyrs in the arena to great heroes celebrated in the legends of Rome's foundation; in so doing he claims a Christian monopoly on virtue in Roman terms. The heroes of Roman tradition were cited as proof of Rome's inherent qualities of dedication and selflessness, which served to justify Rome's political prominence: obviously, Rome deserved to rule because of the moral virtue of the Roman people. Minucius, however, claims that these qualities demonstrated by Christians proved that the Christian god, not mighty Rome, was the true source of liberty, power, and militant victory.

Source: Minucius Felix, *Octavius* 37.1–6:[17] How beautiful a spectacle for god, when a Christian measures his strength with pain; when he is in the jaws of threats and punishments and tortures; when, with a scornful smile, he looks down upon the rattling instruments of death and the grim executioner; when, in the face of kings and princes, he esteems his liberty above all things; when he yields to God alone, whose he is; when he, triumphant victor, defies the very one who has pronounced sentence on him! That man has gained the victory who has obtained that for which he strove. What soldier does not court danger more boldly under the eyes of his general? For, none receives the prize before standing the test. Yet, the general cannot give what he does not own; he cannot prolong life, though he can grant distinction for good service. Besides, the soldier of God neither is forsaken when in pain nor is his life ended by death. Thus, the Christian, though he may seem wretched, cannot be found so. You yourselves extol to the sky men visited by great misfortunes, like Mucius Scaevola, who, after his abortive attempt on the king's life, would have perished among the enemy, had he not sacrificed his right hand. How many of our brethren, without cry of pain, have allowed not only their right hand but their whole body to be scorched and turned to ashes, when it depended entirely on them to gain their release. Am I comparing only men with Mucius or Aquilius or Regulus? Why, even our boys and tender women, fortified against pain by heaven, scoff at crosses and tortures, wild beasts, and all the terrors of punishment. And you, miserable wretches, you do not see that, without reason, no one would undergo punishment of his own accord, or be able to endure the tortures without divine assistance.

In Tertullian, the coming apocalypse and final judgment are specifically imagined as an extraordinary spectacle, held to celebrate the triumph of Christ. The justified Christians will be the audience for a variety of events, fatal charades featuring the righteous punishment of deified emperors, Jupiter, and the persecuting administrators of the Roman empire.

Source: Tertullian, *On the Spectacles* 30.1–2:[18] Moreover, what a spectacle is already at hand – the second coming of the Lord, now no object of doubt, now exalted, now triumphant! What exultation will that be of the angels, what glory of the saints as they rise again! What a kingdom, the kingdom of the just thereafter! What a city, the new Jerusalem! But there are yet other spectacles to come – that day of the Last Judgment with its everlasting issues, unlooked for by the heathen, the object of their derision, when the hoary age of the world and all its generations will be consumed in one fire. What a panorama of spectacle on that day! Which sight shall excite my wonder? Which, my laughter? Where shall I rejoice, where exult – as I see so many and so mighty kings, whose ascent to heaven used to be made known by public announcement, now along with Jupiter himself, along with the very witnesses of their ascent, groaning in the depths of darkness? Governors of provinces, too, who persecuted the name of the Lord, melting in flames fiercer than those they themselves kindled in their rage against the Christians braving them with contempt?

Cyprian was Bishop of Carthage in the mid-third century and was himself caught up in the empire-wide persecutions begun by the emperor Decius. His letter to the martyrs completely recasts the arena by removing it from the historical context entirely. The martyrs here are represented as soldiers in the battle against evil, a battle that has been going on since the days of the Hebrew prophets. Cyprian emphasizes how pleasing the wounds of the martyrs are to the Christian god, who is both the main spectator in the cosmic arena and the internal source of strength for the combatants. The blood of the martyrs was a weapon against hellfire in an arena constructed not by Rome but by the Judeo-Christian deity.

Source: Cyprian, *Letter* 7.2–3, 9:[19] The multitude of those who were present saw with admiration the heavenly contest, the contest of God, the spiritual contest, the battle of Christ, saw that His servants stood with free voice, with unyielding mind, with divine virtue – bare, indeed, of weapons of this world, but believing and armed with the weapons of faith. The tortured stood more bravely than the torturers; and the limbs, beaten and torn as they were, overcame the hooks that beat and tore them. The scourge, often used again and again with all its rage, could not conquer invincible faith, even though the membrane which enclosed the guts were broken, and it was no longer the limbs but the wounds of the servants of God that were being tortured. Blood was flowing which would quench the blaze of persecution, which would overcome the flames of Gehenna with its glorious gore. Oh, what a spectacle was that to the Lord, how sublime, how great, how acceptable to the eyes of God in the allegiance and devotion of His soldiers! This fight, therefore, predicted of old by the prophets, begun by the Lord, waged by the apostles, Mappalicus promised again to the proconsul . . . he exhibited the fight to which he had pledged himself, and he received the reward which he deserved. I not only beseech but exhort the rest of you, that you all follow that martyr now most blessed, and the other partners of that engagement – soldiers and comrades . . . If the battle call you out, if the day of your contest come, engage bravely, fight with constancy, knowing that you are fighting under the eyes of a present Lord, that you are attaining by the confession of His name to His own glory . . . He only looks on His servants, but He Himself also wrestles in us, Himself is engaged, Himself also in the struggles of our conflict not only crowns, but is crowned.

Martyr Acts

The narratives circulated within the Christian community that celebrated the martyrs offer an intriguing perspective on the arena, written from the viewpoint of those unsympathetic to the Roman power structure. They focus on the impact that condemnation to the arena or to the beasts had on the community of the person condemned. Though the lens of the Christian interpreters has a specific ideological bent, nevertheless it has a distinct take on the relationship between Rome and its subjects at a local level. Martyr Acts capture the judicial procedure in the provinces in the wake of Trajan's rescript. They reconfigure the meaning of the arena, however, claiming martyrdom as a demonstration of Christian authority rather than that of Rome. In doing so, they drew upon Jewish experience of martyrdom under Seleucid authority, when death for one's belief was considered a righteous act and a demonstration of particular holiness. The strong Christian strain of asceticism powered the Martyr Acts as well, referencing its exhortations to disregard the body and the things of this world as distractions from the proper focus on the world to come. Christian tradition could make use of Roman ethical interpretations of the arena as well, both praise of gladiators as moral exemplars and condemnation of the crowd as irrationally carnal. The circulation of the Martyr Acts throughout the Mediterranean consolidated these identity-forming patterns within the group; it also made them part of a vicarious audience to a re-imagined Christian spectacle.

Ignatius, Bishop of Antioch, is thought to have been martyred later in the reign of Trajan, not too distant in time from the correspondence between that emperor and Pliny, and thus one of the earlier martyr texts circulating among Christian groups. The existence of these letters suggests the deliberate use by Ignatius of his judicial experience as a teaching opportunity, in which

Ignatius himself interprets the looming execution in accordance with Christian belief. The congregations receiving his letters become vicarious audiences in the arena, who are meant to revisualize the spectacle as affirmation of their convictions instead of confirmation of the Roman structure of power. Imagery of the arena runs throughout Ignatius' letter, as he identifies his struggle in parallel with someone *damnatus ad bestias*. For him, the fight is not just the resistance to the criminalization of Christianity, but resistance to efforts by friends and colleagues to intercede with Roman authorities on his behalf, for a lifting of the sentence.

Source: Eusebius, *Ecclesiastical History* 3.36:[20] The story goes that [Ignatius] was sent from Syria to Rome to be eaten by beasts in testimony to Christ. He was taken through Asia under most careful guard, and strengthened by his speech and exhortation the diocese of each city in which he stayed . . . He wrote one letter to the church at Ephesus . . . another to the church at Magnesia on the Meander . . . he also wrote to the church at Rome, and to it he extended the request that they should not deprive him of the hope for which he longed by begging him off from his martyrdom . . . He writes as follows: "From Syria to Rome I am fighting with wild beasts, by land and sea, by night and day, bound to ten 'leopards' (that is, a company of soldiers), and they become worse for kind treatment . . . I long for the beasts that are prepared for me; and I pray that they may be found prompt for me; I will even entice them to devour me promptly; not as has happened to some whom they have not touched from fear; even if they be unwilling of themselves, I will force them to it. Grant me this favor. I know what is expedient for me; now I am beginning to be a disciple. May I envy nothing of things seen or unseen that I may attain to Jesus Christ. Let there come on me fire, and cross, and struggles with wild beasts, cutting, and tearing asunder, rackings of bones, mangling of limbs, crushing of my whole body, cruel tortures of the devil, may I but attain to Jesus Christ!"

Polycarp, Bishop of Smyrna, had received one of Ignatius' letters, but scholars agree that some decades lapsed before Polycarp himself was martyred, an event which took place sometime in the 150s. The account circulated after his death has features typical of Martyr Acts, such as the introduction and conclusion that exhort the faithful to become like the martyrs, who are assimilated to Jesus. The courage and stamina of the martyrs are praised, qualities also praised in gladiators by pagan authors. Here, however, these qualities are seen as clear indications of the direct intervention of divinity. Miracles pepper the narrative, as does fulfillment of prophecy, situating the martyrdom as part of the great plan of the Christian god, rather than an assertion of control by Rome over a marginalized group. The interactions between the martyrs and the non-Christians fall into two categories: the frustrated rage of the mob against the imperturbable Christians and the dialogue between the magistrate and the martyr, in which standardized judicial procedure is made into an articulation of belief by the accused Christian. Notable in this Martyr Act is the prominence of the spectators; as seen above, the audience chants judicial petitions in the stands of the arena, petitions granted by Rome's agents in Smyrna who obediently arrest Polycarp at their demand. The frenzy of the audience, however, is much in line with the condemnations of spectacle mobs pronounced by Seneca and other Roman analysts; here the passion of the crowd is not a moral failing but a tool of cosmic evil.

Source: *The Martyrdom of Polycarp* 1–3, 9–16:[21] We are writing to you, dear brothers, the story of the martyrs and of blessed Polycarp who put a stop to the persecution by his own martyrdom as though he were putting a seal upon it . . . Just as the Lord did, he too waited that he might be delivered up, that we might become his imitators . . . Who indeed would not admire the martyrs' nobility, their courage, their love of the Master? For even when they were torn by whips until the very structure of their bodies was laid bare down to the inner veins and arteries, they endured it, making even the bystanders weep for pity. Some indeed attained to such courage that they would utter not a sound or a cry, showing to all of us that in the hour of their torment these noblest of Christ's witnesses were not present in the flesh, or rather that the Lord was there present holding converse with them. Fixing their eyes on the favor of Christ, they despised the tortures of this world, in one hour buying themselves an exemption from the eternal fire . . . The most noble Germanicus gave them encouragement by the perseverance he showed; he even fought manfully with the beasts. The governor tried to persuade him, telling him to spare his young manhood; but he with a show of force dragged the beast on top of him, intending to be freed all the more quickly from this unjust and lawless life. At this then all the mob was astonished at the courage of this pious and devoted race of Christians, and they shouted out: "Away with these atheists! Go and get Polycarp!"

. . . As Polycarp entered the amphitheater[22], a voice from heaven said: "*Be strong*, Polycarp, *and have courage.*"[23] No one saw who was speaking, but those of our people who were present heard the voice.

Then, as he was brought in, a great shout arose when the people heard that it was Polycarp who had been arrested. As he was brought before him, the governor[24] asked him: "Are you Polycarp?" And when he admitted he was, the governor tried to persuade him to recant, saying: "Have respect for your age"; (and other similar things that they are accustomed to say); "swear by the Genius of the emperor. Recant. Say, 'Away with the atheists!'"

Polycarp, with a sober countenance, looked at all the mob of lawless pagans who were in the arena, and shaking his fist at them, groaned, looked up to heaven, and said: "Away with the atheists!"

The governor persisted and said: "Swear and I will let you go. Curse Christ!"

But Polycarp answered: "For eighty-six years I have been his servant and he has done me no wrong. How can I blaspheme against my king and savior?"

But the other insisted once again, saying: "Swear by the emperor's Genius!"

He answered: "If you delude yourself into thinking that I will swear by the emperor's Genius, as you say, and if you pretend not to know who I am, listen and I will tell you plainly: I am a Christian. And if you would like to learn the doctrine of Christianity, set aside a day and listen."

The governor said: "Try to move the people."

And Polycarp said: "I should have thought you worthy of such a discussion. For we have been taught to pay respect to the authorities and powers that God has assigned us (for this does not harm our cause). But as for the mob, I do not think they deserve to listen to a speech of defence from me."

The governor said: "I have wild animals, and I shall expose you to them if you do not change your mind."

And he answered: "Go and call for them! Repentance from a better state to one that is worse is impossible for us. But it is good to change from what is wicked to righteousness."

And [the governor] said again to him: "Since you are not afraid of the animals, then I shall have you consumed by fire – unless you change your mind."

But Polycarp answered: "The fire you threaten me with burns merely for a time and is soon extinguished. It is clear you are ignorant of the fire of everlasting punishment and of the judgement that is to come, which awaits the impious. Why then do you hesitate? Come, do what you will."

As he said these and many other words he was filled with a joyful courage; his countenance was filled with grace, and not only did he not collapse in terror at what was said to him, but rather it was the governor that was amazed. He sent his herald into the center of the arena to announce three times: "Polycarp has confessed that he is a Christian."

After the herald had spoken, the entire mob of pagans and Jews from Smyrna shouted out aloud in uncontrollable rage: "Here is the schoolmaster of Asia – the father of the Christians – the destroyer of our gods – the one that teaches the multitude not to sacrifice or do reverence!"

And while they were saying all this they shouted and asked Philip the Asiarch[25] to have a lion loosed on Polycarp. But he said that he was not allowed to do this since the days of the *venationes* were past. Next they decided to shout out all together that Polycarp should be burnt alive. For the vision he had seen regarding his pillow had to be fulfilled, when he saw it burning while he was at prayer and he turned and said to his faithful companions: "I am to be burnt alive."

All of this happened with great speed, more quickly than it takes to tell the story: the mob swiftly collected logs and brushwood from workshops and baths, and the Jews (as is their custom) zealously helped them with this. When the fire was prepared, Polycarp took off all his clothing, loosed his belt and even tried to take off his own sandals . . . Straightway then he was attached to the equipment that had been prepared for the fire. When they were on the point of nailing him to it, he said: "Leave me thus. For he who has given me the strength to endure the flames will grant me to remain without flinching in the fire even without the firmness you will give me by using nails."

> They did not nail him down then, but simply bound him; and as he put his hands behind his back, he was bound like a noble ram chosen for an oblation from a great flock, a holocaust prepared and made acceptable to God . . . A great flame blazed up and those of us to whom it was given to see beheld a miracle. And we have been preserved to recount the story to others. For the flames, bellying out like a ship's sail in the wind, formed into the shape of a vault and thus surrounded the martyr's body as with a wall. And he was within it not as burning flesh but rather as bread being baked, or like gold and silver being purified in a smelting-furnace. And from it we perceived such a delightful fragrance as though it were smoking incense or some other costly perfume.

The Martyrs of Lyons met their end in 177 CE, the same year that the emperor Marcus Aurelius issued the *senatus consultum* on the reduction of costs for arena performers. Like the account of Polycarp's end, this narrative claims to be a letter circulated by the Christian congregations in Gaul for the benefit of their co-religionists. The congregation was reeling from what seems to have been a mass martyrdom of unusually large proportions, directed specifically against a group of Christians recently emigrated from the eastern Mediterranean; one of their number, a Pergamene named Attalus, seems to have been particularly disliked by some of the locals. At any rate, these Christians may have been especially visible in the community, not yet assimilated to local customs. Some of the typical features are present in this account: the role of the demon-inspired crowd in promoting the persecution and the spectacle as a manifestation of the power of the divine. There is much less emphasis on the trial as a setting for the accused to declare the truth of his belief; instead, the narrative spends much time on torture in prison, intended by the Roman authorities to make the Christians knuckle under to religious conformity. Torture was regularly applied to witnesses in Roman judicial procedure, as it was believed to elicit truth by pushing the body to the limits of endurance; here, torture has that effect among the Christians, although the "truth" being witnessed to here is not held as such by the officials. Particulars of administrative procedure prolong the executions into two phases and may reflect a genuine reluctance on the part of the praefect to submit to the will of the crowd. Present also is an investigation into allegations of cannibalism, not unlike the inquiry launched years earlier by Pliny in Bithynia. The focus on particular martyrs, such as the female slave Blandina, particularly serves as a striking example for the reader, who is not meant to feel horror and pity for her wounds: these are beautiful, badges of honor. The weak female body of a lowly slave raised to such spiritual strength heightens the lesson to be learned by the contemporary Christian. The surprising contrast recalls pagan praise for gladiators, whose shameful bodies yet are able to reveal nobility of character.

Source: *The Martyrs of Lyons* 1.4–7, 12–15, 18–19, 33–35, 37–42, 47, 53–56:[26]
The intensity of our afflictions here, the deep hatred of the pagans for the saints, and the magnitude of the blessed martyrs' sufferings, we are incapable of describing in detail; indeed, it would be impossible to put it down in writing. The Adversary swooped down with full force, in this way anticipating his final coming which is sure to come. He went to all lengths to train and prepare his minions against God's servants . . . they heroically endured all that the people en masse heaped on them: abuse, blows, dragging, despoiling, stoning, imprisonment, and all that an enraged mob is likely to inflict on their most hated enemies. They were dragged into the forum and interrogated before the entire populace by the tribune and the city council. When they confessed, they were locked up in prison to await the arrival of the governor . . . But the arrests continued, and every day the finest were taken to fill up the number of the martyrs. The result was that they collected all the most zealous Christians of the two communities and those on whom everything most depended.

Arrested too were some of our servants who were pagans. For the prefect had publicly ordered a full-scale investigation of all Christians. This the servants, ensnared by Satan and terrified of the tortures they saw the faithful suffering, at the soldiers' instigation falsely accused the Christians of Oedipean marriages and dinners in the manner of Thyestes[27], and many other things that it would be sinful for us even to think of or speak about – indeed, one doubts whether such things ever happened among men at all. But these stories got about and all the people raged against us, so that even those whose attitude had been moderate before because of their friendship with us now became greatly angry and gnashed their teeth at us. Thus the Lord's saying was proved true: *The time is coming when whoever kills you will think he is doing a service to God.*[28]

All of us were in terror; and Blandina's earthly mistress, who was herself among the martyrs in the conflict, was in agony lest because of her bodily weakness she would not be able to make a bold confession of her faith. Yet Blandina was filled with such power that even those who were taking turns to torture her in every way from dawn to dusk were weary and exhausted. They themselves admitted that they were beaten, that there was nothing further they could do to her, and they were surprised that she was still breathing, for her entire body was broken and torn. They testified that even one kind of torture was enough to release her soul, let alone the many they applied with such intensity. Instead, this blessed woman like a noble athlete got renewed strength with her confession of faith: her admission, "I am a Christian; we do nothing to be ashamed of," brought her refreshment, rest, and insensibility to her present pain . . .

At the first arrest those who denied their faith were locked up with the others and shared their privations; at this point they had gained nothing by their denial. On the other hand, those who admitted what they were were detained as Christians, but no other charge was preferred against them. The others, however, were held on the charge of being murderers and criminals[29] and were punished twice as much as the rest. . . . The former advanced joyously, with majesty and great beauty mingled on their countenances, so that even their chains were worn on them like some lovely ornament . . . but the others were dejected, downcast . . . the pagans taunted them . . . their resistance was stiffened and those who were arrested straightway confessed their faith without one thought for the Devil's suggestions . . . Maturus, then, Sanctus, Blandina, and Attalus were led into the amphitheater to be exposed to the beasts and to give a public spectacle of the pagans' inhumanity, for a day of gladiatorial games was expressly arranged for our sake. Once again in the amphitheater Maturus and Sanctus went through the whole gamut of suffering as though they had never experienced it at all before – or rather as though they had defeated their opponent in many contests and were now fighting for the victor's crown. Once again they ran the gauntlet of whips (according to the local custom), the mauling by animals, and anything else that the mad mob from different places shouted for and demanded. And to crown all they were put in the iron seat, from which their roasted flesh filled the audience with its savour. But that was not enough for them, and they continued to rage in their desire to break down the martyrs' resistance. But from Sanctus all they would hear was what he had repeated from the beginning, his confession of faith.

Though their spirits endured much throughout the long contests, they were in the end sacrificed, after being made all the day long a spectacle to the world to replace the varied entertainment of the gladiatorial combat. Blandina was hung on a post and exposed as bait for the wild animals that were let loose on her. She seemed to hang there in the form of a cross, and by her fervent prayer she aroused intense enthusiasm in those who were undergoing their ordeal, for in their torment with their physical eyes they saw in the person of their sister him who was crucified for them, that he might convince all who believe in him that all who suffer for Christ's glory will have eternal fellowship in the living God.

But none of the animals had touched her, and so she was taken down from the post and brought back to the prison to be preserved for another ordeal . . . tiny, weak, and insignificant as she was she would give inspiration to her brothers, for she had put on Christ, that mighty and invincible athlete, and had overcome the Adversary in many contests, and through her conflict had won the crown of immortality.

Now it was the emperor's order that these should be beheaded, but that those who had denied their faith should be released. Thus at the outset of the festival[30] here (and it was one that was crowded with people who had come to it from all countries) the governor brought the blessed martyrs before the tribunal to make a show and a spectacle of them before the crowds. This was the reason why he had them questioned once again, and all those who were thought to possess Roman citizenship he had beheaded; the rest he condemned to the animals. . . .

Finally, on the last day of the gladiatorial games, they brought back Blandina again, this time with a boy of fifteen named Ponticus. Every day they had been brought in to watch the torture of the others, while attempts were made to force them to swear by the pagan idols. And because they persevered and condemned their persecutors, the crowd grew angry with them, so that they had little pity for the child's age and no respect for the woman. Instead, they subjected them to every atrocity and led them through every torture in turn, constantly trying to force them to swear, but to no avail.

Ponticus, after being encouraged by his sister in Christ so that even the pagans realized that she was urging him on and strengthening him, and after nobly enduring every torment, gave up his spirit. The blessed Blandina was last of all: like a noble mother encouraging her children, she sent them before her in triumph to the King, and then, after duplicating in her own body all her children's sufferings, she hastened to rejoin them, rejoicing and glorying in her death as though she had been invited to a bridal banquet instead of being a victim of the beasts. After the scourges, the animals, and the hot griddle, she was at last tossed into a net and exposed to a bull. After being tossed a good deal by the animal, she no longer perceived what was happening because of the hope and possession of all she believed in and because of her intimacy with Christ. Thus she too was offered in sacrifice, while the pagans themselves admitted that no woman had ever suffered so much in their experience.

Perpetua is one of the best-known among early Christian martyrs, due to the wide circulation of the account of her trial and execution in 202 CE at Carthage. It is also valuable in that so much of it comes from Perpetua herself, written or dictated while she was in prison; little female-authored material survives from the ancient Mediterranean. This also offers us a first-person perspective on the experience of martyrdom and the anticipation of the arena. The Act follows the pattern of arrest, trial and spectacular execution, with sprinklings of the typical Christian interpretation of these events. Some distinctive features should be noted: first, the strong presence of Perpetua's family, especially her father, who is much more an opposing force to her confession of belief than the Roman authorities. This reflects the power of the *paterfamilias* in Roman society, the fact that, as a woman, Perpetua was much more likely to have her daily choices circumscribed by her father than by Roman administrators. Her conversion is a rebellion more against the domestic power structure than the emperor; she has redirected her family loyalties toward the family of Christian believers. The removal of her baby becomes a small miracle, demonstrating the worthiness of her choice. Unusual here as well is the sequence of elaborate visions Perpetua had in prison, which become expressions of her sanctity and power as a confessor-martyr. The form these visions take is interesting; near-cinematic in their imagery, they present tangible (and spectacle-oriented) metaphors for sanctity and they feature an extremely dynamic heroine who transcends gender boundaries and works for the salvation of herself and those around her. Her interactions with the military tribune demonstrate her social power as well; despite the fact that she has been condemned and, by Roman law, is now *serva poenae*, she argues for better treatment and gets it.

Source: *The Martyrdom of Saints Perpetua and Felicitas* 2, 4–6, 10, 16–18, 20–21:[31]
A number of young catechumens were arrested, Revocatus and his fellow slave
Felicitas, Saturninus and Secundulus, and with them Vibia Perpetua, a newly
married woman of good family and upbringing. Her mother and father were
still alive and one of her two brothers was a catechumen like herself and she
had an infant son at the breast. She was about twenty-two years old. From this
point she herself told the whole story of her martyrdom and left an account
written by her own hand and with her interpretation.

... Then my brother said to me: "Dear sister, you are greatly privileged;
surely you might ask for a vision to be shown whether you are to suffer or
to be freed." And I faithfully promised that I would, for I knew that I could
speak with the Lord, whose great blessings I had come to experience. And so
I said: "I shall tell you tomorrow." Then I made my request and this is the
vision I had.

I saw a ladder of tremendous height made of bronze, reaching all the way to
the heavens, but it was so narrow that only one person could climb up at a
time. To the sides of the ladder were attached all sorts of metal weapons: there
were *gladii, lanceae,* hooks, *machaerae,* and spikes; so that if anyone tried to
climb up carelessly or without paying attention, he would be mangled and his
flesh would adhere to the weapons.

At the foot of the ladder lay a dragon of enormous size, and it would attack
those who tried to climb up and try to terrify them into not climbing. And
Saturus was the first to go up, he who was later to hand himself over of his own
accord. He had been the builder of our strength, although he was not present
when we were arrested. And he arrived at the top of the staircase and he looked
back and said to me: "Perpetua, I am waiting for you. But watch out and don't
let the dragon bite you."

"He will not harm me," I said, "in the name of Jesus Christ."

Slowly, as though he were afraid of me, the dragon stuck his head out from
underneath the ladder. Then using his head as my first step, I stepped on it and
climbed up.

Then I saw an immense garden, and in it a grey-haired man sat in the clothes
of a shepherd, a tall man, milking sheep. And standing around him were many
thousands of people dressed in white. He raised his head, looked at me, and
said: "I am glad you have come, my child."

He called me over to him and gave me, as it were, a mouthful of the milk he
was drawing; and I took it into my cupped hands and drank it. And all those
who stood around said: "Amen!" At the sound of this word I came to, with the
taste of something sweet still in my mouth. I at once told this to my brother,
and we realized that we would have to suffer, and that from now on we would
no longer have any hope in this life.

A few days later a rumor made the rounds that we would be given a hearing.
My father also arrived from the city, worn out with worry, and he came up to
me in order to persuade me, saying: "Daughter, have pity on my gray head,
have pity on your father, if I deserve to be called your father, if I have raised
you with these hands to this prime of life, if I have favored you over your
brothers; do not abandon me to the reproach of men. Think of your brothers,

think of your mother and your aunt, think of your son, who will not be able to live after your death. Give up your pride! You will destroy all of us! None of us will ever be able to speak freely again if anything happens to you."

This was the way my father spoke out of family feeling for me, kissing my hands and throwing himself at my feet, and, weeping, he called on me now not as his daughter but as a woman. I was sorry for my father's sake, because he alone of all my kin would be unhappy to see me suffer.

I tried to comfort him, saying "It will all happen in the prisoner's dock as God wills; for you may be sure that we are not left to ourselves but are all in his power."

And he left me in great sorrow.

One day while we were eating breakfast we were suddenly taken off for a hearing. We arrived at the forum, and immediately the rumor went around the neighborhood of the forum and a huge crowd gathered. We walked up to the prisoner's dock. All the others when questioned confessed. Then, when it came my turn, my father appeared with my son and dragged me down from the step saying, "Make the sacrifice! Have pity on your baby!"

Hilarianus the procurator, who as the successor to the late proconsul Minucius Timinianus had received his judicial powers, said to me: "Have pity on your father's gray head; have pity on your baby son. Make the sacrifice for the health of the emperors."

"I won't do it," I responded.

"Are you a Christian?" said Hilarianus.

"I am a Christian." I said.

And when my father continued trying to persuade me, Hilarianus ordered him to be thrown down and beaten with a stick, and I felt sorry for my father, as if I had been beaten. I felt sorry for his wretched old age.

Then Hilarianus passed sentence on all of us; we were condemned to the beasts, and we returned to prison happily. But my baby had gotten used to being nursed at the breast and to staying with me in prison. So I sent the deacon Pomponius immediately to my father to ask for the baby. But father refused to give me the baby. And as God willed, the baby had no further desire for the breast nor did I suffer from any anxiety for my child and any discomfort in my breasts.

The day before we were to fight with the beasts I saw the following vision: Pomponius the deacon came to the prison gates and began to knock violently. I went out and opened the gate for him. He was dressed in an unbelted white tunic, wearing elaborate sandals. And he said to me: "Perpetua, we are waiting for you; come."

Then he took my hand and we began to walk through rough and broken country. At last we came to the amphitheater out of breath, and he led me into the center of the arena and said to me: "Do not be afraid. I am here with you and struggle alongside you." And he left.

I looked at the huge crowd who watched in astonishment. I was surprised that no beasts were let loose on me; for I knew that I was condemned to die by the beasts. Then out came an Egyptian to fight against me, of vicious appearance, with his supporting fighters. And some handsome young men came up to me as my supporters. My clothes were stripped off and I was made into a man. My supporters began to rub me down with oil, as they do before a contest. Then I saw the Egyptian on the other side rolling in the dust. Next a man of amazing size came out, so large that he rose above the top of the amphitheater. He was dressed in a beltless purple tunic with two stripes, one on either side, running down the middle of his chest. He wore sandals that were extravagantly made of gold and silver, and carried a rod like a *lanista* and a green branch on which there were golden apples. And he asked for silence and said "This Egyptian, if he defeats her, will kill her with the sword. But she, if she defeats him, will receive this branch." Then he went out.

We drew close to one another and began to let loose with punches. He wanted to get hold of my feet, but I kept kicking him in the face with my heels. Then I was raised up into the air and I began to strike him without as it were touching the ground. Then when I noticed there was a lull, I put my two hands together, joining the fingers of one with the other and I grabbed his head. He fell onto his face and I stepped on his head.

The crowd began to shout and my seconds to sing psalms. Then I walked up to the *lanista* and took the branch. He kissed me and said to me: "Daughter, peace be with you." And I began to walk in glory to the Gates of Life. And I woke up. And I realized it was not against beasts but against the devil that I would be fighting, but I knew the victory would be mine. So much for what I did up until the eve of the contest . . . [Perpetua's first-person account ends here; the story of what happened in the arena is given by the witness-editor of the Martyr Act.[32]]

. . . The military tribune had treated them with extraordinary severity because, due to the warnings of certain very foolish people, he became afraid that they would be spirited out of the prison by magical incantations. Perpetua spoke to him directly. "Why can you not even allow us to refresh ourselves properly? For we are the most distinguished of the condemned prisoners, as we belong to Caesar, and will fight on his birthday. Would it not be to your credit if we were brought forth on the day in a healthier condition?" The tribune was disturbed and turned red. And so he gave the order that they were to be treated more humanely . . .

On the day before, when they had their last meal, which is called the free banquet, they celebrated not a free banquet but the love feast.[33] They spoke to the populace with the same steadfastness, warned them of God's judgment, stressing the joy they would have in their suffering, and ridiculing the curiosity of those who came to see them . . .

The day of their victory dawned, and they processed from the prison into the amphitheater happily as if they were going into heaven, with calm faces, trembling with joy not fear. Perpetua followed with bright face and calm step, as the wife of Christ, as the darling of God, putting down everyone's stare with her own intense gaze. With them also was Felicitas, glad that she had safely given birth so that now she could fight the beasts, going from one bloodbath to another, from the midwife to the *retiarius*, ready to wash after childbirth with a second baptism.

They were then led up to the gates and were forced to put on outfits, clothing of the priests of Saturn for the men, of the priestesses of Ceres for the women. But the noble Perpetua strenuously resisted this to the end.

She said: "We came to this of our own free will, that our freedom should not be violated. We agreed to pledge our lives in order not to do such a thing. We agreed upon this with you."

Even injustice recognized justice. The military tribune agreed. They were to be brought into the arena just as they were. Perpetua then began to sing a psalm: she was already stepping on the head of the Egyptian. Revocatus, Saturninus, and Saturus began to give dire warnings to the crowd of spectators. Then when they came within sight of Hilarianus, they began to say with motions and gestures to Hilarianus: "You have condemned us, but God will condemn you," they were saying. At this, the crowd became enraged and demanded that they be beaten with whips by a group of *venatores*. And they were happy at this, that they be able to copy the sufferings of the Lord. . . .

For the young women, however, the devil had prepared a ferocious cow. This was an unusual animal, but it was chosen so that their sex might be matched with that of the beast.[34] So they were stripped naked, placed in nets and brought out. The crowd was horrified[35] when they saw that one was a delicate young girl and the other had recently given birth and had breasts dripping milk. And so they recalled them and dressed them in unbelted tunics. First Perpetua was thrown by the cow and fell on her back. And when she sat up, she pulled down the tunic that had been torn on the side to cover up her thigh, more mindful of her modesty than of her pain. Then she asked for a pin to fasten her disordered hair: for it was not appropriate that a martyr die with dishevelled hair, lest she seem to be in mourning at the moment of her glory. Then she got up and when she saw that Felicitas had been trampled, she went over to her and gave her a hand and lifted her up. Then the two stood side by side. But the cruelty of the audience was by now appeased, so they were called back through the Gates of Life. There Perpetua was stopped by a certain catechumen named Rusticus who at that time was keeping close to her, and she woke up as if from sleep, so intensely was she in spirit and in ecstasy, and she began to look around her and to the amazement of all said: "When are we going to be thrown to that cow or whatever?" and when she heard that it had already happened, she refused to believe it until she noticed the marks of her rough experience on her body and her dress. Then she called for her brother and that catechumen and addressed them, saying "Stand fast in the faith and all love one another and do not be scandalized by our suffering."

. . . And so the martyrs got up and went to the place the crowd wanted them to go to, and kissing one another they sealed their martyrdom with the ritual of peace. The others took the sword in silence and without moving . . . Perpetua, however, had yet to taste more pain. She screamed as she was struck on the bone and then took the trembling hand of the novice gladiator and guided it to her throat. It was as though so great a woman, feared as she was by the unclean spirit, could not be killed unless she herself were willing.

Fructuosus, Bishop of Tarragona, was executed in 259 CE. The context here is the first empire-wide persecution, originally launched by the emperor Decius. In 249, he demanded that all residents of the empire offer sacrifice to the gods of Rome, a vigorous effort to address the system-wide problems using a traditional solution: seek divine help. Furthermore, everyone needed a *libellus* or ticket affirming that they had done their bit for the empire. Christians were unable to fulfill this requirement and a number, who could not or would not evade enforcement, were imprisoned and executed. In 257, five or so emperors later, the emperor Valerian called for the arrest of church hierarchy and the enforcement of sacrifice, and then for the execution of persistent clerics, along with that of resistant Christian elite converts, whose property was also to be confiscated. The passage of time has seen the expansion of Christianity and has affected the Martyr Act's composition. Here, the arrest and execution of Fructuosus and his companions is not demanded by a local mob, but results from imperial decree. There is no hostile crowd; even the governor's household is filled with Christians and Christian sympathizers. The trial section of the Act is fairly perfunctory, as is the description of the execution in the amphitheater, in which Fructuosus declares his duty to provide an example to the whole Christian community. This is, however, a fairly inarticulate example; presumably the audience for the Martyr Act could supply details from tradition. There is an allusion to "the usual miracles"; this reminder of Christian tradition would also recall more elaborate narratives of the manifestation of divinity called forth by martyrdom. A more imagistic version of Fructuosus' miracle is depicted by Prudentius, writing some years after the event. Prudentius carefully supplies a manic governor and a frenzied demonic crowd.

Source: *Passion of the Holy Martyrs Bishop Fructuosus and his Deacons, Augurius and Eulogius 2–3; 5, 7:*[36] The governor Aemilianus said: "Bring in the bishop Fructuosus, Augurius and Eulogius." A court official said, "They are present."

The governor Aemilianus said to Fructuosus: "Were you aware of the emperors' orders?"

Fructuosus said: "I do not know their orders. I am a Christian."

The governor Aemilianus said: "They have ordered you to worship the gods."

Fructuosus said: "I worship the one God who has made heaven and earth, the sea, and all that is in them.[37]"

The governor Aemilianus said: "Do you know that the gods exist?"

"No, I do not," said Fructuosus.

Aemilianus said: "You will know later."

Fructuosus looked up to the Lord and began to pray within himself. . . .

Aemilianus the governor said to Fructuosus: "You are a bishop?"

"I am," said Fructuosus.

"You were," said Aemilianus. And he sentenced them to be burnt alive.

As Bishop Fructuosus was being taken to the amphitheater with his deacons, the people began to sympathize with him, for he was much beloved of pagans and Christians alike. For he was all that the Holy Spirit, through Paul, "the vessel of election"[38] and "the teacher of the Gentiles"[39], declared that a bishop should be. For this reason his brothers, who knew that he was going on to such great glory, were happy rather than sad.

... When he arrived at the amphitheater, he was approached by one of his readers named Augustalis, who begged him with tears that he might remove his shoes for him. The blessed martyr replied: "No, let it go, my son. I shall remove my own sandals in courage and joy, certain of the Lord's promises." Then, after he had removed his sandals, a fellow soldier and Christian came up named Felix, who grasped his right hand and begged him to remember him. The holy bishop Fructuosus answered him in a loud voice so that all could hear: "I must bear in mind the entire Catholic Church spread abroad in the world from East to West." ... After this the usual miracles of the Lord were not lacking. Babylas and Mygdonius, two of our brethren in the household of the governor Aemilianus, saw the heavens open, and this they also revealed to Aemilianus' daughter, their mistress according to the flesh: there was the saintly bishop Fructuosus together with his deacons rising crowned up to heaven, with the stakes to which they had been bound still intact. They summoned Aemilianus and said: "Come and see how those whom you have condemned to death today have been restored to heaven and to their hopes." But when Aemilianus came, he was not worthy to behold them. ... Ah, blessed martyrs, who were tested in the fire like precious gold, clad in the *lorica* of faith and the *galea* of salvation, crowned with a diadem and a "crown that does not fade"[40] because they trod underfoot the Devil's head!

Prudentius' fourth-century paean to the revered martyrs concentrates especially on those from his native Spain. His version of Fructuosus' martyrdom ratchets up the emotional ambience quite a bit in comparison to the earlier martyr act, making the contrast between Christian martyrs and the pagan persecutors a stark one. The Romans rave and thirst for the blood of beasts and men and the Christians eagerly escape from the body's prison into the eternal light.

Source: Prudentius, *Book of the Crowned* 6.49–50, 61–72:[41] Too mad with passion to defer or check his wrath, [the judge] appoints that they shall be burned with cruel fire. They, rejoicing, bid the throng not weep ... By this time they were entering a place enclosed by tiers of seats in a circle, where frenzied crowds attend and are drunk with much blood of wild beasts, when the din rises from the bloody shows, and as the gladiator, whose life is held cheap, falls under the stroke of the stark sword there is a roar of delight. Here the black official, bidden to make ready the fiery torture on a blazing pyre, had laid the topmost brands on the pile which, by destroying the bodies condemned to the flames, was to break open the prison cell and set free from it the souls which were burning with love of the light.

Christian Rome and the Arena

By the time of Augustine, Christianity had become an officially sponsored religion of the Roman state. The continuation of blood spectacle still made the question of Christians at the games relevant. Here, Augustine reiterates the connection between the shows and polytheism, referring to the traditional pantheon as "demons." The performers in the spectacles, he claims, are actively worshipping the old gods in their performances; the gods are likewise pleased by the marginalized existence of the performers. The terms of the critique have been shifted somewhat; the institution of the spectacles is incongruous in an increasingly Christianized society.

Source: Augustine, *Sermons* 198.3:[42] For such demons are pleased with misleading songs, with worthless shows, with the varied foulness of the theatre, with the frenzy of the games, with the cruelty of the amphitheatre, with the violent contests of those who undertake strife and controversy provocative even of hostility in their support of noxious characters, for instance, of an actor in a mime, a play, or a pantomime, of a charioteer, or of a *venator*. By acting in this way they, as it were, offer incense to the demons within their hearts. For the deceptive spirits rejoice in seduction; they feast upon the evil customs and the notoriously vile life of those whom they have misled and entrapped.

Prudentius wrote in the late fourth and fifth centuries CE, like Augustine at a time when the emperors typically played an active role in the official promotion of Christianity. He draws the explicit connection between the deaths of gladiators and pagan sacrifice, claiming that a variety of chthonic deities are propitiated by blood spectacle, and questions the state support of rituals to please infernal gods.

Source: Prudentius, *Against Symmachus* 1.379–392:[43] Look at the crime-stained offerings to frightful Dis, to whom is sacrificed the gladiator laid low on the ill-starred arena, a victim offered to Phlegethon in misconceived expiation for Rome. For what means that senseless show with its exhibition of sinful skill, the killing of young men, the pleasure fed on blood, the deathly dust that ever enshrouds the spectators, the grim sight of the parade in the amphitheatre? Why, Charon by the murder of these poor wretches receives offerings that pay for his services as guide, and is propitiated by a crime in the name of religion. Such are the delights of the Jupiter of the dead, such the acts in which the ruler of dark Avernus finds content and refreshment. Is it not shameful that a strong imperial nation thinks it needful to offer such sacrifices for its country's welfare and seeks the help of religion from the vaults of hell?

The ambience of the arena retained its power for Christian-era writers. Prudentius' *Psychomachia*, roughly translated as *Spiritual Battle*, makes extensive use of arena imagery to present the cosmic battle between good and evil as combats of pairs in a metaphysical amphitheater. The poet thus appropriates a powerful symbol of Roman authority for the purpose of asserting the eventual victory of Christianity. In *Psychomachia*, female virtues, whose appearance and motivations match those of celebrated Christian martyrs, fight against pagan "vices" or rather pagan customs that a newly Christian Rome must now jettison. These are combats *sine missione*, with much detail on the defeat of the opponents.

Source: Prudentius, *Psychomachia* 21–37:[44] Faith first takes the field to face the doubtful chances of battle, her rough dress disordered, her shoulders bare, her hair untrimmed, her arms exposed; for the sudden glow of ambition, burning for new battles, takes no thought to strap on weapons or armor, but trusting in a brave heart and unprotected limbs challenges the dangers of furious war in order to break them down. Behold first Reverence to the Old Gods dares to match her strength against Faith's challenge and strike at her. But she, rising higher, strikes her opponent's head down, its brows bound with fillets, and pushes to the dust the mouth sated with the blood of beasts and tramples underfoot the eyes, squeezing them out in death. The throat is choked and the scant breath confined by the blocking of its passage and long gasps make a hard and agonizing death. The conquering legion exults, which Queen Faith had assembled from a thousand martyrs and inspired against the enemy.

A strong element of the fatal charade's mortal irony infuses the death of Luxuria in Prudentius' poem, as the essence of self-indulgence is killed in a grotesque parody of self-consumption. Luxury is an *essedaria*, brought down by Sobrietas or Self-Control.

Source: Prudentius, *Psychomachia* 412–429:[45] The driver, leaning backwards and pulling back on the reins, nevertheless is carried along, her dripping hair fouled with dust. And then [Luxuria] is thrown out and the spinning wheels tangle the driver, for she falls forward under the axle and with her mangled body slows the chariot down. Sobrietas gives her the death blow as she lies there, hurling at her a great stone from the rock . . . to smash the breath-passage in the middle of the face . . . the teeth within are loosened, the gullet cut, and the mangled tongue fills it with bloody fragments. Her gorge rises at the strange meal; gulping down the pulped bones she spews up again the lumps she swallowed. "Drink now your own blood, after the many winecups," says the virgin [Sobrietas], upbraiding her. "Let these be your grim morsels, in place of the excessive sweets you enjoyed in time past."

The allure of the spectacles was present for the Christianized audience still; Prudentius capitalized on its powerful combination of blood, excitement and horror in his depiction of the battle between good and evil. Augustine relays the immediacy of the arena's power in a famous story about his student, Alypius, whose Christian convictions did not render him "safe" against the compelling pull of the spectacles. Here, Augustine echoes the misgivings about the impact of the crowd that had been expressed earlier by Seneca in a polytheist context.

Source: Augustine, *Confessions* 7.8:[46] But there was no abandoning of the worldly career which his parents were always talking to him about. He had gone to Rome before me in order to study the law and in Rome he had been quite swept away, incredibly and with a most incredible passion, by the gladiatorial shows. He was opposed to such things and detested them; but he happened to meet some of his friends and fellow pupils on their way back from dinner, and they, in spite of his protests and his vigorous resistance, used a friendly kind of violence and forced him to go along with them to the amphitheater on a day when one of these cruel and bloody shows was being presented. As he went, he said to them: "You can drag my body there, but don't imagine that you can make me turn my eyes or give my mind to the show. Though there, I shall not be there, and so I shall have the better both of you and of the show."

After hearing this his friends were all the keener to bring him along with them. No doubt they wanted to see whether he could actually do this or not. So they came to the arena and took the seats which they could find. The whole place was seething with savage enthusiasm, but he shut the doors of his eyes and forbade his soul to go out into a scene of such evil. If only he could have blocked up his ears too! For in the course of the fight some man fell; there was a great roar from the whole mass of spectators which fell upon his ears; he was overcome by curiosity and opened his eyes, feeling perfectly prepared to treat whatever he might see with scorn and to rise above it. But he then received in his soul a worse wound than that man, whom he had wanted to see, had received in his body. His own fall was more wretched than that of the gladiator which had caused all that shouting which had entered his ears and unlocked his eyes and made an opening for the thrust which was to overthrow his soul – a soul that had been reckless rather than strong and was all the weaker because it had trusted in itself when it ought to have trusted in you. He saw the blood and he gulped down savagery. Far from turning away, he fixed his eyes on it. Without knowing what was happening, he drank in madness, he was delighted with the guilty contest, drunk with the lust of blood. He was no longer the man who had come there but was one of the crowd to which he had come, a true companion of those who had brought him. There is no more to be said. He looked, he shouted, he raved with excitement; he took away with him a madness which would goad him to come back again, and he would not only come with those who first got him there; he would go ahead of them and he would drag others with him.

6

Chariot Races and Water Shows

Chariot Races

Roman tradition hailed the circus races as the oldest of Rome's spectacles, established informally by Romulus, Rome's legendary founder, himself. The first races afforded a key opportunity for the Romans in the extended narrative of the origins of Roman identity. Frustrated by his attempts to arrange inter-marriage with neighboring peoples like the Sabines, Romulus decided to work toward his goal using subterfuge, by hosting a regional festival in honor of the god Consus (a.k.a. Neptune) that included *ludi circenses* or chariot races.

Source: Livy 1.9:[1] Deliberately hiding his resentment, [Romulus] prepared to celebrate the Consualia, a solemn festival in honor of Neptune, patron of the horse, and sent notice of his intention all over the neighboring countryside. The better to advertise it, his people lavished upon their preparations for the spectacle all the resources – such as they were in those days – at their command ...all the Sabines were there too, with their wives and children ... Then the great moment came; the show began, and nobody had eyes or thoughts for anything else. This was the Romans' opportunity: at a given signal all the able-bodied men burst through the crowd and seized the young women.

Source: Ovid, *Art of Love* 1.103–108:[2] You first, Romulus, did disturb the games, when the rape of Sabine women consoled the wifeless men. No awnings then hung over a marble theater, nor was the platform red with the spray of crocuses; there, artlessly arranged, were garlands which the leafy Palatine had brought forth; the stage was unadorned; the people sat on rows of turf, any chance leaves covering their unkempt hair.

Whether chariot races were held in the eighth century BCE or not, certainly they were among the earliest games to be sponsored by the Roman state: they were the highlight of the *Ludi Romani* or *Ludi Magni*, the first ordinary games to be established as part of the Roman calendar. They remained favorite choices for extraordinary games, presented to celebrate victories, to fulfill vows, to mark important achievements.

Like other spectacles, the circus games regularly began with a *pompa* or procession, that typically started atop the Capitoline Hill, wound through the Forum along the Sacred Way then back toward the Forum Boarium near the Tiber. The *carceres* or starting gates of the Circus Maximus abutted the Forum Boarium and the grand entrance into the track was in the middle of these starting gates. The presiding magistrate, *triumphator* or emperor, headed up the *pompa*, typically riding in a *biga* or *quadriga*, a two- or four-horse chariot, typically dressed as a triumphant general. Juvenal lampoons the solemn ceremony of the *pompa*, carried out, it seems to him, by cynical experts in the trappings of public performance.

Source: Juvenal, *Satires* 10.36–46:[3] The praetor borne in his lofty carriage through the midst of the dusty Circus, and wearing full ceremonial dress – the tunic with palm-leaves, the heavy Tyrian toga draped in great folds round his shoulders; a crown so enormous that no neck can bear its weight, and instead it's carried by a sweating public slave, who, to stop the consul getting above himself, rides in the carriage beside him.[4] Then there's the ivory staff, crowned with an eagle, a posse of trumpeters, the imposing procession of white-robed citizens marching so dutifully beside his bridle-rein, retainers whose friendship was bought with the meal-ticket stashed in their wallets.

The *editor* presiding over the games was followed by a group of elites, then the drivers and their chariots, serenaded by musicians, then the priests and the ritual displays, including statues of the gods on litters or in carts. Dionysius describes a *pompa* dating to the Republic era; his tone is considerably less cynical than that of Juvenal as he depicts the parade as a celebration of Rome's present and future strength in leadership.

Source: Dionysius of Halicarnassus 7.72:[5] Before beginning the games the principal magistrates conducted a procession in honor of the gods from the Capitol through the Forum to the Circus Maximus. Those who led the procession were, first, the Romans' sons who were nearing manhood and were of an age to bear a part in this ceremony, who rode on horseback if their fathers were entitled by their fortunes to be knights, while the others, who were destined to serve in the infantry, went on foot, the former in squadrons and troops, and the latter in divisions and companies, as if they were going to school; this was done in order that strangers might see the number and beauty of the youths of the commonwealth who were approaching manhood. These were followed by charioteers, some of whom drove four horses abreast, some two, and others rode unyoked horses.

Once the *pompa* was completed, starting teams went to their gates, assigned to a particular stall by lots rolled in an urn. Much visible ceremony attended this, as a means of building anticipation in spectators. The signal for the race to begin was the dropping of a *mappa* or cloth, done by the presiding magistrate, either from above the starting gates or from the imperial box. This was the sign for the release of the mechanism keeping the gates of the *carceres* closed; a grinding noise, audible to spectators, meant that the horses could now burst from their stalls and begin the race.

Source: Tertullian, *On the Spectacles* 16.2–3:[6] The praetor is too slow for [the fans]; all the time their eyes are rolling as though in rhythm with the lots he shakes up in his urn. Then they await the signal with bated breath; one outcry voices the common madness. Recognize the madness from their foolish behavior. "He has thrown it!" they shout; everyone tells everybody else what all of them have seen just that moment.

The events

Races were usually between *quadrigae*, four-horse chariots, although competitions between other sizes of chariots are also known, from as small as the two-horse vehicle up to the relatively rare ten-horse chariot.

To maximize speed and handling, the chariots were extremely light constructions of wood and leather, with a yoke only for the two middle horses; the outer two were only attached to the vehicle by the traces and were thus a bit more maneuverable. Accidents were called *naufragia*, which literally means "shipwrecks." How common these were is difficult to say; given the techniques of the charioteers coupled with the inherent danger of high speeds, a crowded track, and massed horses, they were probably not unusual. Clearly they were exciting, as almost every representation of a circus race from antiquity incorporates one into the narrative.

The technique and clothing of Roman charioteers differed significantly from those used by Greeks. Roman drivers steered using their body weight; with the reins tied around their torsos, charioteers could lean from one side to the other to direct the horses' movement, keeping the hands free for the whip and such. In any given race, there might be a number of teams put up by each faction, who would cooperate to maximize their chances of victory by ganging up on opponents, forcing them out of the preferred inside track or "helping" them lose concentration and expose themselves to accident and injury. The driver's clothing was color-coded in accordance with his faction, which would help distant spectators to keep track of the race's progress. The charioteer wore a short tunic, wrapped with *fasciae* or padded bands to protect the torso, with additional *fasciae* as well around his thighs. A thick leather helmet provided some protection for his head and he carried a *falx*, a curved knife, to cut the reins and keep from being dragged in case of accident. A mosaic from the third century CE shows four leading charioteers from the different colors, all in their distinctive gear (figure 6.1).

Figure 6.1   Mosaic with charioteers of four colors. Scala/Art Resource, NY

As part of his history of the Punic Wars in poetic form, Silius Italicus presents a version of Scipio Africanus' games at Carthago Nova in 206 BCE (see chapter 1). He features the chariot races in this description, emphasizing the excitement of the crowd and their educated spectatorship as they second-guess the techniques of the drivers. The lead horses for each *quadriga* are likewise a focus of attention, their breeding and temperament assessed as key factors in their potential for success. A *naufragium* and a last-minute surge from behind infuse his running account with much excitement.

Source: Silius Italicus, *Punica* 303–456:[7] Now the appointed day came, and the plain was filled with the noise of a crowd past numbering; and Scipio, with tears in his eyes, led the semblance of a funeral procession with due rites of burial . . . Thence he went back to the race-course and started the first contest – that which was to test the speed of horses. Even before the starting-gate was unbarred, the excited crowd surged to and fro with a noise like the sound of the sea, and, with a fury of partisanship, fixed their eyes on the doors behind which the racers were standing.

And now the signal was given, and the bolts flew back with a noise. Scarcely had the first hoof flashed into full view, when a wild storm of shouting rose up to heaven. Bending forward like the drivers, each man gazed at the chariot he favored, and at the same time shouted to the flying horses. The course was shaken by the enthusiasm of the spectators, and excitement robbed every man of his senses. They lean forward and direct the horses by their shouting. A cloud of yellow dust rose up from the sandy soil, concealing with its darkness the running of the horses and the exertions of the drivers. One man backs with fury the mettled steed, another the charioteer. Some are zealous for horses of their own country, others for the fame of some ancient stud. One man is filled with joyful hope for an animal that is racing for the first time, while another prefers the green old age of a well-tried veteran. At the start, Lampon, bred in Gallicia, left the rest behind; he rushed through the air with the flying car, galloping over the course with huge strides and leaving the winds behind him. The crowd roared with applause, thinking that with such a start their favorite had as good as won. But those who looked deeper and had more experience of the race-course, blamed the driver for putting forth all his strength at the beginning: from a distance they uttered vain protests, that he was tiring out his team with his efforts and keeping no reserve of power. "Where are you careering too eagerly, Cyrnus?" – Cyrnus was the charioteer – "Be prudent! Put down your whip and tighten your reins!" But alas, his ears were deaf: on he sped, unsparing of his horses, and forgetting how much ground had still to be covered.

Next came Panchates, a chariot-length and no more behind the leader. Bred in Asturia, he was conspicuous for the white forehead and four white feet of his sires. Though high-mettled, he was low of stature and lacked comeliness; but now his fiery spirit lent him wings, and he sped over the plain, impatient of the reins; he seemed to grow in stature and size as he ran. His driver, Hiberus, was radiant with scarlet of Cinyphian dye.

Third in order, neck and neck with Pelorus, ran Caucasus, a fractious animal that loved not the caressing hand that patted his neck, but rejoiced to bite and champ the iron in his mouth till blood came with the foam. Pelorus, on the other hand, was more tractable and obedient to the rein; never did he swerve aside and drive the car in crooked lines, but kept to the inside and grazed the turning-post with his near wheel. He was conspicuous for the size of his neck and the thick mane that rippled over it. Strange to say, he had no sire: his dam, Harpe, had conceived him from the Zephyr of spring and foaled him in the plains of the Vettones. This chariot was driven along the course by the noble Durius, while Caucasus relied upon ancient Atlas as his driver. Caucasus came from Aetolian Tyde, the city founded by the wandering hero, Diomede; and legend traced his descent to the Trojan horses which the son of Tydeus, successful in his bold attempt, stole from Aeneas by the river Simoïs. Atlas came last, but Durius was last and also moved no faster: one might have thought the pair were running peaceably side by side and keeping level.

And now, when near half the distance was completed, they quickened over the course; and spirited Panchates, struggling to catch up the team ahead, seemed to rise higher and at each moment to mount upon the chariot in front, and the hooves of his prancing forefeet struck and rattled on the car of the Gallician horse. When Hiberus, who came second, saw that the Gallician team of Cyrnus was tiring, that the chariot was no longer bounding ahead, and that the smoking horses were driven on by severe and repeated flogging, then, as when a sudden storm rushes down from a mountain-stop, he leaned forward quickly as far as the necks of his coursers and hung above their crests, and stirred up Panchates, who was chafing at being second in the race, and plied his whip, even while he called to the horse: "Steed of Asturia, shall any other get in front and win the prize when you are competing? Rise up and fly and glide over the plain with all your wonted speed, as if on wings! Lampon is panting hard; his strength is gone and he grows smaller; he has no breath left to carry the goal." At these words, Panchates rose higher, as if he were just starting in the race; and Cyrnus, though he strove to block his rival by swerving, or to keep up with him, was soon left behind. The sky and the race-course resounded, smitten by the shouts of the spectators. Victorious Panchates raised his triumphant crest still higher as he ran on; and he drew after him his three partners in the yoke.

The two last drivers were Atlas and Durius; and now they swerved aside and resorted to tricks. First, one tried to pass his rival on the left; and then the other came up on the right and strove to get in front; but both failed in their attempted strategy. At last Durius, young and confident, leaning forward and jerking at his reins, placed his chariot athwart his rival's course and struck the other car and upset it. Atlas, no match for the other's youth and strength, protested with justice: "Where are you rushing? or what crazy kind of racing is this? You're trying to kill me and my horses together." As he cried out thus, he fell head first from the broken chariot; and the horses too, a sorry sight, fell down and sprawled in disorder on the ground, while the conqueror shook his reins on the open course, and Pelorus flew up the middle of the track, leaving

Atlas struggling to rise. It did not take him long to catch up the weary team of Cyrnus: he flew past with speedy car, though Cyrnus was learning too late the wisdom of controlling his pace. A shout of applause from his supporters drove the chariot on. And now Pelorus thrust his head over the back and shoulders of terrified Hiberus, till the charioteer felt the horse's hot breath and foam upon his neck. Durius pressed on along the plain, and increased the pace of his team by the whip. Nor was the effort vain: coming up on the right, he seemed to be, or even was, running neck and neck with his rival. Then, amazed by the prospect of such glory, he cried out: "Now, Pelorus, now is the time to show that the West-wind was your sire! Let steeds that spring from the loins of mere animals learn how far superior is the issue of an immortal parent. When victorious, you shall offer gifts to your sire, and raise an altar in his honor." And indeed, had he not, even while he spoke, been beguiled, by too great success and by his fearful joy, into dropping his whip, Durius would perhaps have consecrated to the West-wind the altars he had vowed. But now, as wretched as if the victor's wreath had fallen from his head, he turned his rage against himself, tearing the gold-embroidered garment from his breast, and weeping, and pouring out complaints to heaven. When the lash was gone, the team no longer obeyed the driver: in vain he flogged their backs with the reins for a whip.

Meanwhile, Panchates, sure now of victory, sped on to the goal, and claimed the first prize with head held high. A light breeze fanned the mane that rippled over his neck and shoulders; then with proud step he raised his nimble limbs, and a great shout greeted his victory. Each competitor received alike a battle-axe of solid silver with engraving; but the other prizes differed from one another and were of unequal value. To the winner was given a flying steed, a desirable present from the Massylian king; the second in merit then received two cups overlaid with gold of the Tagus, taken from the great heap of Carthaginian spoil; the third prize was the shaggy hide of a fierce lion and a Carthaginian helmet with bristling plumes; and lastly Scipio summoned Atlas and gave him a prize also in pity for his age and ill-fortune, though the old man had fallen down when his chariot was wrecked. To him was given a beautiful youth, to attend on him, together with a skin cap of Spanish fashion.

Sidonius Apollinaris offers an extended poetic description of a "private" set of races, put together by the emperor and calling on the talents of members of the imperial court of the fifth-century western empire. Much attention is paid to the tactics of chariot racing, such as holding back the horses to keep them from early exhaustion and trying to gain the best inside position on the track or, failing that, keeping careful watch on the positioning of one's competitors, to take advantage of any wavering from the course. Especially to be noted is the "tag team" approach, the alliance between drivers of different colors to crowd their opponents out of a winning position.

Source: Sidonius Apollinaris, *To Consentius* 23.320–425:[8] you chose one of the four chariots by lot and mounted it, laying a tight grip on the hanging reins. Your partner did the same, so did the opposing side. Brightly gleam the colors, white and blue, green and red, your several badges. Servants' hands hold mouth and reins and with knotted cords force the twisted manes to hide themselves, and all the while they incite the steeds, eagerly cheering them with encouraging pats and instilling a rapturous frenzy. There behind the barriers chafe those beasts, pressing against the fastenings, while a vapoury blast comes forth between the wooden bars and even before the race, the arena they have not yet entered is filled with their panting breath. They push, they bustle, they drag, they struggle, they rage, they jump, they fear and are feared; never are their feet still, but restlessly they last the hardened timber. At last the herald with loud blare of trumpet calls forth the impatient teams and launches the fleet chariots into the field. The swoop of forked lightning, the arrow sped by Scythian string, the trail of the swiftly-falling star, the leaden hurricane of bullets whirled from Balearic slings has never so rapidly split the airy paths of the sky. The ground gives way under the wheels and the air is smirched with the dust that rises in their track. The drivers, while they wield the reins, ply the lash; now they stretch forward over the chariots with stooping breasts, and so they sweep along, striking the horses' withers and leaving their backs untouched. With charioteers so prone it would puzzle you to pronounce whether they were more supported by the pole or by the wheels. Now as if flying out of sight on wings, you had traversed the more open part and you were hemmed in by the space that is cramped by design, amid which the central barrier has extended its long low double-walled structure. When the farther *metae* freed you all from restraint once more, your partner went ahead of the two others who had passed you; so then, according to the law of the circling course, you had to take the fourth track. The drivers in the middle were intent that if perhaps the first man, embarrassed by a dash of his steeds too much to the right, should leave a space open on the left by heading for the surrounding seats, he would be passed by a chariot driven in on the near side. As for you, bending double with the very force of the effort, you keep a tight rein on your team and with consummate skill wisely reserve them for the seventh lap. The others are busy with hand and voice, and everywhere the sweat of the drivers and flying steeds falls in drops onto the field. The hoarse roar from applauding fans stirs the heart, and the contestants, both horses and men, are warmed by the race and chilled by fear. Thus they go once round, then a second time; thus goes the third lap, thus the fourth; but in the fifth turn the foremost man, unable to bear the pressure of his pursuers, swerved his vehicle aside, for he had found, as he gave command to his fleet team, that their strength was exhausted. Now the return half of the sixth course was completed and the crowd was already clamoring for the award of the prizes; your competitors, with no fear of any effort from you, were scouring the track in front with no concern, when suddenly you drew taut the curbs all together, tensed up your chest, planted your feet firmly before you, and chafed the mouths of your swift steeds . . . then one of the others, clinging to the shortest route round the turning post, was pressed forward by you and his team, carried away beyond control by their onward rush, could no longer be wheeled around in a harmonious course . . . The other adversary, exulting in the public plaudits, ran too far to the right, close to the spectators; then as he turned aside and all too late after long indifference urged his horses with the whip, you sped straight past your swerving rival. Then the enemy in reckless haste overtook you and, foolishly thinking that his first man had already gone ahead, shamelessly made for your wheel with a sideways rush. His horses were brought down, a multitude of intruding legs entered the wheels, and the twelve spokes were crowded until a crack came from those crammed spaces and the turning rim shattered the entangled feet; then he, a fifth victim, was flung from his chariot, which fell upon him, caused a mountain of manifold havoc, and blood disfigured his prostrate brow. Then arose a riot of renewed shouting . . . the just emperor ordered ribbons to be added to the victors' palms and crowns to the necklets of gold and true merit to have its reward.

Races were interspersed with other displays and diversions, along with a break at noon for lunch. Livy describes a military demonstration presented in circus games of the middle Republic, drawing a contrast between this kind of event and the excessive displays of imperial resources known in the Rome of the early Principate, contemporary with Livy.

Source: Livy 44.9:[9] It was the custom in those days, before the introduction of the modern extravagance of filling the arena with wild beasts from all over the world, to seek out spectacular performances of all kinds; for one race with *quadrigae* and one bareback display scarcely took up an hour for the two events. In one of these displays, groups of about sixty young men (sometimes more in the more elaborate games) entered the arena under arms. Their act was to some extent an imitation of army maneuvers, but in other respects it demanded a more sophisticated skill than that of ordinary soldiers, and it had more in common with the style of gladiatorial combats. After performing various evolutions they would form in order of battle, with shields massed together over their heads, the front rank standing, the second stooping a little, the third and fourth increasing their stoop, and the rear rank kneeling, the whole forming a "tortoise" with a slope like the roof of a house. From this two armed men would rush out, about fifty feet away from each other, and, after making threatening gestures at one another they would climb up from the bottom to the top of the "tortoise" over the close-packed shields. They would then perform a kind of skirmish along the outer edges of the "tortoise," or engage in combat in the center, leaping about just as if on solid ground.

Variations on equestrian skills were also featured at the circus *ludi*, including the acrobatic riding of the *desultores* which Livy compares to that of the Numidian cavalry, known for its special training.

Source: Livy 23.29:[10] [Numidians] had been trained to ride into battle leading a spare horse: such was the quickness of these men, and so highly trained were their mounts that often in the heat of an engagement when the horse they were riding tired, they would leap, like circus riders, fully armed upon the back of the fresh one.

Competition was given a special tingle with the *diversium*, in which a victorious charioteer exchanged teams with the competing faction for another race, to "prove" the superior skill of the driver. An inscription in the hippodrome at Constantinople celebrates the amazing versatility of the late fifth-century charioteer Constantine in his command of the *diversium*.

Source: *Planudian Anthology* 374:[11] Constantinus having won twenty-five races on one morning, changed his team with his rival's, and taking the same horses that he had formerly beaten, won twenty-one times with them. Often there was a great strife between the two factions as to which was to have him, and they gave him two robes to choose from.

This sixth-century CE circus program found among the papyrus collection at Oxyrhynchus, in Egypt, gives a sense of the variety of events offered in the later spectacles outside the major cities of the Roman world. Like the Republican games, these games do not display much in the way of extravagant productions. The "victories" might refer to an acknowledgment of successful competitors from the previous day. Unlike the program for *munera* from Pompeii, there is no indication here of specific drivers or horses with their win-loss records, to build excitement and/or calculate odds for gambling.

Source: *P. Oxy.* 2707:[12] For good fortune. Victories. 1st chariot race. Procession. Singing rope-dancers. 2nd chariot race. The singing rope-dancers. 3rd chariot race. Gazelle and hounds. 4th chariot race. Mimes. 5th chariot race. Troupe of athletes. 6th chariot race.

Charioteers

Victorious drivers, like successful gladiators, were awarded prize money in addition to the contractual pay arranged in advance. Since individual drivers competed in multiple races each day of the *ludi*, there was more opportunity for financial gain for circus performers than for most others. Drivers also stood to gain from gambling, winning a portion of the take from their backers. Martial mentions the example of Scorpus, the Green charioteer whose winnings in one hour alone were extraordinarily high.

> Source: Martial *Epigrams* 10.74:[13] Spare at length the weary congratulator, Rome, the weary client. How long shall I be a caller, earning a hundred coppers in a whole day, among escorts and petty clients, when Scorpus in a single hour carries off as winner fifteen heavy bags of gold hot from the mint?

Juvenal's comparison for the Red charioteer Lacerta also gives a sense of the relative value of a star charioteer's earnings; a winning driver's income dwarfs not just that of a poet like Martial, but vastly overmatches the pay of professional advocates.

> Source: Juvenal, *Satires* 7.105–114:[14] How about advocates then? Tell me the sum they extract from their work in court, those bulging bundles of briefs. They talk big enough . . . yet if you check their incomes (real, not declared), you'll find that a hundred lawyers make only as much as Lacerta of the Reds.

Scorpus was one of the most famous drivers of the first century, known not just for his fabulous prizes but for his outstanding successes as well as his early (and thus tragic) death. Martial's epigrams hint at the deep melancholy of the fans as Scorpus' death is given mythic scope.

> Source: Martial *Epigrams* 10.50:[15] Let sad Victory break the palms of Idumaea. Favor, beat your breast with merciless hand. Let Honor put on mourning. Grieving Glory, cast your crowned tresses on the unkind flames. Ah villainy! Scorpus, cheated of your first youth, you die. So soon you yoke black horses. The goal, ever quickly gained by your hastening chariot – your life's goal too, why was it so close?

> Source: Martial *Epigrams* 10.53:[16] I am Scorpus, the glory of the clamorous circus, your applause, Rome, and brief darling. Envious Lachesis snatched me away ere my thirtieth year, but, counting my victories, believed me an old man.

A number of funeral monuments set up in honor of particularly successful drivers inform us about their individual careers. We are given many career details from the epitaph of the charioteer Diocles, especially known for his Red victories in the mid-second century CE, although he spent two years driving for the Whites and eight years for the Greens before transferring to his final and most successful color. Of the recorded 1,462 wins, just over a hundred predated his joining the Reds. The inscription gives some sense of his career highlights, including references to 502 last-minute victories, again

with colors specified for these. The high number of "last-minute" determina-
tions has been interpreted as evidence for inter-color cooperation, in which
the Red team worked together with White or Blue or Green to exhaust or
foul the other teams in a prearranged deal. There is much specific data about
prize money as well, with different pay rates for different kinds of races.
Diocles accumulated a very impressive career total of more than 35 million
sesterces in prizes, truly a vast fortune.

> Source: *CIL* 14.2884:[17] Gaius Appuleius Diocles, charioteer of the Red faction,
> from the Spanish Lusitanian people, aged 42 years, 7 months, 23 days. He drove
> his first chariot in the White faction, in the consulship of Acilius Aviola and
> Corellius Pansa. He won his first victory in the same faction, in the consulship
> of Manius Acilius Glabrio and Gaius Bellicius Torquatus. He drove for the first
> time in the Green faction in the consulship of Torquatus Asprenas (second term)
> and Annius Libo. He won his first victory in the Red faction in the consulship
> of Laenas Pontianus and Antonius Rufinus. Totals: he drove chariots for 24 years,
> emerged from the starting gate 4,257 times and won 1,462 victories, 110 in
> opening races. In single-entry races he won 1,064 victories, winning 92 major
> prizes, 32 of them (including three with six-horse teams) at 30,000 sesterces,
> 28 (including two with six-horse teams) at 40,000 sesterces, 29 (including 1
> with a seven-horse team) at 50,000 sesterces, and 3 at 60,000 sesterces; in two-
> entry races he won 347 victories, including four with three-horse teams at
> 15,000 sesterces; in three-entry races he won 51 victories. He won or placed
> 2,900 times, taking 861 second places, 576 third places, and one fourth place at
> 1,000 sesterces; he failed to place 1,351 times. He tied a Blue for first place
> ten times and a White 91 times, twice for 30,000 sesterces. He won a total of
> 35,863,120 sesterces. In addition, in races with two-horse teams for 1,000 he
> won three times and tied a White once and a Green twice. He took the lead and
> won 815 times, came from behind to win 67 times, won under handicap 36 times,
> won in various styles 42 times, and won in a final dash 502 times (216 over the
> Greens, 205 over the Blues, 81 over the Whites). He made nine horses 100-time
> winners and one a 200-time winner.

Surviving celebratory inscriptions and paeans in tribute offer us not just
career details but a sense of the emotional attachment between fans and
famous drivers. One high achieving charioteer was Porphyrius Calliopas, star
of the circus. Porphyrius arrived in Antioch in 507, having already achieved
prominence as the best driver in Constantinople. His success allowed him a
great deal of leeway in determining the course of his career, as had been the
case with the earlier Diocles. Porphyrius had been affiliated with both the
Blues and the Greens, having raked in huge number of victories for both and
having been awarded with significant public monuments by his appreciative
clubs. Some of these honors were displayed on the central barrier of the
circus at Constantinople; they celebrated not only Porphyrius' achievement
but the relationship he had with the fans.

Figure 6.2 Mosaic with Polydus the charioteer. Rheinisches Landesmuseum Trier

The surviving inscriptions also document tributes in other media that are no longer extant, like the statues mentioned here. The fabric of the statue, be it gold, silver or bronze, was interpreted as an indication of the merit of the honoree. Some portraits of specific drivers do survive: Polydus, a successful charioteer for the Reds in the third century, was the subject of an enormous mosaic on the floor of the imperial baths at Trier. Compressor, his lead horse, also has his name in the image (figure 6.2).

Source: *Planudian Anthology* 335:[18] The Emperor and the faction erected the statue of Porphyrius, son of Calchas, loaded with many crowns won by skilled toil, the youngest of all the drivers as well as the best, and winner of as many victories as any. This man's statue should have been of gold, not of bronze like the others.

Source: *Planudian Anthology* 338:[19] Victory gave to you, Porphyrius, while still young, this honor which time has given to others late in life and grudgingly; for, having counted the performances that won you many crowns, she found them superior to those of old drivers. Why! Did not the rival faction, in admiration of your glory, applaud you loudly? Blessed is the most free people of the Blues, to whom our great Emperor granted you as a gift.

Source: *Planudian Anthology* 340:[20] To others when they have retired, but to Porphyrius alone while still racing, did the Emperor give this honor. For often he drove his own horses to victory and then took in hand the team of his adversary, and was again crowned. Hence arose a keen rivalry on the part of the Greens, hence a shout of applause for him, O. King, who will give joy both to Blues and to Greens.

Porphyrius' fans solicited the emperor to bring their favorite out of retirement; their success in swaying Porphyrius' professional interest was commemorated with additional statues in commemoration of his new victories.

Source: *Greek Anthology* 15.44:[21] Here they set up again in bronze and silver Porphyrius, who formerly, too, stood here in bronze owing to his merit, when he had ceased from his labors and unbuckled his belt. Old man, after receiving honors from abroad, you did at the loud request of the people take up your whip again and rage furiously on the course, as if in a second youth.

Cassiodorus, the sixth-century official, served several kings of the Ostrogoths in Italy after the breakdown of the empire in the west. His *Variae* or *Compendium* is a collection of model imperial letters that document (literally) the continuation of certain civic and imperial values of the earlier Roman state. He puts in the mouth of King Theoderic an acknowledgment of the value of circus racing and, in particular, the power of the driver Thomas.

Source: Cassiodorus, *Variae* 3.51.1–2:[22] Now, some time ago, my judgement bestowed a reasonable salary on Thomas the charioteer, an immigrant from the east, until I should have tested his skill and character. But, since he has become the champion in this contest, and has willingly left his own country, and chosen to support the seat of my rule, I have decided to confirm him in the monthly allowance . . . For he, in his many victories, has "flitted on the lips" of many, riding more on popularity than on chariots. He took up a constantly defeated faction of the people . . . now overcoming the drivers by skill, now surpassing them in the speed of his horses. From the frequency of his triumphs, he was called a sorcerer – and among charioteers, it is seen as a great honor to attain to such accusations.

Just as the public value of charioteers was recognized by private and public means, the danger they represented could be a target of official action. Some charioteers used their celebrity status to push the envelope in terms of what could be tolerated by the state. This license tacitly granted to more prominent charioteers to misbehave with impunity was occasionally addressed by the authorities; one such instance is cited among the "good" actions of the emperor Nero (alongside his execution of Christians).

Source: Suetonius, *Nero* 16:[23] [Nero] put an end to the diversions of the chariot drivers, who from immunity of long standing claimed the right of ranging at large and amusing themselves by cheating and robbing the people.

Scandal surrounding "bad" emperors alleged that they were not just the unseemly companions of unacceptably degraded people, like gladiators and charioteers, but that they elevated such persons to high office and power. Elagabalus is targeted for such criticism.

Source: Historia Augusta, *Elagabalus* 6, 12:[24] As his associates, first in the chariot-race and then as colleagues in the whole of his life and actions, he had the charioteers Protogenes and Gordius...To the prefecture of the Praetorian Guard he appointed a dancer who had performed as an actor at Rome. He made Gordius, a charioteer, prefect of the vigils and Claudius, a barber, prefect of the grain supply.

Enthusiasm for specific colors and specific charioteers entailed a corresponding hatred for rival drivers and factions. Evidence for this can be found in the hundreds of *defixiones* or curse tablets, found in and around circuses and graveyards of the Roman world. Using these *defixiones*, fans summoned the beings of the underworld to exert their powers against favorite performers, by writing their wishes on small strips of lead which were then rolled up and "delivered" to the infernal spirits by being buried in podium walls, race tracks, *carceres* or being placed in graves. This was a very common form of everyday magic, used primarily against racing performers but also to secure success in business and love. The following curse tablet from Apamea, dating to the fifth or sixth century CE, is very specific in its directions to the underworld deity, particularly urging that the charioteers be hampered in certain tactical maneuvers used against other drivers.

Source: *Supplementum Epigraphicum Graecum*, hereafter *SEG*, 34 (1984) #1437:[25] Most holy Lord Charakteres,[26] tie up, bind the feet, the hands, the nerves, the eyes, the knees, the courage, the leaps, the whip, the victory and the crowning of Porphyras[27] and Hapsicrates, who are in the middle-left, as well as his co-drivers of the Blue-colors in the stable of Eugenius...in the hippodrome at the moment when they are about to compete may they not squeeze over, may they not collide, may they not extend, may they not force [us] out, may they not overtake, may they not break off [in a new direction] for the entire day when they are about to race. May they be broken, may they be dragged, may they be destroyed.

Another curse tablet compels the angry ghost to use his powers against not just the drivers but also the particular abilities of the horses, listed by name, who run for the Red and Blue factions.

Source: *Defixionum Tabellae* 237:[28] I invoke you, spirit of one untimely dead, whoever you are, by the mighty names SALBATHBAL AUTHGEROTABAL BASUTHATEO ALEO SAMMABETHOR. Bind the horses whose names and images/likeness on this implement I entrust to you; of the Red [team]: Silvanus, Servator, Lues, Zephyrus, Blandus, Imbraius, Dives, Mariscus, Rapidus, Oriens, Arbustus; of the Blues: Imminens, Dignus, Linon, Paezon, Chrysaspis, Argutus, Diresor, Frugiferus, Euphrates, Sanctus, Aethiops, Praeclarus . . . Bind their running, their power, their soul, their onrush, their speed. Take away their victory, entangle their feet, hinder them, hobble them, so that tomorrow morning in the hippodrome they are not able to run or walk about, or win, or go out of the starting gates, or advance either on the racecourse, or circle around the turning point; but may they fall with their drivers, Euprepes, son of Telesphoros, and Gentius and Felix, and Dionysius "the biter" and Lamuros. Bind their hands, take away their victory, their exit, their sight, so that they are unable to see their rival charioteers, but rather snatch them up from their chariots and twist them to the ground so that they alone fall, dragged along all over the hippodrome, especially at the turning points, with damage to their body, with the horses whom they drive. Now, quickly.

This use of curses to gain extracurricular advantages became a source of concern in the later empire, when the state sponsored a number of efforts to stop the deployment of magic for social and political purposes. Ammianus Marcellinus notes the indictment of a charioteer in 364 CE, who had had his son trained in magic, no doubt to serve the professional needs of the father.

Source: Ammianus Marcellinus 26.3.3:[29] Finally, after many punishments of the kind, a charioteer called Hilarinus was convicted on his own confession of having entrusted his son, who had barely reached the age of puberty, to a mixer of poisons to be instructed in certain secret practices forbidden by law, in order to use his help at home without other witnesses; he was condemned to death.

Figure 6.3 Lamp with acclaim of horse

The horses

Some horses also had outstanding careers, becoming celebrities alongside their drivers. Tuscus, for example, was a horse favored by Diocles, with whom he won 429 races, celebrated on the monument of Diocles for his tremendous abilities. This is paralleled in figural representations: one victorious horse is commemorated on a terracotta lamp dated to the first century, which depicts the lead horse, bedecked with a wreath, surrounded by celebrating fans. A placard above the horse's head would, in the original event, have displayed the name of the horse (figure 6.3). On the other hand, such resounding achievement also made horses targets for those employing curse tablets, as noted above.

One of the notorious popular stories about the "bad" emperor Caligula concerns "his" horse, Incitatus, being appointed senator. One should bear in mind that Incitatus was a successful circus horse; Caligula's enthusiasm is linked to his passion for racing.

Source: Suetonius, *Caligula* 55:[30] To prevent Incitatus, his favourite horse, from being disturbed [Caligula] always picketed the neighborhood with troops on the day before the races, ordering them to enforce absolute silence. Incitatus owned a marble stable, an ivory stall, purple blankets, and a jeweled collar; also a house, a team of slaves, and furniture – to provide suitable entertainment for guests whom Gaius invited in [the horse's] name. It is said that he even planned to award Incitatus a consulship.

Volucer ("Winged One"), who raced for the Greens, had a fan in the emperor Lucius Verus, who cherished the horse in material ways. The award of prize money to horses attributed to Verus' enthusiasm is an interesting point; who would hold this money in trust for the horse?

Source: Historia Augusta, *Verus* 6:[31] [Verus] had such great interest in the circus-games that he frequently both sent and received letters from his province concerning the games . . . he had a golden statue made of Volucer, a horse who ran for the Greens, which he used to carry around with him. Indeed, he used to put grapes and nuts in Volucer's manger instead of barley, and to order that he should be brought to him in the Palace of Tiberius covered in purple-dyed blankets. He made a tomb for him when he was dead, on the Vatican Hill. It was because of this horse that gold pieces and prizes first began to be demanded for horses.

Relatively few mares raced in the Roman *ludi*; the horses featured in inscriptions and in mosaic portraits almost all have male names, although some ancients thought that mares were a steady choice for the inside positions. Selection of horses for racing depended on development; a certain maturity was necessary to provide the weight and mass desired.

Source: Pliny, *Natural History* 8.162:[32] But a different build is required for the Circus, and consequently though horses may be broken as two-year-olds to other service, racing in the Circus does not claim them before five.

Certain areas of the empire were noted for the speed and strength of the race horses bred there, including Spain, Sicily, Thessaly and North Africa, although Juvenal points out that results mean more than bloodlines or origins, even for the stud-lines of the famous stallions Coryphaeus and Hirpinus.

Source: Juvenal, *Satires* 8.57–63:[33] The horse we most admire is the one that romps home a winner, cheered on by the seething roar of the crowd. Good breeding doesn't depend on a fancy pasturage; the thoroughbred earns his title by getting ahead of the field, by making them eat his dust. But lack of victories means that the auction-ring will claim him, even the one from the flock of Coryphaeus and the posterity of Hirpinus.

The elder Pliny recounts the unusual result of an accident at the races, in which the team of horses carried on without their driver and won the event. Note the tactics described here as typical for a successful team. Pliny attributes the victory to equine pride; we might see the benefits of intensive training.

Source: Pliny, *Natural History* 8.159–160:[34] Horses harnessed to chariots in the circus unquestionably show that they understand the shouts of encouragement and applause. At the races in the Circus, forming part of the Saecular Games of Claudius Caesar [in 47 CE], a charioteer of the Whites named Corax was thrown [out of his chariot] at the start; his team took the lead and kept it by getting in the way of their rivals and jostling them aside and doing everything against them that they would have had to do with a most skilful charioteer in control, and as they were ashamed for human science to be beaten by horses, when they had completed the proper course they stopped dead at the chalk [finish] line.

The colors

From the earliest documented days of chariot racing in Rome, there were four factions or teams in the circus: Red (*russata*), White (*albata*), Blue (*veneta*), and Green (*prasina*). Over time, the professional organizations of the circus would be simply referred to by color, instead of constantly using the formal "faction" designation. The origins of these organizations were not precisely known to authors of the imperial period, who nevertheless claimed cosmic or religious meaning as the inspiration for their formation. Tertullian sees in these connections superstition to be condemned by Christians like himself.

Source: Tertullian, *On the Spectacles* 9.5:[35] For at first there were only two colors: white and red. White was sacred to Winter because of the whiteness of its snow; red, to Summer because of the redness of its sun. But afterwards, when both love of pleasure and superstition had grown apace, some dedicated the red to Mars, others the white to the Zephyrs, the green to Mother Earth or Spring, the blue to Sky and Sea or Autumn.

These groups seem to have broken into pairs of rivals: Reds despised Whites and vice versa, while Blues and Greens went all out to destroy each other in competition. The intensity of this competition, both in the performers and in the fans, is noted as early as the first century BCE, when the fans of the Whites try to minimize the posthumous charisma of a Red driver, who was capable of inspiring self-sacrifice from one fan at least.

Source: Pliny, *Natural History* 7.53:[36] It is found in the *Acta*[37] that at the funeral of Felix the charioteer of the Reds, one of his fans threw himself upon the pyre – a pitiful story – and the opposing fans tried to prevent this score to the record of a professional by asserting that the man had fainted owing to the quantity of scents.

By the time of Augustus, *factiones* were the organizations in charge of the training, supply and maintenance of performers for the chariot races, roughly equivalent to the gladiatorial *ludi*. These *factiones* were run by *domini factionum*, equestrian-status (at least in the early days) entrepreneurs, who acted as liaisons with the sponsors of the games; politician *editores* could contract with the *domini* to rent the horses, charioteers and all necessary equipment and manpower for the circus events.

The great popularity of the chariot races in late Republic spectacle provoked a certain anxiety that equestrian suppliers of performers could hold such power over elite sponsors of circus *ludi*, a tension that is reflected in real-world conflicts with the *domini factionum*. Gnaeus Domitius Ahenobarbus, father of the future emperor Nero, as praetor was responsible for arranging games and may have tried to delay payment of financial prizes to the winners, as a means of controlling cash outlay, perhaps. (Presumably this prize payment was in addition to the contractual payment for the performance itself.) The faction leaders reacted against this effort by demanding that all future prizes be paid immediately, allowing no opportunity for hedging. Ahenobarbus' behavior as *editor* reflects badly on his honor as a leader and is used by Suetonius as an example of his general lack of integrity.

Source: Suetonius, *Nero* 5:[38] [Nero's father] was remarkably dishonest . . . while praetor, swindling victorious charioteers of their prize money . . . when the managers of the teams (*domini factionum*) complained he decreed that in future all prizes must be paid on the spot.

Nero's enthusiasm for chariot races led him to ratchet up the number of competitions in a given day; no doubt a large number of fans would be pleased to maximize the thrills of victory for each set of circus games. In doing so, however, the emperor raised the bar of financial expectations for the professionals. In future, instead of negotiating contracts for part of a day (at a lower cost), faction leaders were able to demand that they be hired for an entire day, minimum.

Source: Suetonius, *Nero* 22:[39] Horses had been Nero's main interest since childhood; despite all efforts to the contrary, his chatter about the chariot races at the Circus could not be stopped . . . [He] came up from the country to attend all the races, even minor ones, at first in secret and then without the least embarrassment . . . He frankly admitted that he wished the number of prizes increased, which meant that more contests were included and that they lasted until a late hour, and the faction managers no longer thought it worth while to bring out their teams except for a full day's racing.

Pliny the Younger doesn't like the circus races, personally, but touches on something important about them: fans had extreme loyalty to the different factions as colors, not as homes of specific drivers or horses. Pliny finds this mindless, confused by and contemptuous of partisanship that focuses on the color of a shirt rather than an interest in technique or in equine bloodlines.

Source: Pliny, *Letters* 9.6:[40] The races were on, a type of spectacle which has never had the slightest attraction for me, I can find nothing new or different in them: once seen is enough so it surprises me all the more that so many thousands of adult men should have such a childish passion for watching galloping horses and drivers standing in chariots, over and over again. If they were attracted by the speed of the horses or the drivers' skill, one could account for it, but in fact it is the racing-colors they really support and care about and if the colors were to be exchanged in mid-course during a race, they would transfer their favor and enthusiasm and rapidly desert the famous drivers and horses whose names they shout as they recognize them from afar. Such is the popularity and importance of a worthless shirt – I don't mean with the crowd, which is more worthless than the shirt, but with certain serious individuals. When I think how this futile, tedious, monotonous business can keep them sitting endlessly in their seats, I take pleasure in the fact that their pleasure is not mine.

By the time of the emperors, however, Blues and Greens were the most prestigious factions, preferred by emperor and populace alike. Indeed, Reds and Whites are only rarely mentioned in the surviving literature, although their continued activity is documented in inscriptions and in curse-tablets, which record the initiative of the professionals rather than just the fans focused on by literary sources. Martial notes that topics of conversation for his dinner party include Scorpus, one of the most successful drivers, and the

Green faction; Martial considers this "safe" discussion, at a time when the encouragement of informers made more overtly political talk dangerous.

> Source: Martial *Epigrams* 10.48:[41] When my guests are satisfied, I shall offer ripe fruit and leesless wine from a Nomentan flagon twice three years old in Frontinus' consulship. To boot there will be merriment free of malice, frank speech that gives no anxiety the morning after, nothing you would wish you hadn't said. Let my guest talk of Scorpus and the Green; let my cups get no man put on trial.

By the height of the circus frenzy in the late Roman period, the Reds and the Whites were overshadowed by the primary organizations of the Blues and Greens, although whether this means that there had been a formal merger of structure to streamline the factions is not entirely certain. Red and White drivers continued to compete in races and to win, but the majority of the best charioteers worked for the Blues and Greens, whose power enabled them to offer the most lucrative deal to good drivers.

During the late Roman empire in Constantinople, greater centralization meant that services like spectacles were funded by public money, at least in the major cities. Shifting economic resources, including the decline of a monetary economy in much of the empire, affected the sustainability of games especially in smaller urban centers. Funding for games was likely to be deprioritized at a time when the payment of taxes stretched a community's resources beyond what it could bear. Fewer centers were able to support festivals, so there was a certain amount of consolidation of games in the later empire. The organization of performances likewise was centralized; by the end of the fifth century, the circus faction had been expanded to become a sort of super-guild, responsible for all kinds of spectacle performance. The imperial bureaucracy expanded to oversee housing, food, training, and salaries of the performers, although a staff of specialists continued to provide more professional services for the organizations.

Circus fans

By the fifth century, there had been a parallel consolidation of fans into what is often called "factions," but which should be distinguished from the *factiones*, the professional organizations of performers. Fan clubs were essentially private groups with a public presence, one of the remaining means of crafting social identity in a world of diminishing traditional affiliations. These fan clubs wore the blue and green colors of their favorites when they attended spectacles, thus providing a highly visible marker of their group identity. They sat in reserved sections where their close proximity made it easier for them to engage in one of the activities in which they excelled:

their group chants. Long practice in operating as a claque enabled the fan clubs to not only express their enthusiastic support for their faction, but also vigorously sneer, *en masse*, at the opponents. They could also articulate issues of public concern, as had been true for the audience claques of the earlier empire. They could chant for relief in times of grain shortage, for easing of taxes, and for enhancements of the spectacle.

Dio Cassius offers an eye-witness account of circus claque activity in 196 CE, during a period of ramped-up competition between a number of rivals for the purple.

Source: Dio Cassius 75.4.2–7:[42] The populace, however, could not restrain itself . . . There had assembled, as I said, an untold multitude and they had watched the chariots racing, six at a time . . . without applauding, as was their custom, any of the contestants at all. But when these races were over and the charioteers were about to begin another event, they first enjoined silence upon one another and then suddenly all clapped their hands at the same moment and also joined in a shout, praying for good fortune for the public welfare. This was what they first cried out; then, applying the terms "Queen" and "Immortal" to Rome, they shouted: "How long are we to suffer such things?" and "How long are we to be waging war?" And after making some other remarks of this kind, they finally shouted "So much for that" . . . in all this they were surely moved by some divine inspiration . . . This demonstration was one thing that increased our apprehensions still more.

Fan clubs had a formal role to play as recognized groups in the late Roman city. The "official" duties of the fan clubs, or at least the designated representatives of the partisans, included the ceremonial welcome and acclamation of newly inaugurated emperors and empresses. Theophylact disapprovingly describes the coronation of Phocas and Leontia in 602 and notes the dispute that rose between Blues and Greens over who would stand where to perform the formal acclamation.

Source: Theophylact Simocatta, *History* 8.10.9–10:[43] Since it is customary for emperors to proclaim their consorts with processions as well, the tyrant [Phocas] openly honored the custom and decided to lead the queen Leontia in triumph. On this day then, there was a conflict between the factions about their station, since they contested the arrangement of places: for the Greens wanted to take up station in the Ampelion, as it is called (this is a forecourt of the emperor's dwelling), and to serenade the queen with the customary applause, but the Blue faction objected, for they regarded this as contrary to custom . . . very great commotion arose.

The distinctive passion of the circus fan was something that was noted in the early empire and even before the imperial monarchy: the example of the fan responding with suicide to the death of a driver comes to mind (see above). Particularly disturbing to a number of authors is the fact that this passion was aroused by "nothing," by a color or a race, rather than a "real" problem that might merit such depth of feeling. Dio Chrysostom, in the late first century, articulates this as an issue of social status.

Source: Dio Chrysostom, *Discourse* 32.75:[44] Why are you so violently disturbed? What the contest? For it is not . . . a question of a kingship or a wife or a death that hangs in the balance, nay, it is only a contest of slaves for a paltry bit of silver, slaves who sometimes are defeated and sometimes victorious, but slaves in any case.

Philostratus' biography of the first-century CE philosopher and ascetic Apollonius includes snapshots of civic events in the Roman provinces, laying a moral overtone on such regular events as circus racing and the intense enthusiasm of the audience. Here, fandom from the early empire is described as the catalyst for civic violence; Apollonius' reaction to such situations emphasizes the waste and frivolity of such partisanship, in comparison to tensions generated by real problems, such as famine or even human competition.

Source: Philostratus, *Life of Apollonius of Tyana* 1.15:[45] Whenever, however, he came on a city engaged in civil conflict (and many were divided into factions over spectacles of a low kind), he would advance and show himself, and . . . would put an end to all the disorder . . . Well, it is not so very difficult to restrain those who have started a quarrel about dances and horses, for those who are rioting about such matters, if they chance with their eyes on a real man, blush and check themselves and easily recover their senses; but a city hard pressed by famine is not so tractable.

Source: Philostratus, *Life of Apollonius of Tyana* 5.26:[46] But because the Alexandrians are devoted to horses, and flock into the racecourse to see the spectacle, and murder one another in their partisanship, he therefore administered a grave rebuke to them . . . " . . . it were quite excusable if one should show an excess of zeal in the rivalry of human beings like himself. But here I see you rushing at one another with drawn swords, and ready to hurl stones, all over a horse race."

Emperors as fans

As seen with other kinds of spectacle, the emperor was ideally supposed to demonstrate a certain balance, to avoid abusing his overweening power on inappropriate targets and causes. The "good" emperors practiced moderation in the enthusiasm for spectacle in general, and the circus events prove no exception to this. Caligula, here as elsewhere, is a negative model for imperial behavior. His fervor leads him to abandon the palace for quarters unfit for his rank and to the use of extreme measures to ensure Green victory.

Source: Suetonius, *Caligula* 55:[47] He supported the Green faction with such ardour that he would often dine and spend the night in their stables and, on one occasion, gave the driver Eutychus presents worth 20,000 gold pieces.

Source: Dio Cassius 59.14:[48] Yet after doing all this he later put the best and most famous of these out of the way by poison. He did the same also with the horses and charioteers of the rival factions; for he was strongly attached to the faction that wore frog-green and from this color was also called the faction of the Leek. Thus even today the place where he used to practice driving chariots is called the Gaianum after him.

Caracalla also was said to have fed his partisanship with murder.

Source: Dio Cassius 78.1:[49] Caracalla put out of the way a man who was renowned for no other reason than for his profession, which made him very conspicuous ... [Caracalla] killed [Euprepes the charioteer] because he supported the faction opposite the one he himself favored. So Euprepes was put to death in his old age, after having been crowned in a vast number of horse-races; for he had won seven hundred and eighty-two crowns, a record equaled by no one else.

Fan clubs and unrest

Consolidation of the organizations of performers in the fifth century may have allowed for more formal relationships between performers and recognizable groups of fans, who now directed their loyalties toward a single faction, rather than a range of performers in different events.

Ammianus Marcellinus' condemnation of the circus crowd emphasizes the parasite role played by the idle poor in the fourth century, whose values have deteriorated to encompass solely their sources of immediate physical pleasure. He makes explicit the nostalgic view that the games, for them, are the equivalent of temple, home, political meeting, and state, all targets of Roman loyalty in a more virtuous time.

> Source: Ammianus Marcellinus 28.4.28–31:[50] Let us now turn to the idle and slothful commons . . . These spend all their life with wine and dice, in low haunts, pleasures, and the games. Their temple, their dwelling, their assembly, and the height of all their hopes is the Circus Maximus. You may see many groups of them gathered in the *fora*, the cross-roads, the streets, and their other meeting-places, engaged in quarrelsome arguments with one another, some (as usual) defending this, others that. Among them those who have enjoyed a surfeit of life, influential through long experiences, often swear by their hoary hair and wrinkles that the state cannot exist if in the coming race the charioteer whom each favors is not first to rush forth from the barriers, and fails to round the turning-point closely with his ill-omened horses. And when there is such a dry rot of thoughtlessness, as soon as the longed-for day of the chariot-races begins to dawn, before the sun is yet shining clearly they all hasten in crowds to the spot at top speed, as if they would outstrip the very chariots that are to take part in the contest; and torn by their conflicting hopes about the result of the race, the greater number of them in their anxiety pass sleepless nights.

Ammianus does not emphasize the danger of mayhem represented by the circus mob in Rome, and there may have been a genuine difference between the western and eastern empire at this time. It's in the east, with its larger cities, its greater concentration of wealth, and the retention of the imperial machinery that we find more active and regular threat generated by the fan clubs. Uncontrolled partisanship generated riots that put the general safety at risk. The fact that social identities were more compressed may also have ramped up the intensity of the connection generated by fan clubs, a factor in the phenomenon of circus riots.

Procopius' contemporary description of the fans' activities in early sixth-century Byzantium highlights the criminality that he suggests is an outgrowth of the indulgence inherent in spectatorship. He also emphasizes imperial corruption at the core of the problem, the cynical manipulation of such groups by the emperor Justinian to create chaos and thus, allegedly, to enhance his own power. Justinian is a target of Procopius' hostility throughout the narrative.

> Source: Procopius, *Secret History* 7.1:[51] The people had for a long time previous been divided . . . into two factions, the Blues and the Greens. Justinian, by joining the former, which had already shown favor to him, was able to bring everything into confusion and turmoil, and by its power to sink the Roman state to its knees before him.

Procopius finds the visible benefits of the Blues' association with the emperor evidence of corruption.

> Source: Procopius, *Secret History* 7.41:[52] Justinian's crime was that he was not only unwilling to protect the injured, but saw no reason why he should not be the open head of the guilty faction [of the Blues]; he gave great sums of money to these young men, and surrounded himself with them: and some he even went so far as to appoint to high office and other posts of honor.

Extreme fans tended to be young men, who, in the earlier empire, might have belonged to associations focused on athletics or the support of particular kinds of performances, including gladiatorial combats and *venationes* (see chapter 3). Procopius acknowledges that only a small and intense minority of the fans formally affiliated with the partisan clubs, to help organize their activities, especially those which were not confined to the arena.

> Source: Procopius, *Secret History* 7:[53] . . . Collecting in gangs as soon as dusk fell, [the Blues] robbed their betters in the open Forum and in the narrow alleys . . . Some they killed after robbing them, so they could not inform anyone of the assault. These outrages brought the enmity of everybody on them, especially that of the Blue partisans who had not taken active part in the discord. . . . the evil progressed; and as no punishment came to the criminals from those in charge of the public peace, their boldness increased more and more.

The Nika revolt

Eventually, the partisan mayhem Procopius describes evolved into a full-scale revolt in 532, one with political weight and likely political causes at heart: this revolt was not about the color of a shirt. Justinian had been sole emperor in Constantinople since the death of his father Justin in 527. There had been an ongoing war with Persia, and in 532 Justinian succeeded in forcing the new Persian king to a negotiated truce to fix the eastern boundaries so Justinian could devote imperial resources to regaining control in the west. Justinian's extensive reform program had had the effect of strengthening the power of the Praetorian Praefect, John the Cappadocian, who was the agent responsible for the enactment of administrative changes. John had been particularly good at maximizing imperial revenues, which proved extremely useful for Justinian's military, diplomatic, and construction needs. John's capacity to accrue personal profit while performing his duties did not make him popular with a number of people. Especially annoyed were wealthy landowners and local officials, who suffered the loss of elite privileges, while being compelled to pay additional taxes and submit to intensified scrutiny of municipal and military accounts. The instability caused by the Nika rebellion would force Justinian to replace John with Phocas, whose sympathy for elite interests was meant to ease tension between the throne and the privileged classes, for the time being at least.

Urban disruption by the more intense, typically young, members of fan clubs had become a standard feature of life in the late Roman world. Once Justinian was solidly established as emperor, however, he attempted to crack down on fan club lawlessness. His intent to follow through on the botched hanging of a Blue and a Green drove rabid fans of both factions to join forces to force the compliance of the emperor. "Nika" or "victory," a word typically screamed by partisans in the circus stands, became their slogan and gave the revolt its name. On January 13, 532, Nika rebels attacked public buildings in Constantinople, damaging such symbols of imperial power as the vestibule of the Palace and Hagia Sophia, the Church of Holy Wisdom. Efforts to distract the rioters with chariot races the next day failed: rebels set fire to the Hippodrome itself. By now the numbers of rebels were being increased with disgruntled opponents to Justinian's reforms, such as displaced small farmers, driven off their lands by increased taxation; the rebels demanded that key agents in Justinian's administration be ousted from their position, then demanded the replacement of the emperor himself, elevating the nephew of Anastasius, the former emperor. Justinian wanted to cut his losses and run. The empress Theodora stood firm. Theodora had allegedly come from the circus herself, daughter of a *bestiarius* who grew up to perform risqué dances that attracted the eye of the emperor. She sneered at the rioting circus fans and recommended vigorous strategy to reclaim power. Justinian drove a wedge between the factions, bribed key players, launched a ruthless counter-assault on the crowd in the Hippodrome and rounded up ringleaders in the wake of the massacre.

Source: Procopius, *The Persian War* 1.24:[54] At this same time [January 1, 532] an insurrection broke out unexpectedly in Byzantium among the populace, and, contrary to expectation, it proved to be a very serious affair . . . In every city the population has been divided for a long time past into the Blue and the Green factions; but within comparatively recent times it has come about that, for the sake of these names and the seats which the rival factions occupy in watching the games, they spend their money and abandon their bodies to the most cruel tortures and even do not think it unworthy to die a most shameful death. And they fight against their opponents knowing not for what purpose they put themselves in danger, but knowing well that, even if they overcame their enemy in the fight, the conclusion of the matter for them will be to be carried off immediately to the prison and finally, after suffering extreme torture, to be killed. So there grows up in them against their fellow men a hostility which has no cause, and at no time does it stop or disappear, for it yields neither to the ties of marriage nor of kinship nor of friendship . . . they care neither for things divine nor human in comparison with conquering in these struggles . . . I, for my part, am unable to call this anything except a disease of the soul . . . At this time the officers of the city administration in Byzantium were leading away to death some of the rioters. But the members of the two factions, conspiring together and declaring a truce with each other, seized the prisoners and then entered the prison and released all those who were in confinement there . . . fire was applied to the city as if it had fallen under the hand of an enemy . . . During this time the emperor and his consort and a few members of the senate shut themselves up in the palace and remained quietly there. Now the watchword which the populace passed around to one another was Nika . . . Now as long as the people were waging this war with each other in behalf of the names of the colors, no attention was paid to the offenses of [the corrupt John of Cappadocia, praetorian praefect at the time, and Tribunianus, a greedy quaestor] against the constitution; but when the factions came to a mutual understanding . . . then openly throughout the whole city they began to abuse the two and went about seeking them to kill. Accordingly the emperor, wishing to win the people to his side, instantly dismissed both these men from office [but his appointment of honest men has no impact] . . . the whole population ran to [Hypatius and Pompeius, nephews of the former emperor Anastasius] and they declared Hypatius emperor and prepared to lead him to the forum to assume the power . . . they proclaimed him Emperor of the Romans . . . now the emperor and his court were deliberating as to whether it would be better for them if they stayed or if they took to flight in ships . . . the empress Theodora also spoke to the following effect: ". . . My opinion is that the present time, more than any other, is not the time for flight, even though it brings safety . . . consider whether it will not turn out that after you have been saved, you would gladly trade that safety for death. As for myself, I approve a certain ancient saying that the purple makes a good burial shroud." When the queen had spoken thus, all were filled with boldness and turned their thoughts toward resistance . . . [loyal generals Belisarius and Mundus try to attack Hypatius in the emperor's box in the circus] But since the soldiers had decided to support neither side, until one of them should be manifestly victorious, they pretended not to hear at all . . . Belisarius returned to the emperor and declared that the day was lost for them, for the soldiers who guarded the palace were rebelling against him . . .

Concluding that he [Belisarius] must go against the populace who had taken their stand in the hippodrome – a vast multitude crowding each other in great disorder – he drew his sword from his sheath and, commanding the others to do likewise, with a shout he advanced upon them at a run . . . Mundus, who was standing not far away . . . when he observed that Belisarius was in the struggle, he immediately made a sally into the hippodrome through the entrance which they call the Gate of Death. From both sides the partisans of Hypatius were attacked and destroyed . . . There perished among the populace that day more than thirty thousand. But the emperor commanded that [Hypatius and Pompeius] be kept in close confinement. Then, while Pompeius was weeping . . . Hypatius reproached him at length and said that those who were about to die unjustly should not lament. For in the beginning they had been forced by the people against their will, and afterwards they had come to the hippodrome with no thought of harming the emperor. And the soldiers killed both of them on the following day . . . the emperor confiscated all their property for the public treasury and also that of all the other members of the senate who had sided with them . . . this was the end of the insurrection in Byzantium.

Water Shows

In an effort to maximize the variety and extravagance of spectacle in the late Republic, Roman sponsors began to make use of water as an innovative medium for events, enhancing both the beauty of water as it cascades or sprays over performers and audience, as well as the capacity for danger as humans negotiate a potentially hostile environment. Spectacle held on water falls into two major categories: mock naval battles or reenactments and what one might call "aquacades" or water ballets, in which narratives, often using mythic themes, are acted out by performers in damp, clinging costumes, with a certain amount of sexual content.

Julius Caesar, in this as in all other spectacle, was notorious for the inventiveness of venue and the sheer scale of his displays. Having built a special *naumachia* facility (see chapter two), the dictator presented a sea battle alongside a variety of events with a military flavor.

Source: Appian, *Civil Wars* 2.102:[55] [Caesar] gave also various spectacles with horses and music, a combat of foot-soldiers, 1,000 on each side, and a cavalry fight of 200 on each side. There was also another combat of horse and foot combined. There was a combat of elephants, twenty against twenty, and a naval engagement of 4,000 oarsmen, where 1,000 fighting men contended on each side.

Domitian's *naumachia* fits the Caesarian model, and for a specific purpose: Domitian's military achievements were contested in antiquity, with allegations that triumphs were claimed for negotiated truces or even for fictional battles. Domitian's militarized spectacle, however, emphasized the martial mindset of the emperor *editor*, more so than might have been the case had he simply presented the more usual races or *munera*. This plan backfired when the emperor refused to yield to an act of nature, requiring that he hold additional public events to make up for the debacle.

Source: Dio Cassius 67.8:[56] In the course of holding what purported to be triumphal celebrations, [Domitian] arranged numerous contests. In the Circus, for example, he exhibited battles of infantry against infantry and again battles between cavalry, and in a new place he produced a naval battle. At this last event practically all the combatants and many of the spectators as well perished. For, though a heavy rain and violent storm came up suddenly, he nevertheless permitted no one to leave the spectacle; and though he himself changed his clothing to thick woolen cloaks, he would not allow the others to change their attire, so that not a few fell sick and died. By way, no doubt, of consoling the people for this, he provided for them at public expense a dinner lasting all night.

One of the largest *naumachia* spectacles was that presented at the Fucine Lake by Claudius. As one of his many public works projects, Claudius had ordered the draining of the lake, a land reclamation effort designed for public benefit. He combined celebrating the completion of the drain facilities with a grand naval battle, presented at nearly full-scale, using both real military and condemned criminals as participants. Seating was set up for the spectators on the hilly terrain surrounding the lake.

Source: Tacitus, *Annals* 12.56:[57] Nearly at this date, the tunnelling of the mountain between Lake Fucinus and the river Liris had been achieved; and, in order that the impressive character of the work might be viewed by a larger number of the visitants, a naval battle was arranged upon the lake itself . . . Claudius equipped triremes, quadriremes, and nineteen thousand combatants: the lists he surrounded with rafts, so as to leave no unauthorized points of escape, but reserved space enough in the center to display the vigor of the rowing, the arts of the helmsman, the impetus of the galleys, and the usual incidents of an engagement. On the rafts were stationed companies and squadrons of the praetorian cohorts, covered by a breastwork from which to operate their catapults and ballistae: the rest of the lake was occupied by marines with decked vessels. The shores, the hills, the mountain-crests, formed a kind of theater, soon filled by an untold multitude, attracted from the neighboring towns, and in part from the capital itself, by curiosity or by respect for the sovereign. He and Agrippina presided, the one in a gorgeous military cloak, the other – not far distant – in a Greek mantle of cloth of gold. The battle, though one of criminals, was contested with the spirit and courage of freemen; and, after much blood had flowed, the combatants were exempted from destruction.

Caligula is depicted by Dio Cassius as an emperor whose inappropriate enthusiasms lead him to test boundaries, indulging capricious whimsy in governing Rome and involving the emperor too much in the presentation of spectacle. Here, he conflates the realms of sea and land in a lavish engineering feat in which the Mediterranean was converted to an arena and the emperor starred in his own water show. The capacity to mount an extraordinary show is explicitly compared to military conquest; Caligula's references to Alexander the Great play on this as well, suggesting that Caligula's achievement in making the world his showcase is fully equal to Alexander's conquest of the world.

Source: Dio Cassius 59.17:[58] [Gaius rejected the "normal" kind of triumph], as he did not consider it any great achievement to drive a chariot on dry land; on the other hand, he was eager to drive his chariot through the sea, as it were, by bridging the waters between Puteoli and Baiuli. [he makes arrangements for a pontoon-style bridge to be constructed across the Bay of Naples, using what boats were available, with added features such as rest areas and running water available for his use] . . . when all was ready, he put on the breastplate of Alexander, or so he claimed it was, and over it a purple silk *chlamys*, adorned with much gold and many precious stones from India; moreover he donned a sword, took a shield, and put on a garland of oak leaves. Then he offered sacrifice to Neptune and some other gods and to Envy, in order, as he put it, that no jealousy should attend him, and entered the bridge from the end at Baiuli, taking with him a multitude of armed horsemen and foot-soldiers, and he dashed fiercely into Puteoli as if he were in pursuit of an enemy . . . then [the next day] wearing a gold-embroidered tunic, he returned in a chariot over the same bridge, being drawn by race-horses accustomed to win the most victories. A long train of what purported to be spoils followed him, including Darius, a member of the Arsacid family, who was one of the Parthians then living in Rome as hostages. His friends and associates in flowered robes followed in vehicles and then came the army and the rest of the throng, each man dressed according to his individual taste . . . after so magnificent a victory[59] he had to deliver a harangue; so he ascended a platform which had been erected on the ships near the center of the bridge. First he extolled himself as an undertaker of great enterprises, and then he praised the soldiers as men who had undergone great hardships and perils, mentioning in particular this achievement of theirs in crossing the sea on foot . . . since the place was crescent-shaped, fires were lighted on all sides, as in a theater, so that the darkness was not noticed at all; indeed it was his wish to make the night day, as he had made the sea land.

Nero's aquacade was a combination of different events; both banquet and water pageant, the show was presented with the intent of winning favor by sharing the luxury of the emperor's private life with the people of Rome. It's unclear that the emperor actually distributed food to the populace outside the invited guests, but the fact that the water spectacle took place in a public space enabled the people to vicariously enjoy the emperor's pleasures. Tacitus' disapproval rests on the excess involved, as well as the too-nuanced provisions for carnal fulfillment. Nero here, as elsewhere, is depicted as a violator of status, making private behavior public and degrading the dignity of high rank.

Source: Tacitus, *Annals* 15.37:[60] Nero himself now tried to make it appear that Rome was his favorite abode. He gave feasts in public places as if the whole city were his own home. But the most prodigal and notorious banquet was given by Tigellinus. To avoid repetitious accounts of extravagance, I shall describe it, as a model of its kind. The entertainment took place on a raft constructed on Marcus Agrippa's lake.[61] It was towed about by other vessels, with gold and ivory fittings. Their rowers were degenerates, assorted according to age and vice. Tigellinus had also collected birds and animals from remote countries, and even the products of the ocean. On the quays were brothels stocked with high-ranking ladies. Opposite them could be seen naked prostitutes, indecently posturing and gesturing. At nightfall the woods and houses nearby echoed with singing and blazed with lights.

Water events were a part of Titus' shows arranged to inaugurate the Flavian Amphitheater in 80 CE. Martial's description suggests that these included a range of displays, from synchronized swimming by women in water nymph costumes, to mythicized combats between performers dressed as divinities, to lavish naval combats, likewise given a supernatural tone. As with the other spectacle poems, Martial here emphasizes that Titus' achievement outstrips those of earlier emperors, both virtuous and excessive ones.

Source: Martial, *Spectacles* 30:[62] The well-trained bevy of Nereids sported all over the surface and in various conformations decorated the yielding waters. The trident menaced with upright tooth, the anchor with curved. We thought we saw an oar, we thought we saw a boat, and the Laconians' star shining, welcome to the seamen, and broad sails bellying in conspicuous folds. Who invented such devices in the clear water? Thetis either taught these games or learned them.

Source: Martial, *Spectacles* 34:[63] It had been Augustus' labor to pit fleets against each other here and rouse the waters with naval clarion. How small a part is this of our Caesar! Thetis and Galatea saw in the waves beasts they never knew. Triton saw chariots in hot career in the sea's dust and thought his master's horses had passed by. As Nereus prepared fierce battle for ferocious ships, he was startled to find himself walking on foot in the liquid expanse. Whatever is viewed in the Circus and the Amphitheater, that, Caesar, the wealth of your water has afforded you. So no more Fucinus and the lake of direful Nero; let this be the only sea fight known to posterity.

Timeline of Roman History

753 BCE	Legendary foundation of Rome by Romulus, its first king. Story of Rape of Sabine women located at site of Circus Maximus.
	Succeeded by series of kings of doubtful historicity.
616 to 510 BCE	So-called "Etruscan" monarchy in Rome, including the reign of Tarquinius Priscus, remembered in Rome as major developer of urban infrastructure, and Tarquinius Superbus, much-maligned tyrant and last of Rome's kings.
	First formal structure for Circus Maximus.
	Alleged introduction of some kind of gladiatorial combat.
509 BCE	Establishment of Republican form of government, with policy-shaping capacity distributed between the Senate and a number of executive magistrates elected from among them. Popular will is registered through elections and up or down votes on legislation and major issues, but the senatorial wealthy maintain the institutionalized power to dominate voting.
390 BCE	Celtic tribes sack Rome.
366 BCE	*Ludi Romani* become first set of "ordinary" games.
343 to 290 BCE	Rome fights three wars against the Samnites. Expansion of Roman influence outside Latium in central Italy.
280 to 275 BCE	War against Tarentum and Pyrrhus, mercenary/adventurer king of Epirus. With victory, Rome dominates Italian peninsula.
264 to 241 BCE	First Punic war against Carthage.
	Sicily comes under Roman influence.
264 BCE	First *munera* in Rome presented by D. Junius Brutus.
252 BCE	Elephants appear in triumph of L. Caecilius Metellus.
218 to 201 BCE	Second Punic war (Hannibalic war).
	Rome becomes pre-eminent power in western Mediterranean.

216 BCE	Second *munera* in Rome held for M. Aemilius Lepidus.
213 BCE	Scipio Africanus presents impressive *Ludi Romani*.
206 BCE	Scipio Africanus holds *munera* and chariot races in Spain; funeral games for family members thus serve to commemorate his own success in returning area to Roman control.
211 to 133 BCE	Major Roman military involvement in Greek East. Spread of Roman political control through much of the Mediterranean.
	Expansion of opportunities for power afforded by this expansionism leads to heightened competition among the ruling class; presentation of elaborate games becomes a tool for persuading a broader constituency.
194 BCE	Segregation of senatorial class to "best" seats at *Ludi Romani*.
168 BCE	Aemilius Paullus defeats Perseus, King of Macedonia, at Battle of Pydna. Triumphal monuments and celebrations service the building of Rome's (and Paullus') image in the east.
166 BCE	Celebration of victory by Antiochus IV Epiphanes, King of Syria, takes on Roman cast with incorporation of gladiatorial events.
146 BCE	Destruction of Corinth and of Carthage by Rome.
133 to 50s BCE	Increasing political interest among different groups in the larger Roman state spurs tension over broader distribution of power; resistance by conservative Senators generates periodic political violence and outbreaks of civil war. Spectacle is normalized as a political tool and standard feature of competing for and holding public office.
91 to 88 BCE	Italian War, fueled by discontent among Italian allies over differential access to power and benefits of empire.
81 to 79 BCE	Dictatorship of Sulla, established by military coup.
73 to 71 BCE	Spartacus spearheads revolt of slaves and others, catalyzed by grievances of gladiators but drawing on sociopolitical tensions of late Republic.
70 BCE	Stone amphitheater built at Pompeii by veterans of Italian war.
65 BCE	Julius Caesar organizes lavish games as aedile; the Senate places legal limits on how many gladiators can be kept within city limits.
63 BCE	M. Tullius Cicero sponsors Lex Tullia to prohibit presentation of *munera* during campaign for public office.
57 BCE	P. Clodius Pulcher uses troupe of gladiators as "muscle" in inciting riot over specific legislation, expanding the political usefulness of *munera* beyond the venue of spectacles.

55 BCE	Pompey the Great celebrates the dedication of his theater with huge spectacle; the exuberant suffering of elephants provokes disapproval of audience.
52 BCE	G. Scribonius Curio gives elaborate funeral games for his father, some of which are housed in a mechanized double theater or "amphitheater."
49–44 BCE	Dictatorship of Julius Caesar, which ends with his assassination. Caesar's consolidation of influence provides an instructive model for political successors, as the Senate never regains dominant authority over Roman state. Caesar's popular building program and spectacle organization also set a standard for emperors. Monumentalization of Circus Maximus, provision of more elaborate venues for *munera, naumachia*, and other events.
43 to 31 BCE	Rule of the Second Triumvirate: M. Antonius, G. Julius Caesar Octavianus, and M. Aemilius Lepidus are formally granted extraordinary powers for the duration of civil strife.
42 BCE	Rome's aediles substitute gladiatorial combats for the usual chariot races at the *Cerealia* festival: this is the first appearance of *munera* in the "ordinary" games.
31 BCE	Antony and Cleopatra defeated at the Battle of Actium. Octavian is the sole remaining political competititor; consolidation of his peacetime authority begins, with an official conferral of powers along with the title of "Augustus" in 29 BCE.

Julio-Claudian Dynasty: 29 BCE to 68 CE

29 BCE to 14 CE	Reign of Augustus. Augustus establishes the *munus legitimum*, the pattern for presentation of gladiatorial combats, *venationes* and executions. Institutionalizes emperor's control of extraordinary spectacle, as part of his elimination of competition for political power among the elite. The Lex Julia Theatralis reasserts the legal mandate for hierarchical seating at spectacle, with sections reserved for the elite placed closer to the action. Imperial cult in the west to incorporate spectacle as ritual of loyalty.
27 BCE	First stone amphitheater in the city of Rome built by Statilius Taurus.
14 to 37 CE	Reign of Tiberius.
19 CE	Senatorial decree is passed to renew limits placed on appearance of elites as performers in the arena.

27 CE	Disastrous collapse of temporary arena at Fidenae.
Circa 30 CE	Death of Jesus of Nazareth.
37 to 41 CE	Reign of Gaius (Caligula).
41 to 54 CE	Reign of Claudius.
	Quaestors are designated the magistrates responsible for presenting the December *munera*.
	Naval battles staged on the Fucine Lake celebrate the emperor's organizational skills, in putting together huge spectacle and in sponsoring the planned drainage project.
54 to 68 CE	Reign of Nero.
59 CE	Riot involving fights among spectators in stands of Pompeii's amphitheater provokes the passage of a ten-year senatorial ban on local *munera*.
64 CE	Great Fire of Rome; search for targets to blame for conflagration focuses on the Christian cult, leading to the first state-sponsored persecution and the criminalization of Christianity.
69 CE	"Year of Four Emperors": Galba, Otho, Vitellius, and Vespasian.

Flavian Dynasty: 69 to 96 CE

67 to 74 CE	Judaean war; effort to suppress rebellion commanded first by Vespasian and then by Titus. Titus' series of victory celebrations in area feature prisoners of war as targets of spectacle ferocity and demonstrations of imperial retribution.
79 CE	Eruption at Vesuvius preserves broad range of evidence about life in Roman town, including particulars of spectacle presentation.
80 CE	Flavian Amphitheater (Colosseum) dedicated by the emperor Titus with extremely elaborate games; construction of this largest of amphitheaters is a signature piece for the dynasty.

"The Good Emperors": 96 to 180 CE

107 CE	Emperor Trajan gives greatest set of imperial games: 123 days of spectacle to celebrate victory over the Dacians.
Circa 110 CE	Rescript of Trajan establishes formal procedure for dealing with accused Christians.
	Martyrdom of Ignatius, Bishop of Antioch, around this time.
150s	Martyrdom of Polycarp, Bishop of Smyrna.

177 CE	Emperor Marcus Aurelius sponsors legislation to control prices of gladiators, designed to ensure that spectacle can continue throughout the empire.
	Persecution and death of the Martyrs of Lyons.
180 to 192 CE	Reign of Commodus.
192 CE	Provocative imperial games held by Commodus feature the emperor himself as a performer.

Severan Emperors: 193 to 235 CE

193 to 211 CE	Reign of Septimius Severus.
	Competing claims to imperial power until 197 inspire unrest among crowds at the Circus Maximus.
202 CE	Martyrdom of Perpetua.
211 to 217 CE	Reign of Caracalla.
213 CE	Caracalla extends citizenship to all free residents of the empire.
218 to 222 CE	Reign of Elagabalus.

The Third-century Mess

235 to 284 CE	Serious economic and political instability of the empire, marked by external pressure and repeated episodes of civil war. Series of usurpers, regional and militarized claimants hold imperial power on brief and insecure basis.
249 to 251 CE	Emperor Decius authorizes first empire-wide persecution of Christians as part of an effort to enlist Graeco-Roman pantheon to heal devastation of the third century.
259 CE	Martyrdom of Fructuosus, Bishop of Tarragona.

The Late Empire

| 284 to 305 CE | Reign of Diocletian, sharing imperial power with colleague Maximian (286 to 305) and junior colleagues Galerius and Constantius Chlorus (293 to 305). Administrative division of empire paves the way for later permanent separation between east and west. Extraordinary efforts to extend imperial oversight into especially the economic life of the Roman world, to regain order and control after the chaos of much of the third century. Diocletian's planned retirement, undertaken to ensure orderly transfer of imperial powers, fails to ward off renewed civil war over succession. |
| 303 to 311 CE | "Great Persecution" of Christians. |

312 CE	Constantine defeats rival Maxentius at Battle of Milvian Bridge, thus becoming major holder of western imperial power during period of contested rule following retirement of Diocletian.
313 CE	Edict of Milan legalizes Christianity.
323 to 337 CE	Reign of Constantine alone over entire empire.
330 CE	Capital of imperial administration transferred to Constantinople; continuing deterioration in status and resources for city of Rome and western empire in general will make it impossible to resist the later invasions, leading eventually to western separation into tribal kingdoms. Eastern empire sees ongoing elaboration of imperial bureaucracy, which will include the consolidation of all spectacle production and performance under the umbrella organization of the factions of circus professionals.
378 CE	Defeat of Emperor Valens at Adrianople by Ostrogoths and Visigoths opens floodgates for invasions of western empire by increasing multitudes of tribal groups.
378 to 395 CE	Reign of Theodosius.
391 CE	Theodosius fatally undermines polytheistic practices by cutting off public financing and official recognition.
395 CE	Empire permanently divided east and west when Theodosius' will splits realm between his juvenile heirs, Honorius (west) and Arcadius (east).
410 CE	Visigoths sack Rome, the first time that the city has been ravished by foreign invaders since 390 BCE.
455 CE	Vandals sack Rome.
476 CE	Romulus Augustulus, last western claimant to title of "emperor," is ousted by Odoacer; Italy will become an Ostrogothic kingdom.
493 CE	Theoderic establishes himself as King of Italy; having been educated in Constantinople, he deploys symbols and ceremony of imperial Rome, including circus races observed by court official Cassiodorus.
Circa 500 CE	Clovis, King of the Franks, converts to Catholic Christianity and uses this connection to imperial norms in his consolidation of an expanded realm.
527 to 565 CE	Reign of Justinian in eastern empire.
529–533 CE	Publication of the *Code*, the *Institutes* and the *Digest*, compilations of Roman law and commentary done under the auspices of Justinian.
532 CE	Circus fans catalyze Nika revolt, an outburst against alleged corruption and favoritism in Justinian's administration. The destruction caused by the rebellion provides an

opportunity for Justinian to sponsor a large-scale building program in Constantinople. Justinian's efforts to reclaim the entire Mediterranean basin as the seat of the Roman Empire also begin within a year of recovery after the Nika revolt.

Glossary of Terms and Names

aedile Lower magistracy. Responsible for infrastructures, such as public buildings, utilities, streets, and eventually ordinary festivals of religious calendar.

amphitheatrum Latin word derived from the Greek for "theater on both sides." Used for a building type developed by Rome: an elliptical arena with seating (typically) on all sides of the performance area; lower seats separated from arena by podium wall.

biga Two-horse chariot.

censor High honor during Republic. Took census of citizens every five years and supervised ceremonial purification. Responsible for building and other public contracts. Duties eventually absorbed by emperor.

circus Area for chariot racing, roughly the shape of an elongated horseshoe, with starting gates at short, straight end. Similar in outline to the Greek stadium, but much larger. Also refers to the event itself.

comitia Name given to popular voting assemblies in Rome, organized by wealth or neighborhood.

consul Two chief executive magistrates of Roman government. Commanded armies of Rome. Initiated agenda for senate, summoned popular assemblies for voting.

contio Informal political meetings, best known from the late Republic.

damnatus Someone condemned on capital charges.

dictator Originally an appointed official that took charge of Rome in time of emergency, with overriding powers especially in military matters. Eventually pushed beyond traditional limits of six months by Sulla and Caesar. Outlawed by Second Triumvirate.

doctor Trainer at gladiatorial school, often an ex-gladiator specializing in certain combat technique.

editor Producer of a spectacle, typically a member of the sociopolitical elite using this public service as a means of securing status.

eques A type of armature for gladiators.

equestrian   Top class in Roman society, determined by wealth and "morals." Marked by narrow purple stripe on the toga. Status of "equestrian" necessary to be elected to the Senate.

essedarius   A type of armature for gladiators.

euripus   Ancient name for central barrier in circus.

factio   Originally refers to professional organization for chariot racing, by late Antiquity this term refers to fan organizations as well.

familia   Professional organization of gladiators, trainers, and owner-investors.

flamen   Member of one of the Roman state's major priestly colleges.

gladius   Short sword. Root of the word "gladiator."

hoplomachus   A type of armature for gladiators.

imperator   Title given to a successful general in the Republic, later absorbed by Augustus and successors as basis of term "emperor."

lanista   Manager-owner of a gladiatorial training school, responsible for acquisition of new combatants and their training. Negotiates terms of performance with editor.

ludus   Two important meanings: (1) games presented in association with religious festivals or thanksgiving celebrations, and (2) training school for gladiators and *bestiarii*.

maeniana   Section of seating in amphitheater.

meridianus   Noon events at *munus legitimum*, when executions took place.

munus, munera   Literally "duty," came to be term for gladiatorial games in reference to the pious duty the heir owed the deceased, to be served by the presentation of proper funeral rites that might include gladiatorial combats. Used in Roman towns to refer to magistrates' civic duties that might include the arrangement of gladiatorial spectacle.

murmillo   A type of armature for gladiators.

ordo   Row of seating at an amphitheater.

podium   Wall surrounding performance area at arena; protects spectators from potential danger of blood events.

pompa   Parade at Roman festival; involves political and religious personnel as well as performers at spectacle.

praetor   Second highest magistracy. Primary responsibility for judicial procedure, but also could serve as military commander if necessary. During the empire, presented ordinary gladiatorial games.

princeps   Literally "chief." Leader of the Senate was Princeps Senatus. Became important title for emperor.

quadriga   Four-horse chariot, typical vehicle for circus races.

quaestor   Lowest magistracy. During the Republic, quaestors were in charge of Rome's finances and also served as aides to consuls in wartime and proconsular governors in the provinces. During the empire, alternated with praetor in presenting ordinary *munera*.

retiarius   A type of armature for gladiators, using net and trident.

samnite   A type of armature for gladiators.

secutor   A type of armature for gladiators.

senate   Deliberative and advisory body in Roman constitution. During Republic, debated legislation, oversaw expenditure, considered policy.

Ex-magistrates took up lifetime post as Senators. Policy-making capacity superseded by that of emperor.

spina   Literally "backbone," modern term for *euripus*, the central barrier in the circus.

theatrum   Building type originally developed in Greek world for dramatic presentations, modified under Roman influence to house range of spectacles. Included *scaenae* or stage proper with backdrop rising behind it, orchestra, roughly semi-circular flat area between stage and seating, and rows of seating rising up in semi-circle around the orchestra.

thraex   A type of armature for gladiators.

tyro   Novice gladiator.

venatio   A show purporting to be a wild animal hunt combined with display of exotic creatures. Combats between animals or between men and animals.

venator   Roughly synonymous with *bestiarius*; performer specializing in animal combat.

Notes

Chapter 1: The Politics of the Arena

1   Loeb translation by L. H. G. Greenwood.
2   Loeb translation by E. T. Sage.
3   Loeb translation by B. O. Foster.
4   Loeb translation by J. D. Duff.
5   Translation by P. Halsall, online at www.hagiographa.com/LostBooks/tertullian_spectacles.htm.
6   This is the father of P. Licinius Crassus, who would be consul in 171 BCE.
7   Unpublished translation by Matt Roller.
8   The dead father here is T. Quinctius Flamininus, the "Liberator of Greece"; the son, producer of this event, would be consul in 150 BCE.
9   Penguin translation by J. Healy.
10 Loeb translation by F. G. Moore.
11 Penguin translation by H. Bettenson.
12 Loeb translation by E. T. Sage and A. C. Schlesinger.
13 Loeb translation by C. B. Gulick.
14 The *triclinium* is the Roman banqueting couch; the choice of this Latin word within Athenaeus' Greek text has been interpreted to indicate Antiochus' specific use of the Roman version of the couch, and not the Greek.
15 Translation by D. H. Berry, ed., *Cicero Defence Speeches* (Oxford: Oxford University Press, 2000).
16 Penguin translation by R. Graves.
17 Loeb translation by E. Cary.
18 Penguin translation by R. Warner.
19 Loeb translation by W. H. S. Jones.
20 Loeb translation by D. R. Shackleton-Bailey.
21 Penguin translation by R. Graves.
22 Penguin translation by I. Scott-Kilvert.
23 L. Aemilius Paullus Macedonicus was the natural father of both Q. Fabius Maximus Aemilianus and P. Cornelius Scipio Aemilianus, who had been adopted

by childless friends of his but honored their birth family by retaining the cognomen "Aemilianus." Aemilius Paullus died in 160; his other two, non-adopted, sons had predeceased him.

24 Thirty talents is about 750,000 sesterces; compare to the 80,000 sesterces Nobilior maxed out on below.

25 Penguin translation by M. Grant.

26 Translation by E. Shuckburgh, ed., *The Letters of Cicero: The Whole Extant Correspondence in Chronological Order* (London: G. Bell and Sons, 1909–15).

27 Loeb translation by N. H. Watts.

28 Loeb translation by D. R. Shackleton-Bailey.

29 Here, Cicero is drawing on the meaning of *"munus"* as gift or obligation, as well as gladiatorial show.

30 Translation by H. G. Edinger, ed., *Cicero de Officiis/On Duties* (Indianapolis: Bobbs-Merrill Company Inc., 1974).

31 Loeb translation by D. R. Shackleton-Bailey.

32 Ibid.

33 Ibid.

34 Ibid.

35 Penguin translation by H. Bettenson.

36 This is the priestly college of the pontiffs, one of the more politically prominent of Rome's priesthoods.

37 Loeb translation by E. T. Safe and A. C. Schlesinger.

38 The *ius imaginum* was the right to display images of family ancestors who were acknowledged for their high level of service to Rome.

39 Translation by D. H. Berry.

40 Adapted from Loeb translation by C. D. Yonge.

41 Samnite and *provocator* were gladiatorial armatures. See chapter 3 for more details.

42 Penguin translation by R. Graves.

43 Loeb translation by E. Cary.

44 Loeb translation by R. Gardner.

45 Cicero here refers to Clodius' brother, Appius Claudius Pulcher, praetor that year and still a patrician.

46 Loeb translation by E. Cary.

47 Adapted from Penguin translation by J. Carter.

48 Loeb translation by D. R. Shackleton-Bailey.

49 Loeb translation by R. Gardner.

50 Ibid.

51 Translation by E. Shuckburgh, *Letters*.

52 I.e. the "First Triumvirate" of Pompey, Caesar, and Crassus.

53 Loeb translation by R. Gardner.

54 P. Lentulus Spinther was the consul.

55 Adapted from Loeb translation by R. Gardner.

56 P. Cornelius Scipio Nasica, adopted by Q. Metellus Pius, consul in 80, and thus becoming Q. Caecilius Metellus Pius Scipio, tribune in 59, praetor in 55, games given in 57, exactly within the window permitted by law.

57 Loeb translation by D. R. Shackleton-Bailey.

58 Penguin translation by J. Healy.

59 Adapted from C. D. Yonge, trans., *The Orations of Marcus Tullius Cicero* (London: George Bell and & Sons, 1891). L. Calpurnius Piso had supported Cicero's exile.

60 Adapted from Loeb translation by H. White.

61 Penguin translation by M. Grant.

62 The calendar of Furius Dionysius Filocalus, dating to 354 CE, has ten days (December 2, 4–6, 8, 19–21, 23 and 24) for the *munera* out of a total of 177 days devoted to various *ludi*.

63 Actual competition for offices was controlled as well under the *princeps*; Augustus regularly submitted lists of names of appropriate candidates for the annual magistracies, who were routinely approved by the Senate. It soon reached the point that popular elections were no longer held.

64 Loeb translation by E. Cary.

65 Ibid.

66 Ibid.

67 By becoming poorer, they would give Caligula less reason for jealousy and thus less reason to target them for particular abuse.

68 Loeb translation by E. Cary.

69 Translation by A. J. Church and W. J. Brodribb, in M. Hadas, ed., *Complete Works of Tacitus* (New York: Modern Library, 1942).

70 Ibid.

71 Ibid.

72 Penguin translation by P. Green.

73 Adapted from Loeb translation by E. Cary.

74 Ibid.

75 Loeb translation by E. Cary. This section of Dio only exists in fragmentary quotations in later authors, such as Xiphilinus.

76 Adapted from Loeb translation by E. Cary.

77 Loeb translation by C. R. Haines.

78 Loeb translation by B. Radice.

79 Adapted from Loeb translation by J. C. Rolfe.

80 An undignified gesture. He should have kept his left hand inside his toga.

81 Translation by A. J. Church and W. J. Brodribb, *Tacitus*.

82 Ibid.

83 Penguin translation by R. Graves.

84 Loeb translation by B. Radice.

85 Adapted from Penguin translation by M. Grant.

86 Loeb translation by C. R. Haines.

87 The extreme nature of these descriptions reflects the tradition of criticism that had developed around notoriously bad emperors.

88 Loeb translation by E. Cary.

89 Adapted from W. Whiston, trans., *The Works of Flavius Josephus* (Auburn and Buffalo: John E. Beardsley, 1895).

90 Penguin translation by A. Birley.

91 Translation by M. H. Crawford, ed., *Roman Statutes* (London: Institute of Classical Studies, 1996).

92 Local-born citizens of Pompeii were enrolled in the Menenia voting tribe.

93 This would be April 8 through 12.

94 This is a different date: March 28 here.

95 Ellius is identified as a famous contemporary gladiator.

96 Such panels were recovered in eighteenth-century excavations at Pompeii, but exist today only in artists' renderings of the originals.

97 It has been argued, however, that a visit to Pompeii by Nero in 64, hinted at by references to Poppaea and acclamations for the "judgments" of the emperor, may have been an opportunity for a lifting of the ban by imperial fiat.

98 Penguin translation by B. Radice.

99 Penguin translation by R. Graves.

100 Translation by J. H. Oliver and R. E. A. Palmer, "Minutes of an Act of the Roman Senate," *Hesperia* 24 (1955): 320–349.

101 Ibid.

102 HS is the standard abbreviation for "sesterces."

103 The Telegenii are apparently the *familia* of *bestiarii* hired for Magerius' games. See chapter 4.

Chapter 2: The Venue

1 Compared to around twenty such structures in the Greek eastern Mediterranean.

2 Adapted from Penguin translation by I. Scott Kilvert.

3 Loeb translation by A. W. Mair.

4 Translation by A. J. Church and W. J. Brodribb, in M. Hadas, ed., *The Complete Works of Tacitus* (New York: Modern Library, 1942).

5 This is the theater built by Pompey the Great in 55 BCE.

6 Penguin translation by J. Healy.

7 Loeb translation by E. Cary.

8 The word "amphitheater" is derived from Greek: "amphi" means "on both sides" and "theatron" is the architectural term for the seating area in the standard Greek theater complex. "Hunting theater" is often used by Greek authors to refer to amphitheaters.

9 "This" refers to the dedication of the Temple of Venus Victrix.

10 Penguin translation by R. E. Latham.

11 Adapted from Loeb translation by J. W. Duff and A. M. Duff.

12 Although the word "theater" is used here, the description matches the amphitheater building type, with elliptical arena and special provisions for blood games.

13 *Balteus* literally means "belt"; here Calpurnius may be referring to a sparkling decorative stripe spanning the arena.

14 Translation by A. J. Church and W. J. Brodribb, *Tacitus*.

15 27 CE.

16 400,000 sesterces (HS) was the minimum property requirement for equestrian status.

17 Loeb translation by E. Cary.

18 This structure was not known as the Colosseum in antiquity. The name came to be used for the Flavian Amphitheater in the medieval period; scholars believe this refers not to the "colossal" size of the spectacle structure but rather the surviving colossal statue of the sun-god that stood next to it. The statue was part of Nero's Domus Aurea that was re-incorporated into the Flavian reworking of the area.

19 It did not, however, have the largest performance space; its arena was about two-thirds the size of that at Caesarea in Mauretania. Tarraco and Luca also had arenas somewhat larger than the Flavian Amphitheater.

20 Loeb translation by D. R. Shackleton Bailey.

21 The "colossus" here is the 120-foot tall statue built by Nero and originally given the facial features of that emperor. It was apparently recast as a generic representation of the sun god, Sol or Helios. This is the Colossus that in medieval times would inspire the "Colosseum" nickname for the structure.

22 Translation by S. J. B. Barnish, ed., *The Variae of Magnus Aurelius Cassiodorus Senator* (Liverpool: Liverpool University Press, 1992).

23 Adapted from Loeb translation by J. W. Duff and A. M. Duff.

24 Adapted from Penguin translation by Aubrey de Sélincourt.

25 Adapted from Loeb translation by E. Cary.

26 *Curiae* were one of the older means of categorizing the Roman populace for voting purposes. Each *curia* was a specific neighborhood, granted one bloc vote in the curial assembly.

27 Penguin translation by R. Graves.

28 This moat at the edge of the track in the Circus Maximus was a means of keeping animals inside the performance space, done in response to Pompey's elephant debacle of 55 BCE (see chapter 1), in which uncontrolled animals spoiled the spectacle.

29 Loeb translation by E. Cary.

30 The *plethron* and *stadion* are Greek measurements: a *plethron* is approximately 100 feet in length, while a *stade* is 6 *plethra*: the length of a stadium.

31 103 CE.

32 The surviving Circus Maximus, mostly from the Trajanic reconstruction, has an arena about 580 meters by 80 meters.

33 The modern usage depends on Cassiodorus' description, part of which appears below, in which he describes the victory monuments, presumably statues of war captives with backs (*spinae*) bent in submission. The term *euripus* is a bit confusing, as its first connection with the Circus Maximus is in reference to Julius Caesar's water barrier around the perimeter of the track. After this was removed by Nero, the use of the watery *euripus* term probably acknowledges the presence of fountains in the barrier.

34 Loeb translation by E. Cary.

35 There was also a link to Augustan image-building, as Apollo, one of the Graeco-Roman sun gods, had long been the patron of Augustus.

36 This god is the deified Julius Caesar, adopted father of Augustus.

37 Penguin translation by J. Healy.

38 Possibly a conflation of the two pharaonic names Psamtik (or Psammetichus) and Neferibre. Neferibre Psammetichus II was a pharaoh of the Twenty-sixth (Saite) dynasty and ruled 595–589 BCE. Pythagoras was thought to have been born in the mid-sixth century.

39 This is the obelisk Augustus set up as part of his enormous sundial.

40 Translation by S. J. B. Barnish, *Variae*.

41 The translation of the piece is disputed. Some suggest it should be rendered as "Farewell Hierax . . . Olympus . . . Antiocus," the "*va*" inscribed to be understood as "*vale*" rather than "*vade*," as I have taken it.

42 Translation by P. Halsall, online at www.hagiographa.com/LostBooks/
    tertullian_spectacles.htm.
43 Translation by S. J. B. Barnish, *Variae.*
44 Loeb translation by H. White.
45 Penguin translation by R. Graves.
46 The Greater and Lesser Codetae were low-lying areas in the Campus Martius,
    named after the marshy plants that grew there and resembled the *codae* or tails
    of horses. The *Naumachia* of Augustus was located at the Greater Codeta.
47 Penguin translation by R. Graves.
48 Adapted from Loeb translation by E. Cary.
49 Ibid.
50 Penguin translation by R. Graves.
51 Loeb translation by D. R. Shackleton Bailey.
52 Penguin translation by R. Graves.
53 Loeb translation by E. T. Sage.
54 Loeb translation by J. Bostock and H. T. Riley.
55 Penguin translation by R. Graves.
56 Loeb translation by D. R. Shackleton Bailey.
57 Lesser and greatest here are the equestrians and the senatorials.
58 Adapted from Loeb translation by D. R. Shackleton Bailey.
59 Leitus is identified as the attendant who removes pretenders from the elite seats.
60 Adapted from Loeb translation by D. R. Shackleton Bailey.
61 This is Attis, youthful paramour in myth of Cybele, the Great Goddess. To ensure
    the continuity of the vegetation cycle, Attis dies to signal the coming growing
    season.

Chapter 3: A Day at the Games

1   Translation by J. H. Oliver and R. E. A. Palmer, "Minutes of an Act of the Roman
    Senate," *Hesperia* 24 (1955): 320–349.
2   The order in which the information appeared varied, as seen above, in accordance
    with the emphasis determined by the *editor.*
3   Adapted from Loeb translation by B. Einarson and P. H. de Lacy.
4   Translation by P. Halsall, online at www.hagiographa.com/LostBooks/
    tertullian_spectacles.htm.
5   Loeb translation by E. Cary.
6   Adapted from Loeb translation by J. W. Duff and A. M. Duff.
7   The unsophisticated rustic may be here describing buffalo, dugongs, polar bears
    and hippopotamus.
8   Penguin translation by R. Campbell.
9   Loeb translation by H. L. Jones.
10 Adapted from Loeb translation by B. Einarson and P. H. de Lacy.
11 Loeb translation by D. R. Shackleton Bailey.
12 Ibid.
13 Loeb translation by M. D. MacLeod.
14 Whether the fish-man regularly fought the net-man is disputed. This is the
    claim made by a number of ancient authors, including Valerius Maximus and
    Quintilian, and the heavy armature would balance the light weapons of the

retiarius well. But visual representations set the *murmillo* against the *Thraex* and the *provocator*.

15 The armature of the *retiarius* derives from the tools of the fisherman, not from military gear of foreign nationals. This is unusual. Some have suggested that the *retiarius* first appeared in water pageants before being embraced by the *ludus*.

16 Adapted from Penguin translation by J. P. Sullivan.

17 This is probably a reference to a public banquet also offered by the *editor* as part of the games package; see chapter 1.

18 Adapted from translation by J. Lindsay.

19 Penguin translation by R. Graves.

20 Translation by R. Humphries, ed., *The Loves, The Art of Beauty, The Remedies for Love, and the Art of Love* (Bloomington: Indiana University Press, 1957).

21 The reference here is to *"Hoc habet!"* or "He's had it!," the shout given by the spectators when one of the gladiators receives a final blow.

22 Penguin translation by R. Warner.

23 Translation by P. Halsall, online (see note 4).

24 Translation by A. Roberts and J. Donaldson, eds., *The Ante-Nicene Fathers*, vol. 2 (New York: C. Scribner's Sons, 1899–1900).

25 Adapted from Penguin translation by J. P. Sullivan.

26 Adapted from Penguin translation by M. Grant.

27 Adapted from translation by A. Watson in T. Mommsen, P. Krueger, and A. Watson, eds., *The Digest of Justinian* (Philadelphia: University of Pennsylvania Press, 1985).

28 Translation by A. J. Church and W. J. Brodribb, in M. Hadas, ed., *Complete Works of Tacitus* (New York: Modern Library, 1942).

29 Ibid.

30 Loeb translation by H. Rackham and W. S. Jones.

31 Q. Lutatius Catulus, consul of 78 BCE.

32 P. Cornelius Lentulus Spinther, consul of 57 BCE and a supporter of Cicero's return from exile. See chapter 1.

33 Adapted from Loeb translation of J. H. Mozley.

34 Pontus and Idume produced famous dates, Damascus grew plums on the boughs, Caunus had renowned figs and Ameria, a region of Gaul, grew apples and pears.

35 Annona is the personification of the grain dole (*annona*) in which Rome's neediest male citizens were eligible for distributions of rations of grain, oil and wine, not, however, in sufficient quantities to support a family.

36 Penguin translation by R. Campbell.

37 Loeb translation by E. Cary.

38 Adapted from Loeb translation by R. M. Grummere.

39 Loeb translation by E. Cary.

40 Loeb translation by D. R. Shackleton Bailey.

41 Ibid.

42 Ibid.

43 Ibid.

44 The "law" referred to here is the custom that combat continues until one of the gladiators has been made to yield and asks for *missio* with a raised finger.

45 Loeb translation by E. Cary.

46 The club was the favorite weapon of the hero Hercules, to whom Commodus frequently compared himself. Indeed, his many displays of animal slaughter are probably a reference to his Herculean qualities.

47 Commodus and his opponent both use wooden weapons; this may have been a demonstration match, then, with blunted weapons, held prior to the "real" combats.

48 Literally, "servant of the bedchamber" or valet. Here, the intimation of shared bed is present, as Commodus' sexual liberality was a source of criticism.

49 If Commodus were using the *secutor's* helmet, with its complete enclosure from forehead to shoulder, these "kisses" were more head-bumps than smooches.

50 This is a reference to a standard depiction of the gigantomachy, the mythic war between the Olympian gods and an earlier generation of gods. Giants, as monstrous sons of the earth, were depicted as anguipeds, i.e. with legs like snakes, to show their connection to the earth and the underground.

51 Adapted from Penguin translation by R. Campbell.

52 Adapted from Loeb translation by W. C. F. Wright.

Chapter 4: The Life of the Gladiator

1 Loeb translation by F. R. Walton.

2 Loeb translation by E. Cary.

3 After Augustus, only members of the imperial family were allowed to celebrate triumphs per se. Others could be awarded the lesser honor of the ovation, which is formal thanks and recognition without the glamorous parade and spectacle.

4 Adapted from Loeb translation by H. St. J. Thackeray.

5 Loeb translation by H. St. J. Thackeray.

6 The "brother" referred to here is of course the future emperor Domitian.

7 Adapted from translation by A. Watson, in T. Mommsen, P. Krueger, and A. Watson, eds., The *Digest of Justinian* (Philadelphia: University of Pennsylvania Press, 1985).

8 M. Hyamson, ed., *Mosaicarum et Romanarum legum Collatio* (London: Oxford University Press, 1913).

9 Penguin translation by R. Graves.

10 Loeb translation by E. Cary.

11 Ibid.

12 Loeb translation by H. White.

13 Penguin translation by R. Warner.

14 Ibid.

15 Loeb translation by H. White.

16 Ibid.

17 Penguin translation by R. Warner.

18 Although Appian does seem to contradict himself about Spartacus' openness to formerly Roman soldiers.

19 Loeb translation by H. White.

20 Penguin translation by R. Warner.

21 Ibid.

22 Loeb translation by H. White.

23 Adapted from Loeb translation by E. Cary.

24 Translation by A. Watson, *Digest*.
25 Adapted from translation by A. Watson, ibid.
26 Ulpian notes that the difference between being condemned to the mines and to the mine-works (*opus metelli*) is in the weight of the chains: those in the mines have heavier chains and, presumably, have committed more serious offenses.
27 Penguin translation by R. Graves.
28 Adapted from Penguin translation by A. Birley.
29 Translation by A. Watson, *Digest*.
30 Loeb translation by R. M. Gummere.
31 Translation by J. H. Oliver and R. E. A. Palmer, "Minutes of an Act of the Roman Senate," *Hesperia* 24 (1955): 320–349.
32 Adapted from translation by J. E. Ryland, in A. Roberts and J. Donaldson, eds., *The Ante-Nicene Fathers*, vol. 2 (New York: C. Scribner's Sons, 1899–1900).
33 Loeb translation by A. M. Harmon.
34 Translation by J. P. Toner, *Leisure and Ancient Rome* (Cambridge: Polity Press, 1995).
35 Adapted from translation by C. Dodgson, trans., *Tertullian: Apologetic and Practical Treatises* (London: J. G. and F. Rivington, 1842).
36 Penguin translation by J. Healy.
37 Loeb translation by D. R. Shackleton Bailey.
38 Translation by P. Halsall, online at www.hagiographa.com/LostBooks/tertullian_spectacles.htm.
39 Adapted from translation by A. Watson, *Digest*.
40 Loeb translation by H. E. Butler.
41 Translation by T. W. Higginson, ed., *The Works of Epictetus* (New York: Thomas Nelson and Sons, 1890).
42 Translation by J. P. Toner in Toner, *Leisure and Ancient Rome*.
43 Loeb translation by J. E. King.
44 Translation by J. Walsh, "Galen's *Exhortatio ad Artes Addiscendas*," *Medical Life* 37 (1930): 507–529.
45 Translation by E. Wallis in A. Roberts and J. Donaldson, eds., *The Ante-Nicene Fathers*, vol. 5 (New York: C. Scribner's Sons, 1899–1900).
46 Loeb translation by H. Rackham and W. S. Jones.
47 Penguin translation by P. Green.
48 Hadrian's legislation cited above suggests that even a gladiator condemned to the school as a criminal penalty did not necessarily expect to die.
49 Penguin translation by R. Graves.
50 Ibid.
51 Ibid.
52 Unpublished translation by Martha Jenks.
53 Adapted from translation by R. J. White, ed., *Artemidorus: The Interpretation of Dreams* (Park Ridge, NJ: Noyes Press, 1975).
54 Penguin translation by A. Birley.
55 A graffito from the *ludus* at Pompeii claims that Seneca was opposed to spectacle as a whole: "The philosopher Annaeus Seneca is the only Roman writer to condemn the bloody games." (*CIL* 4.4418) Some modern scholars have made much of Seneca's Letter 7 on the noon executions, finding here a more universal denunciation than is warranted by the text. See chapter 3.

56 Adapted from Loeb translation by R. M. Gummere.

57 Romans did not have toilet paper.

58 This epitaph from Thessalonika is topped by a relief sculpture with a horseman above a bust of a beardless youth on the left and a left-advancing image of a gladiator on the right, with a sword in the left hand and a large rectangular shield in the right, helmet covering his head.

59 Adapted from translation by C. Roueché.

60 Ibid.

61 Adapted from Penguin translation by R. Graves.

62 Loeb translation by D. R. Shackleton Bailey.

63 Ibid.

64 Penguin translation by R. Graves.

65 Adapted from Loeb translation of J. H. Mozley.

66 Translation by A. J. Church and W. J. Brodribb, in M. Hadas, ed., *Complete Works of Tacitus* (New York: Modern Library, 1942).

67 Penguin translation by P. Green.

68 Loeb translation by E. Cary.

69 Ibid.

70 Translation by B. Levick, "The *Senatus Consultum* from Larinum," *Journal of Roman Studies* 73 (1983): 97–115.

71 Penguin translation by P. Green.

72 Translation by A. J. Church and W. J. Brodribb, *Tacitus*.

73 Loeb translation by E. Cary.

Chapter 5: Christians and the Arena

1 Translation by A. J. Church and W. J. Brodribb, in M. Hadas, ed., *Complete Works of Tacitus* (New York: Modern Library, 1942).

2 Loeb translation by K. Lake.

3 Eusebius quotes Tertullian *Apology* 5 here.

4 Penguin translation by B. Radice.

5 But see the situation in Lyons below for an instance where the "other" crimes become part of the dispute.

6 Those holding the Roman citizenship were sent to Rome; one of the benefits of citizenship was the right to appeal against summary action taken by Rome's magistrates. In Rome, the emperor, as holder of tribunician power, would be responsible for securing their rights to lawful judicial procedure.

7 Loeb translation by K. Lake.

8 Translation by R. Arbesmann, E. J. Daly, and E. A. Quain, trans., *Tertullian: Apologetical Works and Minucius Felix* (New York: Fathers of the Church, 1950).

9 Ibid.

10 Ibid.

11 Translation by P. Halsall, online at www.hagiographa.com/LostBooks/tertullian_spectacles.htm.

12 Translation by B. P. Pratten, in A. Roberts, and J. Donaldson, eds., *The Ante-Nicene Fathers*, vol. 2 (New York: C. Scribner's Sons, 1899–1900).

13 Translation by P. Halsall, online (see note 11).

14 Ibid.

15 Adapted from translation by J. E. Ryland, in A. Roberts and J. Donaldson, eds., *The Ante-Nicene Fathers*, vol. 2 (New York: C. Scribner's Sons, 1899–1900).

16 Quoted by Eusebius *Ecclesiastical History* 4.8. Loeb translation by K. Lake.

17 Translation by Arbesmann, Daly, and Quain, *Tertullian*.

18 Translation by P. Halsall, online (see note 11).

19 Adapted from translation by E. Wallis, in A. Roberts and J. Donaldson, eds., *The Ante-Nicene Fathers*, vol. 5 (New York: C. Scribner's Sons, 1899–1900).

20 Loeb translation by K. Lake.

21 Translation adapted from H. Musurillo, ed., *The Acts of the Christian Martyrs* (Oxford: Oxford University Press, 1972).

22 Note that the trial is placed in the spectacle building here.

23 Paraphrase of Joshua 1: 6, 7; biblical references are frequently scattered through the Martyr Acts.

24 L. Statius Quadratus is identified later in the text as the governor in question.

25 The Asiarch is a Roman official associated with the cult of the divine emperor in the province of Asia. This is probably to be identified with G. Julius Philippus, whom an inscription of 149 mentions as an Asiarch.

26 Translation adapted from Musurillo, *The Acts*.

27 A paraphrase for incest and cannibalism from the common vocabulary of Greek mythology. Oedipus, in his efforts to confound prophecy, unknowingly married his mother Jocasta, and Thyestes unknowingly was made to eat his own children, cooked into a meaty stew, as part of an extended series of atrocities and counter-atrocities that resulted from his accursed feud with his brother Atreus.

28 John 16: 2.

29 That is, of being incestuous cannibals.

30 This is the celebration held annually on August 1 at Lyons, as a major celebration of the cult of the emperor not just in Lyons but in "the Three Gauls." This served as a regular demonstration of loyalty to the emperor and the empire.

31 Adapted from Musurillo, *The Acts*. A catechumen is in the process of undergoing conversion to Christianity, engaged in the preparation and study needed before the final step of baptism.

32 Who may have been the Christian author Tertullian.

33 One of the rituals of the early Christian church, a commemoration of Jesus' last meal with his followers. Here it is a reinterpretation of the gladiators' banquet (see chapter 4), at which the expected resignation and anticipation of the games to come is replaced by joyous anticipation of martyrdom fulfilled.

34 Perhaps a variation on the standard practice of offering female animals in sacrifice to female divinities.

35 Emotion-driven mood swings of the crowd, here from outrage at the unrepentant condemned to outraged modesty on behalf of the condemned, are noted for other contexts as well.

36 Translation by H. Musurillo, *The Acts*.

37 Acts 4:24.

38 Acts 9:15.

39 2 Timothy 1:11

40 1 Peter 1:4.

41 Loeb translation by H. J. Thomson.

42 Translation by M. S. Muldowney, ed., *Saint Augustine: Sermons of the Liturgical Seasons* (New York: Fathers of the Church, 1959).

43 Loeb translation by H. J. Thomson.
44 Adapted from Loeb translation by H. J. Thomson.
45 Ibid.
46 Translation by R. Warner, ed., *The Confessions of St. Augustine* (New York and Scarborough, Ontario: New American Library, 1963).

Chapter 6: Chariot Races and Water Shows

1   Penguin translation by A. de Sélincourt.
2   Adapted from Loeb translation by J. H. Mozley.
3   Penguin translation by P. Green.
4   This refers to the tradition demanding a slave ride in the general's chariot in the triumphal parade, whispering "Remember, you are only a man."
5   Loeb translation by E. Cary
6   Translation by P. Halsall, online at www.hagiographa.com/LostBooks/tertullian_spectacles.htm.
7   Adapted from Loeb translation by J. D. Duff.
8   Adapted from Loeb translation by W. B. Anderson.
9   Penguin translation by H. Bettenson.
10 Penguin translation by A. de Sélincourt.
11 Loeb translation by W. R. Paton.
12 Translation by J. R. Rea, *The Oxyrhynchus Papyri* XXXIV (1968): 91–92.
13 Loeb translation by D. R. Shackleton Bailey.
14 Adapted from new Penguin translation by P. Green.
15 Loeb translation by D. R. Shackleton-Bailey.
16 Ibid.
17 Adapted from translation by N. Lewis and M. Reinhold, eds., *Roman Civilization, Selected Readings: The Empire* (New York: Columbia University Press, 1990).
18 Loeb translation by W. R. Paton.
19 Ibid.
20 Ibid.
21 Adapted from Loeb translation by W. R. Paton.
22 Translation by S. J. B. Barnish, *Variae*.
23 Loeb translation by J. C. Rolfe.
24 Penguin translation by A. Birley.
25 Translation by J. G. Gager, "Curse and Competition in the Ancient Circus," in H. W. Attridge, J. J. Collins, and T. H. Tobin, eds., *Of Scribes and Scrolls* (Maryland: University Press of America, 1990), pp. 215–228.
26 This is a reference to the signs or "characters" written on the tablet and the supernatural beings whose symbols these were.
27 Porphyrius, the famous charioteer of late fifth-/early sixth-century Constantinople, may be the driver meant here.
28 Translation by J. G. Gager, *Curse Tablets and Binding Spells from the Ancient World* (Oxford: Oxford University Press, 1992), #9.
29 Loeb translation by J. C. Rolfe.
30 Penguin translation by M. Grant.
31 Adapted from Penguin translation by A. Birley.
32 Loeb translation by H. Rackham.
33 Adapted from new Penguin translation by P. Green.

34 Loeb translation by H. Rackham.

35 Translation by P. Halsall, online (see note 6).

36 Loeb translation by H. Rackham.

37 This is likely the *Acta Diurna*, a gazette published in Rome from the mid-first century BCE with news of official events, ceremonies and so forth.

38 Penguin translation by M. Graves.

39 Ibid.

40 Penguin translation by B. Radice.

41 Loeb translation by D. R. Shackleton Bailey.

42 Loeb translation by E. Cary.

43 Translation by M. and M. Whitby, eds., *The History of Theophylact Simocatta* (Oxford: Clarendon Press, 1986).

44 Loeb translation by J. W. Cohoon and H. Lamar Crosby.

45 Loeb translation by F. C. Conybeare.

46 Ibid.

47 Penguin translation by M. Grant.

48 Loeb translation by E. Cary.

49 Adapted from Loeb translation by E. Cary.

50 Loeb translation by J. C. Rolfe.

51 Adapted from translation by R. Atwater, ed., *Procopius Secret History* (Ann Arbor: University of Michigan Press, 1961).

52 Ibid.

53 Translation by R. Atwater, *Procopius*.

54 Adapted from Loeb translation by H. P. Dewing.

55 Adapted from Loeb translation by H. White.

56 Loeb translation by E. Cary.

57 Loeb translation by J. Jackson.

58 Loeb translation by E. Cary.

59 The "victory" here is Caligula's conquest of the sea, by means of the bridge.

60 Penguin translation by M. Grant.

61 This is the ornamental pool or Stagnum constructed by Agrippa as part of his bath complex on the Campus Martius, first in a series of increasingly elaborate imperial bath facilities.

62 Loeb translation by D. R. Shackleton Bailey.

63 Ibid.

Suggestions for Further Reading

Auguet, R., *Cruauté et civilization: les jeux romains* (Paris: Flammarion, 1970). (English translation published in 1972 by Allen and Unwin.)

Balsdon, J. P. V. D., *Life and Leisure in Ancient Rome* (New York: McGraw-Hill, 1969).

Barton, C., *The Sorrows of the Ancient Romans* (Princeton: Princeton University Press, 1993).

Beacham, R. C., *Spectacle Entertainments of Early Imperial Rome* (New Haven: Yale University Press, 1999).

Bergmann, B. and C. Kondoleon, eds., *The Art of Ancient Spectacle* (Washington, DC: National Gallery of Art, 1999).

Bomgardner, D. L., *The Story of the Roman Amphitheater* (London: Routledge, 2000).

Brown, S., "Death as Decoration: Scenes from the Arena on Roman Domestic Mosaics," in A. Richlin, ed., *Pornography and Representation in Greece and Rome* (New York: Oxford University Press), pp. 180–211.

Cameron, A., *Bread and Circuses: The Roman Emperor and His People* (Oxford: Clarendon Press, 1974).

Cameron, A., *Circus Factions: Blues and Greens at Rome and Byzantium* (Oxford: Clarendon Press, 1976).

Cameron, A., *Porphyrius the Charioteer* (Oxford: Clarendon Press, 1973).

Carcopino, J., *Daily Life in Ancient Rome* (London: Penguin, 1956).

Castrén, P., *Ordo Populusque Pompeianus: Polity and Society in Roman Pompeii* (Rome: Instituti Romani Finlandiae, 1975).

Coleman, K., "Fatal Charades: Roman Executions Staged as Mythological Enactments," *Journal of Roman Studies* 83 (1993): 44–73.

Coleman, K., "Launching into History: Aquatic Displays in the Early Empire," *Journal of Roman Studies* 80 (1990): 48–74.

Coleman, K., "Ptolemy Philadelphus and the Roman Amphitheater," in W. J. Slater, ed., *Roman Theater and Society* (Ann Arbor: University of Michigan Press, 1996), pp. 49–68.

Dudley, D. R., *Urbs Roma* (Phaidon Press: Aberdeen, 1967).

Dunbabin, K. M. D., *The Mosaics of Roman North Africa: Studies in Iconography and Patronage* (Oxford: Clarendon Press, 1978).

Edmondson, J. C., "The Cultural Politics of Public Spectacle in Rome and the Greek East, 167–166 BCE," in Bergmann, B. and C. Kondoleon, eds., *The Art of Ancient Spectacle* (Washington, DC: National Gallery of Art, 1999), pp. 77–96.

Edmondson, J. C., "Dynamic Arenas: Gladiatorial Presentations in the City of Rome and the Construction of Roman Society during the Roman Empire," in W. J. Slater, ed., *Roman Theater and Society* (Ann Arbor: University of Michigan Press, 1996), pp. 69–112.

Favro, D., "The City Is a Living Thing: The Performative Role of an Urban Site in Ancient Rome, the Vallis Murcia," in B. Bergmann and C. Kondoleon, eds., *The Art of Ancient Spectacle* (Washington, DC: National Gallery of Art, 1999), pp. 205–220.

Favro, D., *The Urban Image of Augustan Rome* (Cambridge: Cambridge University Press, 1996).

Feldherr, A., "Ships of State: *Aeneid* 5 and Augustan Circus Spectacle," *Classical Antiquity* 14 (1995): 245–265.

Franklin, J. L., "Cn. Alleius Nigidius Maius and the Amphitheatre: *Munera* and a Distinguished Career at Ancient Pompeii," *Historia* 96 (1997): 434–447.

Franklin, J. L., *Pompeis difficile est: Studies in the Political Life of Imperial Pompeii* (Ann Arbor, MI: University of Michigan Press, 2001).

Friedländer, L., *Roman Life and Manners under the Early Empire* (translation of *Sittengeschichte Röms*) (London: Routledge and Kegan Paul, 1965).

Futrell, A., *Blood in the Arena: The Spectacle of Roman Power* (Austin, TX: University of Texas Press, 1997).

Gager, J. G., "Curse and competition in the ancient circus," in H. W. Attridge, J. J. Collins and T. H. Tobin, eds., *Of Scribes and Scrolls* (Baltimore: University Press of America, 1990), pp. 215–228.

Gager, J. G., *Curse Tablets and Binding Spells from the Ancient World* (Oxford: Oxford University Press, 1992).

Golvin, J.-Cl., *L'amphithéâtre romain* (Paris: E. de Boccard, 1988).

Golvin, J.-Cl. and C. Landes, *Amphithéâtres et gladiateurs* (France: CNRS, 1990).

Grant, M., *Gladiators* (New York: Delacorte Press, 1967).

Heintz, F. "Circus Curses and their Archaeological Contexts," *Journal of Roman Archaeology* 11 (1998): 337–342.

Hopkins, K., *Death and Renewal* (Cambridge: Cambridge University Press, 1983).

Humphrey, J., *Roman Circuses: Arenas for Chariot Racing* (London: B. T. Batsford Ltd., 1986).

Hyamson, M., *Mosaicarum et Romanarum Legum Collatio* (London: Oxford University Press, 1913).

Junkelmann, M., *Das Spiel mit dem Tod* (Mainz: Verlag Philipp von Zabern, 2000).

Köhne, E. and C. Ewigleben, eds., *Gladiators and Caesars* (Berkeley: University of California Press, 2000).

Kyle, D., *Spectacles of Death in Ancient Rome* (London: Routledge, 1998).

Levick, B., "The *Senatus Consultum* from Larinum," *Journal of Roman Studies* 73 (1983): 97–115.

Lim, R., "'In the Temple of Laughter': Visual and Literary Representations of Spectators at Roman Games," in B. Bergmann and C. Kondoleon, eds., *The Art of Ancient Spectacle* (Washington, DC: National Gallery of Art, 1999), pp. 343–365.

Lyle, E. B. "The Circus as Cosmos," *Latomus* 43 (1984): 827–841.

Oliver, J. H. and R. E. A. Palmer, "Minutes of an Act of the Roman Senate," *Hesperia* 24 (1955): 320–349.

Parker, H., "The Observed of All Observers: Spectacle, Applause, and Cultural Poetics in the Roman Theater Audience," in B. Bergmann and C. Kondoleon, eds., *The Art of Ancient Spectacle* (Washington, DC: National Gallery of Art, 1999), pp. 163–180.

Plass, P., *The Game of Death in Ancient Rome* (Madison: University of Wisconsin Press, 1995).

Poliakoff, M., *Combat Sports in the Ancient World: Competition, Violence and Culture* (New Haven: Yale University Press, 1987).

Potter, D. S., "Martyrdom as Spectacle," in R. Scodel, ed., *Theater and Society in the Classical World* (Ann Arbor: University of Michigan Press, 1993), pp. 53–88.

Potter, D. S., "Performance, Power and Justice in the High Empire," in W. J. Slater, ed., *Roman Theater and Society* (Ann Arbor: University of Michigan Press, 1996), pp. 129–159.

Potter, D. S. and D. J. Mattingly, eds., *Life, Death and Entertainment in the Roman Empire* (Ann Arbor, MI: University of Michigan Press, 1998).

Rawson, E., "Chariot-racing in the Roman Republic," *Papers of the British School at Rome* 49 (1981): 1–16.

Rawson, E., "Discrimina ordinum: the Lex Julia Theatralis," *Papers of the British School at Rome* 55 (1987): 508–545.

Riccobono, S., ed., *Acta Divi Augusti pars prior* (Rome: Regia Academia Italica, 1945).

Richardson, L., *A New Topographical Dictionary of Ancient Rome* (Baltimore: Johns Hopkins University Press, 1992).

Robert, L., *Les gladiateurs dans l'Orient grec* (Paris: Bibliothèque de l'École des Hautes Études, 1940).

Roueché, C., *Performers and Partisans at Aphrodisias* (London: Society for the Promotion of Roman Studies, 1993).

Sabbatini Tumolesi, P., *Gladiatorum Paria: Annunci di spettacoli gladiatorii a Pompeii* (Rome: Instituto di Epigrafia ed Antichità Greche e Romane dell' Università di Roma, 1980).

Scobie, A., "Spectator Security and Comfort at Gladiatorial Games," *Nikephoros* 1 (1988): 191–243.

Syme, R., "Scorpus the Charioteer," *American Journal of Ancient History* 2 (1977): 86–94.

Veyne, P., *Bread and Circuses* (London: Penguin, 1990).

Ville, G., *La gladiature en occident des origins à la mort de Domitien* (Rome: Écôle française de Rome, 1981).

Welch, K., "Negotiating Roman Spectacle, Architecture in the Greek World: Athens and Corinth," in B. Bergmann and C. Kondoleon, eds., *The Art of Ancient Spectacle* (Washington, DC: National Gallery of Art, 1999), pp. 125–146.

Welch, K., "The Roman Arena in Late-Republican Italy: A New Interpretation," *Journal of Roman Archaeology* 7 (1994): 59–80.

Wiedemann, T., *Emperors and Gladiators* (London: Routledge, 1992).

Wistrand, M., *Entertainment and Violence in Ancient Rome* (Göteborg, Sweden: Acta Universitatis Gothoburgensis, 1992).

Zanker, P., *The Power of Images in the Age of Augustus* (Ann Arbor: University of Michigan Press, 1988).

Index

CPSIA information can be obtained
at www.ICGtesting.com
Printed in the USA
BVHW071344111218
535290BV00015B/108/P